LESS THAN MEETS THE EYE

The Twentieth Century Fund is a research foundation undertaking timely analyses of economic, political, and social issues. Not-for-profit and nonpartisan, the Fund was founded in 1919 and endowed by Edward A. Filene.

BARBARA HINCKLEY

LESS
THAN MEETS
THE EYE

◆ ◆ ◆

Foreign Policy Making
and the Myth
of the
Assertive Congress

A Twentieth Century Fund Book

The University of Chicago Press ◆ *Chicago and London*

BARBARA HINCKLEY is professor of political science at Purdue University. She is the author of several books on Congress and the presidency. Her recently published book *Follow the Leader*, coauthored with Paul Brace, won a prize from the American Political Science Association for the best book on the presidency published in 1992.

The University of Chicago Press, Chicago 60637
The University of Chicago Press, Ltd., London
© 1994 by The Twentieth Century Fund
All rights reserved. Published 1994
Printed in the United States of America
03 02 01 00 99 98 97 96 95 94   1 2 3 4 5

ISBN (cloth): 0-226-34143-7
ISBN (paper): 0-226-34144-5

Library of Congress Cataloging-in-Publication Data

Hinckley, Barbara, 1937–
    Less than meets the eye : foreign policy making and the myth of
the assertive Congress / Barbara Hinckley.
        p.   cm.
    "A Twentieth Century Fund book"
    Includes bibliographical references and index.
    1. United States. Congress.   2. United States—Foreign
relations administration.   I. Title.
JK1081.H56   1994
328.73'0746—dc20   93-36084
                                                       CIP

∞ The paper used in this publication meets the minimum requirements of the American National Standard for Information Sciences—Permanence of Paper for Printed Library Materials, ANSI Z39.48-1984.

CONTENTS

✦ ✦ ✦

FOREWORD

✦ ✦ ✦

SINCE THE BIRTH OF THE REPUBLIC, the President and Congress have debated over the balance of powers regarding foreign policy. The area in dispute covers trade policy, arms sales, foreign aid, and intelligence, but the greatest clamor always emerges over the decision to send American troops abroad. With the end of the Cold War, the consensus that underpinned American foreign policy during the long struggle with the Soviet Union has dissolved, awakening arguments long forgotten or muted when America confronted a clear and menacing "enemy."

All parties now have a greater latitude to fight for turf without facing the accusation of compromising national security. Thus, today's arguments often are drawn across partisan lines. The same Republicans who spent twenty years decrying the War Powers Act as an infringement of the President's powers because it demands congressional approval within sixty to ninety days of sending troops onto foreign soil are demanding that President Clinton seek prior congressional approval for sending American troops to Haiti or Bosnia.

This renewed outcry over the relative powers of Congress and the President is, in keeping with much of the focus of the debate over the past twenty years, centered on the War Powers Act and Congress's oversight role. Barbara Hinckley, professor of political science at Purdue University and author of *Follow the Leader: Opinion Polls and the Modern Presidents*, *The Symbolic Presidency*, and *Problems of the Presidency*, here turns her attention to the congressional side of the conflict. A noted political scientist, she is probing the claims that Congress's authority has expanded during the past three decades. Her conclusion, after examining foreign policy legislation, military action, and foreign assistance authorizations over a thirty-year period, is that the conflict is in large part an illusion, a symbolic display mounted to cover what is really a lack of deliberate foreign policy making on either side. After putting forth a careful case in support of this position, Hinckley presents suggestions for reforming the process to ensure that both Congress and the President address important substantive questions in a serious fashion in the future.

This book is an outgrowth of the Twentieth Century Fund's long-standing interest in the role played by our national legislature, joining an impressive list of publications including Fred R. Harris's *Deadlock or Decision: The U.S. Senate and the Rise of National Politics,* Barry Blechman's *The Politics of National Security: Congress and U.S. Defense Policy,* I. M. Destler's *American Trade Politics,* and Dennis Ippolito's *Congressional Spending,* as well as the Report of the Twentieth Century Fund Task Force on covert action, *The Need to Know.*

Hinckley's conclusions are likely to broaden the scope of future debate over the relative roles of the executive and legislative branches in foreign policy making. As an institution devoted to bringing important international and national issues to public prominence, we thank her for helping us fulfill our mission.

Richard C. Leone, President
The Twentieth Century Fund
November 1993

AUTHOR'S PREFACE

♦ ♦ ♦

W E CANNOT LEARN from history if we do not know what the history is or if we make up imaginary accounts to fit the political positions of the time. I was constantly surprised in the writing of this book how little information was available on U.S. foreign policy making. It was not a problem of classified information: it was the *public records* of presidential and congressional activities that had not been gathered together, analyzed, and thought about. Yet, all the while people were confidently debating the "role" of the Congress and of the President as if they knew what these roles had been.

How very curious. This phenomenon is not only the result of an information culture running too fast for itself—where media commentators each day must seem informed and original, and books are to be talked about rather than read. These pressures are important surely. It appears to stem more fundamentally, however, from the foreign policy subject itself in a way relevant to the book's thesis. This book argues that symbolism takes precedence over substance in the foreign policy making of elected representatives. There is less of a "struggle" for influence than meets the eye. The too easy acceptance of this optical illusion by popular commentators and others, the unwillingness to look for information that might contradict it, suggests that the idea is an important one. If our representatives *fight* each other to make foreign policy because they care so much, everything must be fine. It is best not to let any stray facts spoil the aura of accountability and democratic debate.

What growth has occurred in substantive foreign policy legislation voted in Congress between the 1960s and the 1980s? How many times has the War Powers thirty-day (or sixty-day) clock, so hotly debated in the past, actually been invoked? When did the military assistance component of the foreign aid budget more than double? What legal restrictions on CIA activities existed by the end of the Bush administration? The answers, respectively, are no growth, none, during the Reagan years, and very few. (Congress set an eighteen-month clock once, more than a year after the use of force occurred.) Americans might support or disagree with these outcomes of the legislative process, but they have to know about them first to do so. Needless to say, a symbolic debate on the "constitutional prerogatives" of the two branches can lead attention away from these issues. Thus while the book targets the President and Congress as co-contributors to the illusion of struggle, a wider responsibility is projected. A basic reading of democratic theory suggests that presidents and members of Congress will be as responsible as they are asked to be by a wider informed opinion.

An informed historical perspective should become more important than ever in the years ahead. Instances of the U.S. use of force abroad have sharply increased from the mid-1980s through the years of the Bush administration. If the reduced threat to national and global security in the post–Cold War era lowers the stakes of these potential engagements—making them more likely—the same relaxation of tensions makes the events more debatable and less obviously a matter to be decided only by the President. It is not a question of *whether* these issues will be debated but *where*. Debate will take place within the executive bureaucracy and with representatives of foreign governments. Presidents always have the benefit of this advice. But if these issues are to be deliberated in Congress, which shares the constitutional war-making power, they must transcend claims of assertiveness and the counterclaims of meddling. To understand what Congress is and is not able to do, it will be important to see how the institution has been weakened by its own past reforms and why the very hard work of individual members does not add up to accomplishments of the Congress as a whole. Some lessons in this regard from the debate on Somalia in the fall of 1993 are noted in the Afterword to this book.

The same historical perspective is needed if Congress begins to revise the War Powers Act or to establish special consultative committees to meet with presidents on occasions of the use of force. The War Powers Act, enacted under very atypical conditions, has become an acute embarrassment, a kind of legislative albatross, because it does not address the reality of typical occasions of force. One can imagine a rousing debate in which all members might join on the constitutional prerogatives at issue. However, the desired outcome—of revision or repeal—should not change the typical patterns of congressional support for presidents on these occasions. History also tells us that the clearest guidelines to consultation (with the special intelligence committees, for example) are not sufficient if the executive officers choose not to consult. After the necessary apologies and handwringing, the legislators agree that perhaps their guidelines could be clarified. In each of these cases Congress will seem to be asserting itself.

While attention focuses on a few very visible events, other policy goes forward. *Less than Meets the Eye* attempts to give a sense of this larger agenda: the periodicity of trade policy, the ups and downs of intelligence oversight, the fragile nature of the foreign aid bill, with its implications for the power of the purse. The book also seeks to point out, for the scholarship of the future, the kinds of data which could be systematically researched. Clearly, an informed and responsible foreign policy cannot be limited to the few events awarded a public display.

Given the scarcity of information, the acknowledgment of debts I incurred in preparing this book is anything but pro forma. I would first of all like to thank the board and staff of the Twentieth Century Fund for making the project possible, and particularly the efforts of Ronald Repogle, former project director John Samples, Jason Renker, Beverly Goldberg, and Stephen Greenfield. Colleagues who read the manuscript at critical points, supplying their insight and expertise, include Robert Browning, Timothy Cook, Leah Haus, Miroslav Nincic, Randall Ripley, and Bruce Russett. To Browning also, who was present at the beginning of the project, my appreciation for making available at the conclusion the resources of the C-SPAN Video Archives at Purdue University. The highly skilled research assistance of Ellen Carnaghan and Edward Muir was indispensable. Carnaghan not only supplied her own foreign policy expertise but exhibited a unique talent for tracking buried government documents. Martha Williams, legislative assistant at the Office of Management and Budget, provided important assistance at the beginning of the research. The University of Chicago Press has been a pleasure to work with through all the stages of the book's publication. My thanks in particular to senior editor John Tryneski for his essential advice and support and to Jo Ann Kiser for such an intelligent job of copyediting.

None of these individuals, of course, should agree with all the statements of such a complex and controversial subject matter. I see this as merely a first book of many to follow by other scholars. My thanks are due for making this first account possible.

Barbara Hinckley
October 1993

1

✦ ✦ ✦

THE CURRENT
DEBATE

P EOPLE LIKE TO SAY that there is a "struggle" between President and Congress over the making of foreign policy, a
struggle built in by the constitutional sharing of power
between the branches. They point out that the birth of the Republic was immediately followed by a clash between the first President
and the first Congress over who was to conduct the nation's foreign policy. George Washington argued for neutrality in the war
between Britain and France, while Jefferson and the Republicans
in Congress sided with France and the French Revolution. They
go on to indicate the many occasions since then where conflict has
flared, in matters large and small, in war making, peace making,
and the conduct of routine affairs. Writing on the eve of World
War II, presidential scholar Edwin Corwin observed that both
branches were given an "invitation to struggle" by the treatment
of foreign policy in the Constitution.[1] A modern account of foreign policy making uses Corwin's phrase as its title, stressing the
conflict between the branches.[2] Other accounts, too, have pointed
to a Congress more active and assertive in recent years than it
was before.[3] Reagan Republicans began to worry in print about
"the fettered presidency" and the usurping by Congress of the
President's constitutional role. Books appeared describing *The
Growing Power of Congress* and *The Imperial Congress.*[4] It seems
that half a century after Corwin and many wars later, the struggle
goes on.

Or does it? In today's debate over who should hold the foreign
policy reins, those on one side argue that the nation needs a president able to exercise discretion in foreign affairs unhampered by

535 congressional secretaries of state. To them, assistance to guerrilla fighters or a standoff in the Middle East is an executive matter that should be free of congressional interference. Indeed, they would argue (as did several witnesses in the Iran-contra hearings) that when Congress interferes trouble is sure to follow. In the words of one editorial, the nation must be delivered from the "mayhem caused by the would-be Metternichs on Capitol Hill."[5] On the other side, people contend that a congressional role in foreign policy is basic to democratic government. Only an active and assertive Congress can hold the executive accountable and ensure that policy choice, whether critical or routine, is subject to evaluation and review.

The arguments follow lines of party and ideology for the most part. The presidential advocates who were Federalists in 1793 became Kennedy Democrats in 1960 and Reagan-Bush Republicans some two decades later. The Congress, filled with its safe senior members and charged with meddling and interference, was disliked by the liberals in the 1960s and by the conservatives in the 1990s. Times of divided-party control, with a president of one party facing a Congress controlled by the opposite party, give each branch special incentive to argue its own prerogatives.

So former administration staffer John Lehman asks "Who Should Be on Top: Congress or the President?" in a lively argument for presidential primacy in war making.[6] Lehman admits there may be problems of executive secrecy and delegation, but he saves his most colorful characterizations for Congress:[7]

> In contrast, the deficiencies of Congress are so obvious as to need little repetition; yet its characteristic multifarious interests, diffuse authority, paucity of resources, thinness of expertise, lack of hard data available to the executive, plodding and workaday procedures, freedom from secrecy, lack of continuity, and, above all, localism and parochialism are, ironically, also the bases of its power.

A congressional restriction on funds, soon to be compromised and then removed, is described as a "heel on the executive throat."[8] Lehman's book, of course, is intended to offer a point of view rather than any serious study of foreign policy. It includes accounts from his years in Washington, although it emphasizes the Bush wars in Panama and the Gulf, during which time he was not part of the administration, and includes brief selected historical synopses from George Washington to the present. But are we being asked the right questions in this or other examples of the now popular genre on the foreign policy "debate"? Is it a matter of who is on top? Are we really talking about war making or something else? While writers, including former members of government, play King of the Mountain, what other questions might be obscured?

Beneath the ideological sparring lie issues of the gravest importance. As James Madison pointed out in a letter to Thomas Jefferson in 1798, it is generally true that the loss of liberty at home is to be charged to the provisions against real or imagined dangers from abroad. If foreign policy is handled badly, the nation faces threats to its security from abroad. But if foreign policy is managed by abuses of power at home, the nation faces the equally grave danger of being destroyed from within. So, people ask whether democracies are necessarily disadvantaged in the conduct of foreign policy by the demands that policy be deliberated by elected officials. But they also ask whether, in the pursuit of executive power to correct the disadvantage, these nations face another danger—that they will cease to be democracies, no matter how well their foreign policy is conducted.

Most matters of policy do not raise national security risks: a White House decision to wiretap an American journalist, the invasion of the island of Grenada, a secret arms sale of defunct weapons. Each, however, has been justified on national security grounds. Indeed, decisions involving the highest stakes typically find President and Congress in a united stand: it is not in times of crisis but in times of calm that the debate is heard most clearly. Most decisions also allow time for the President to consult with a wide circle of advisers. In the Cuban Missile Crisis, perhaps the one event in recent American history posing a direct threat to the security of the United States, Kennedy took one week to make the decision in consultation with some two dozen advisers.[9] Key decisions by Eisenhower and Johnson on Vietnam,[10] by Reagan in Lebanon and Libya, by Bush in the Persian Gulf—all were weeks or months in the making. If presidents can handpick two dozen or so advisers, clearly they can include key committee members and leaders in this select grouping without compromising the nation's security in the process.

If Congress is criticized for not keeping secrets, the executive bureaucracy, too, has been a source of leaks of classified information, as presidents from Eisenhower to Bush were keenly aware of. Leaks of classified information within the executive branch have traditionally been used to mobilize media and public opinion in support of particular policies, or as a weapon in intra-bureaucratic factional battles. If there are a few occasions when presidents do not have time to engage congressional consultation, there are many occasions when they do. As foreign policy expert Miroslav Nincic argues, "Arguments applicable to infrequently occurring events should not be made to cover a much broader area of international behavior."[11]

In other words, on most matters of foreign policy in the past quarter of a century, it is not that the risks are so great or that the time is so short or that the secrecy is in danger of being compromised. The solemn debate continues, but the real issues have moved to another level—of executive convenience versus accountability. Most would grant that presidents must act unilaterally on some exceptional occasions, but who is to say when the boundaries are crossed? How do we distinguish matters of security from controversies in need of debate? When does executive prerogative become presidential convenience or worse? In Madison's words, when do the real dangers become the pretended ones?

Nor is it a coincidence that Secretaries of State so often argue that Congress should not meddle in foreign affairs. Congress should not meddle in State Department business, they are effectively saying, by demanding reports, questioning provisions, or making changes in normal routine. The President in these arguments becomes the shield behind which the agencies hide. In a verbal sleight of hand, "President" becomes "executive branch." While the rhetoric remains the same, the real issues have changed again, this time weighing bureaucratic convenience against accountability. "The business of Congress is to stay out of my business," CIA Director William Casey snapped to an audience in 1984. And when asked why he had withheld information from the intelligence committees, Vice Admiral John Poindexter responded, "I simply didn't want any outside interference."[12] Presidents can watch only a few issues at a time; so if Congress is warned away from "meddling," the Caseys and Poindexters are free from any interference by elected representatives in what they perceive as their business.

We need to ask, therefore, if there really is a struggle between the President and the Congress, if this popular wisdom is correct.

It gives comfort, certainly, by suggesting that our democratic officials are vigorous and alert. If President and Congress *fight* to make policy, they must care very much about these issues. Therefore we do not need to worry about them, but can debate the particular constitutional divisions. If the struggle is in large part illusory, we are missing the point. We not only must balance presidential power with safeguards against the abuse of that power, but ask about the proper divisions between bureaucratic and elected officeholders. We would have to ask how elected officials could be made as active as they seem to be and what institutional and electoral mechanisms could make them so. Attention would shift from general constitutional discussions to a closer look at the institutions themselves.

This book argues that the conflict is in large part an illusion, perhaps at times deliberately encouraged. We will find agendas filled with highly selected debates and symbolic issues, with demands for reports that are not read and tough restrictions with built-in escape provisions. The two branches support each other in this symbolic display, staging dramatic last-minute compromises or complaining about each other's usurpation or meddling. Officials hotly contest the restrictions and then invoke the escape clauses—routinely, year after year. Some work gets done, but overall there is more illusion and less policy making than meets the eye.

Why, for example, would William Casey and other administration officials go *four* times to Congress, with apologies, admitting they had lied again on the same issue? Each time, Congress expressed shock and outrage that it had been lied to, and then accepted the apology. (See chapter 7.) Why would Casey make the trip to apologize if he knew he was going to lie again? And why would Congress accept the apology each time without any improved guarantees? Do we elect officials who can actually be fooled four times in a row in the same way? It will become clear that both the CIA director and the intelligence committees he is lying to need each other and need the process to continue in the same way. Both need the illusion that intelligence activity is being watched by elected representatives in Congress.

SOME QUESTIONABLE ASSUMPTIONS

For all its importance, the current debate proceeds with little in the way of information. Central to the debate is the notion of an assertive Congress. Both sides assume that Congress became more active in foreign policy in the mid-1970s, a combined product of internal reforms and reaction against the presidency of Watergate and the Vietnam War. Since no equivalent countershift occurred, it must still be in the assertive phase.[13] Somehow twenty years of American history are telescoped, so that the Congress of the 1990s is still the Congress of Watergate, debating impeachment and passing the War Powers Act. Nothing has changed in the interim. The question then becomes whether this increased role is good or bad for the country.

Put in those terms, the debate misses the mark in several important ways. *First, it assumes that foreign policy is a single category, consistent in itself.* There are many kinds of foreign policy, however —war, diplomacy, trade, international development, foreign assistance. These policy areas vary in their stakes, in their visibility to the American public, and in their ties to domestic politics. It follows that Congress might be more assertive—and more changeable in its influence—in some of these areas than in others. The debate could change sharply depending on what we find the range and variation to be. If, for example, Congress defers to the President on matters of the highest stakes (a surprise U.S. attack), but insists on a role in the more normal course of policy making (a problem in the Caribbean), then claims of the need for executive secrecy and dispatch are greatly weakened. We should then be asking whether Congress should have more of a role in one area and less of a role in the other, if such debate were found to be necessary at all.

Second, *the debate assumes that the roles are adversarial*—that the two branches are locked in a struggle for power and that Congress as well as the President seeks predominance in foreign policy making. It is worth remembering that Congress is not a single entity but is composed of 535 members of very different points of view and widely differing constituencies. In the famous debate preceding the war in the Persian Gulf, 52 senators supported the President while 47 opposed him. The vote in the House was 250 to 183. The debate, like the vote, was sharply divided, ranging from those who equated the President with the nation to those who spoke of a separate congressional responsibility in considering matters of war. As one writer puts it, "Congress does not speak with one voice; it has no unitary position or statement of institutional interest."[14]

Moreover, to the extent it does speak with its many voices, the outcome is often to support the President, as it was in the Gulf debate. So Congress has repeatedly indicated that it does not want to see the CIA budget or know what that agency is doing. It has said that it does not have the information to question Pentagon decisions, and then has voted against gaining the information. It has asked to see all executive agreements, but has voted not to be able to agree or disagree with them. This does not sound like an organization hungry for more power, at least as far as foreign policy is concerned. Speaker of the House Thomas Foley was repeatedly asked by an interviewer after the Gulf debate why Congress did not itself declare war, which it had the constitutional power to do, but instead gave the President the discretion to do so. Foley called the decision the "moral equivalent" of such a declaration, but he never really answered the question.[15]

Third, *the debate assumes that the presidential role is known and active,* that the President equals the executive branch. Presidents are individuals, however, with the normal human limits on time and attention: for every item they are briefed on daily, scores of others will be decided elsewhere. Indeed, students of presidential decision making point out just how large is the gap between executive and presidential information.[16] It may be that *neither* the President nor Congress makes much of the nation's foreign policy. They are not natural antagonists in a fight for increased influence, but collaborators in a routine policy process whose origins are the bureaucratic agencies and the policies of the past. Claims of an adversarial relationship therefore obscure the real problem that no one is minding the store.

Dichotomies can be slippery when used to support the argument of the moment. The dichotomy of executive versus legislature includes people who are and are not elected in one branch and people who are elected in the other branch. It includes people who possess a great deal of foreign policy information (bureaucrats) and people (the presidents) who may have little information and are highly dependent on particular bureaucratic sources. Thus arguments about who should make foreign policy—those with more or less factual information or more or less democratic support—are wrongly cast as a battle between executive and legislature.

Finally, *the debate assumes that the congressional role is known*—that there has been a marked shift in policy followed by no further substantial change. To illustrate the confusion, imagine a president in the following situation. He seeks to expand foreign assistance to new regions of the world and to institute a limited degree of long-term aid to help in the nations' economic planning. Congress, however, refuses the request for long-term aid and lists more than a dozen countries for whom aid is prohibited. *That* will be the U.S. foreign policy on the subject, Congress asserts. The President is also trying to win a major treaty in the Senate. The treaty passes narrowly only after extensive lobbying with the Congress and close collaboration with two very powerful committees. Overall, the President gains a mixed record of victory on his foreign policy requests.

Who is the President confronting such an assertive Congress? The answer of course is Kennedy, in the 1960s, facing a Congress with both houses controlled by his own party. Has Congress become more assertive since that time or less so?

The notion of an assertive Congress is itself an assertion—stated as fact and not investigated. Oddly, no systematic comparison exists of congressional foreign policy action in the modern period. No one has actually researched systematically whether it has or has not changed. In a review essay on research in foreign policy making in Congress, political scientists James Lindsay and Randall Ripley describe just how small the body of literature is. While *commentary* on the congressional role abounds, few systematic studies exist, with most of these at least a quarter of a century old. Even when scholars do turn their attention to the subject, the authors observe, they do so less to add to our knowledge of the subject than to argue about Congress's constitutional prerogatives, debate whether Congress is gaining or losing power relative to the President, or dispute whether congressional action helps or hinders U.S. foreign policy.[17]

Past studies have looked at a small number of cases at one point in time. Holbrook Carroll studied the House Foreign Affairs Committee in the 1960s. Alton Frye and Thomas Franck and Edward Weisband looked at the newly assertive Congress in the 1970s. Charles Whalen, Jr., criticized House foreign policy making in the 1980s. Each book concentrates on its own time pe-

riod for the most part, drawing comparisons only by implication.[18] Although people have compared particular policies over
time—defense spending, oversight, the making of international
agreements—these studies primarily end with the 1970s.[19]

What then is the evidence for this heightened assertiveness,
supposedly lasting now for nearly two decades? There is little
clear evidence one way or the other. Circumstantial evidence
exists of course. Exhibit A is the War Powers Act of 1973, under which Congress sought to limit the President's war-making
powers. Under the statute, presidents must inform Congress
within forty-eight hours when U.S. combat troops are sent to foreign nations. This sets a sixty-day (or extended ninety-day) clock
ticking during which time Congress must act either to continue
or terminate the situation. Exhibit B is the internal changes in
the 1970s that increased staff, created a Congressional Budget
Office, and required that each committee designate a subcommittee for purposes of oversight. These reforms were intended
to strengthen Congress's policy-making capacity generally in its
interactions with the executive branch: by this reasoning, domestic policy should be as assertive as foreign policy. Since neither
the War Powers Act nor the internal changes have been revoked,
one can then argue—circumstantially—that the condition they
sought to create is continuing. One needs to assume, of course,
that the changes on paper were changes in fact, that Congress did
change its role in oversight and military involvement.

Many people discuss whether the sixty-day clock provision of
the War Powers Act is a good or bad thing. Few may know that the
provision is virtually unused. A president used it once—when the
use of force was already over. Congress invoked it once, a year after the force had occurred, and changed the clock to an eighteen-
month clock. On most occasions of force, the sixty-day clock is ig-
nored by both branches. Rather than disputing the value of the
provision, shouldn't we be asking why Congress is *not* using it, and
why it will do anything, even go to the courts, to avoid it? On a
closer look the circumstantial evidence is not that convincing.

For each example of the new congressional activism, one can
find an earlier matching example. Look at the nuclear-freeze
movement in Congress, someone might say. Here were members
of Congress during the Carter and early Reagan years willing to
make policy on a matter of the highest stakes. But look at the Joint
Committee on Atomic Energy during the early post–World War

II years, when the Committee felt the Atomic Energy Commission was not doing enough to build a nuclear arsenal or to keep the nuclear secrets. The Joint Committee engaged in hearings, forced the resignation of presidential appointees to the Commission, and harassed other commissioners until it finally got its way. Unlike the modern intelligence committees, the Joint Committee had no problem demanding information prior to actions taken on issues of the highest secrecy. Or, someone else might say, see Congress target particular missile programs, micromanaging defense. But see Kennedy try to cut the same programs or their predecessors against a then-reluctant Congress. Watch him walk Armed Services Committee Chair Carl Vinson around the Rose Garden until Vinson agreed to a compromise in one congress. (The proposal would be back the following year.) Look at Congress refusing Reagan aid for the Nicaraguan contras and see all the trouble that caused. Congress has always targeted nations that could or could not receive aid since the beginning of the foreign assistance programs. Few presidents persisted, however, as long as Ronald Reagan in the face of this opposition. The exercise not only shows the pitfalls of arguing from examples, it points to a dangerous foreshortening of our historical memories. People think Congress is different now because they do not know what it was like before.

And what is the "now" that follows this unremembered history of "before"? The "now" begins to stretch across a quarter of a century. Are writers in the 1990s signaling a current trend when they speak of the passage of the War Powers Act? Is the congressional assertiveness of the Nixon administration the same as that in the Bush or Clinton administration? Bush, we will see, not only compiled a new record for separate uses of force by a modern president but also scored other foreign policy victories in Congress. Clinton's air strike against an Iraqi intelligence headquarters in June of 1993 brought the expected immediate congressional support. Minority Leader Robert Dole was quick to approve. Even liberal and antiwar critic Patricia Schroeder (D., Colo.) found something to praise, observing that Clinton had spared civilian lives by not bombing during the day.[20] Perhaps there is more than one series of changes in this period that we should be remarking upon.

There is another difficulty with the evidence besides its failure to make comparisons across time. Expertise in policy and expertise in the institutions that make policy do not usually go together:

the policy people do not understand the institutions in depth while the institutional experts stay free of policy content. At the extreme, advice can be offered in which the wrong situation is perceived and the wrong prescriptions given. Students of Congress today do not talk about its assertiveness, they speak of its near-incapacity to make any decisions.[21] Students of the presidency discuss the malfunctions of executive decision making and the difficulty of bringing information to the White House level.[22] They suggest that war making is virtually the only area where presidents can act freely and the only one assured of public support.[23] This raises the risk that national security will be used as a cover for non-security-related issues, while it suggests that presidents are more active at some times and in some policies than in others. Again, the question is not which branch of elected representatives makes foreign policy, but whether either does.

Altogether, four patterns of foreign policy making are possible. In one type, an active president faces an inactive Congress. This is assumed to be the conventional pattern, engaged in before the mid-1970s: presidents propose new policies and Congress accedes in large part to the White House requests. In a second type, an active president faces an active Congress, in the reform pattern thought to be common in recent years. Presidents propose policies, but Congress opposes them or offers its own initiatives: controversy is the result. A third type, the reverse of the conventional pattern, would find an inactive president matched with an active Congress. The fourth type, virtually unmentioned, is the default pattern. Here, both President and Congress support past programs or fail to enact any program. The debate assumes we have shifted from type one to type two and argues about which is to be preferred. This book contends we are closer to type four. Some initial support for the argument is shown by the contexts within which President and Congress make their decisions.

The Congressional Context

The popular wisdom assumes increased congressional foreign policy activity from the middle of the 1970s. Yet, a closer look at Congress suggests influences working for and against activity that hold across time.

To begin, assume members of Congress can hold any of three

primary and overlapping goals, as Richard Fenno suggests.[24] They seek to be reelected, to make good public policy, and to gain influence, or prestige, within the institution. All members need to seek reelection of course, although some must pursue this goal more continually, more intensely, and with higher priority than others do. Yet, the senator with a six-year term and the safe House incumbent need to follow their own reelection routines, keeping in touch with local opinion, making visits home, attending the necessary fundraisers.[25] Indeed, they can be reelected, they would argue, because they keep in touch—that is, "represent"— so well. At the same time, members can pursue the making of public policy, primarily by work in committees and subcommittees. In addition, they can cosponsor bills, engage in a range of floor activity, and give interviews to the national media on issues important to them. Some members also pursue institutional prestige, working with the party leadership or gaining top seniority on committees, like a Carl Vinson in the 1960s or a Sam Nunn in the 1980s. The routes to influence in the contemporary Congress are more varied than in the past; yet, members as different in style and objectives as Thomas Foley and Newt Gingrich can seek and attain institutional prestige.

What can we expect of members, pursuing these goals, in the way of foreign policy making? Congressional interest in foreign policy should follow (1) the public's interest and opinion (reelection), (2) the interests of the committee experts (policy), and (3) the broader strategies developed by the party leadership (prestige). At any one time all of these influences can be operative: some policies would be pursued because they captured public attention; others because they represented long-standing interests of a few committee members; still others because they fit with the leadership strategies of the time. Leaders would be mindful of the larger party agenda, the extent of conflict expected in their own and the other chamber, and the party in the White House. For example, Congress should be more likely to "interfere and meddle" in foreign policy in times of divided-party control of the White House and Congress and on policies gaining broad agreement in the House and Senate.

These same influences, however, suggest that assertiveness will not be the congressional norm. Activity should not be expected in cases where House and Senate committee experts disagree, on issues the leadership feels it cannot address, and on many issues far from public attention. This is a legislative body where time and influence must be carefully expended, where conflict must be kept within tolerable levels, and where many other policies can fulfill the goals of members better than foreign policy programs do. Seen in this light, foreign policy making by Congress should be the exception and not the*rule.

It is also important to see the policy environments that Congress works within: the pattern of relationships formed as members work along with other policy makers.[26] These environments include the constituency, clientele groups, bureaucratic agencies, the congressional institution itself, as well as the presidency. So, members acting alone or as part of a committee might make tariff policy to support local products or work with lobbyists on Japanese-American trade policies. They might keep a watchful eye on agency programs, or help the institution manage conflict in conference or on the floor. One study group interviewed House members about their participation in matters of foreign policy. According to the majority of the members, the decision whether to participate or not was shaped by constituency concerns, while the extent of their participation was shaped by the Congress and by their own position in the institution.[27] Unlike the president-centered view popularized by news media and held by the public at large, *the President is not the center of the congressional universe.* (Some say it has no center—only an axis stretching from the home base to Capitol Hill.) It follows that decisions whether or not to act and how to act will be products of many separate influences and not primarily statements about presidential power.[28] Since many of these environments are stable, the decision not to take action need not mean acquiescence to the White House or a failure of congressional will. It can mean that a substantial number of members prefer the policy the way it is.

Most critically, the congressional environment will mediate how much policy-making activity can actually get done. Congress's diverse representational basis has always made stopping a policy easier than building the majorities necessary to pass a new one: that is, to get a bill that will pass in the House and Senate committees and in the two chambers. As one student of Congress summarizes in an article published in 1989:[29]

> Congress shows a disturbing tendency—not always, but often enough—toward . . . delay, incoherence, ineffectiveness . . . as it

grapples with public policy challenges. These failures can be traced in large measure to the generic legislative characteristics of Congress: its representativeness, its collegiality, its openness, and the nonspecialized nature of its membership. The viability of the activist model to which Congress ostensibly conforms is therefore called into question.

But as influence is further dispersed and decentralized by structural changes and reforms, this disturbing tendency for delay and ineffectiveness should *increase*. It will become more difficult to form and hold the necessary majorities to pass legislation. So Catherine Rudder, another congressional scholar, points out that tax policy became difficult to pass once it was brought outside the closed doors of the House Ways and Means Committee. The change increased the responsiveness of members to various interests but decreased the chances of any effective tax legislation.[30]

The changes of the 1970s—in staff, oversight, war powers— were part of a larger reform package engineered in the Senate and House, the Senate by 1972 and the House by the middle of the decade. The reforms made committee practices more democratic in the calling of meetings, designation of subcommittees, and election of subcommittee chairs. Both chambers introduced the secret ballot for the election of committee chairs, making the seniority rule less automatic as a selection criterion. An increase in the number of subcommittees meant that virtually all senators and one-third of the House members in their majority parties could have a subcommittee to chair. In matters of policy making, however, the two reform strands worked against each other. One set of reforms sought to strengthen the Congress in policy making in relation to the executive branch, while the other set of reforms decentralized influence to such an extent that it was difficult to make any policy. A committee chair in the pre-reform days, ruling his committee and protected by seniority, could fight the White House to a stalemate. The reforms took away this congressional power vis-à-vis the executive, in the interests of democratization. So Charles Whalen, Jr., subtitles his book on House foreign policy "The Irony of Congressional Reform." While each member was more able to take part in some policy making, the chamber as a whole was less able to make policy. As one senior House member remarked who had chaired a committee before and after the reform era, "Changes have slowed down the process . . . to a point where it is difficult to get anything done."[31]

These effects are seen throughout the Congress, as Norman Ornstein and colleagues point out. There is "more and more activity . . . combined with fewer and fewer products."[32] Dramatic increases in the number of staff hired, recorded votes taken, committee and subcommittee meetings held stand in marked contrast to the steady decline in the number of bills passed. While the staff hirings, votes, and meetings have now stabilized or been cut back, there is no corresponding upturn in the finished products of legislation.

We might therefore expect *less,* rather than more, foreign policy making in the post-reform Congress, although this effect could be moderated somewhat by the divided-party government characteristic of recent years. A further irony can be seen. While the reforms cut back the power of committees, they did not provide any alternative power center. Hence despite the increased fragmentation and dispersion of power, committees and the leadership remain the only routes for congressional foreign policy making. It is easier now to stop action, by passing controversial floor amendments or rejecting a conference committee report. Where action does go forward it will do so in large part by the efforts of the leadership and the committee members. In short, the impact on foreign policy making of constituency opinion, committee interest, and party leadership strategies should be seen in both pre-reform and post-reform years.

THE PRESIDENTIAL CONTEXT

When we say that the President makes foreign policy, what do we mean by "President"? Surely we do not mean the entire executive branch. Agencies have their own bureaucratic incentives and routines, while their ties to Congress and to clientele groups outlast any one sitting president. For every covert activity a president authorizes, we assume many others are going forward. Foreign policy is made within agencies in State, at points in Defense, Treasury, Agriculture, the Agency for International Development, the U.S. International Trade Commission, and the U.S. Information Agency, among others. It is made in the many intelligence agencies existing within, or outside of, the traditional department structures: the Defense Intelligence Agency, the Central Intelligence Agency, the National Security Agency, for a few examples. Presidents are chief in name only of such a vast operation, as writers have observed before. "Surely it is arbitrary to highlight the unifying quality of the President," constitutional scholar Louis Fisher states. "Just as easily we can look at the fragmentation of the executive branch and the many groups within it competing for control."[33]

Nor do we mean the individuals in office when we say presidents make foreign policy—a Mr. Ronald Reagan or Mr. Gerald Ford. Presidents are political experts, not foreign policy experts. They might not understand a key defense agreement or know much of the world's geography. Besides, their ceremonial schedule allows only selected attention to foreign affairs. Their speeches to groups, to take only one example—church groups, the Boy Scouts, the Future Farmers of America—average one for every working day through their first three years in office.[34] Other ceremonial events, travel time, the arranging of photo opportunities, meeting with interest-group representatives in the White House must also be scheduled. Naming an individual president as foreign policy maker is a convenience for the reporting of complex issues. It is also symbolically important and a psychological comfort for the American people to feel there is someone "in charge."

Ideally, when we say the President makes foreign policy, we refer to a small and shifting group of advisers who *meet with* the President: a National Security Adviser, a Secretary of State, a few other advisers depending on the occasion, plus two or three more in the White House who either attend the meetings or schedule the events. The group is larger or smaller depending on the President's preferences and his relations with advisers. The difficulty of this definition is that we cannot always know who is in the group or how well they carry messages to others. The power of appointment does not mean the power to make policy, only to have an influence on the policy, to a greater or lesser degree. When we say "the White House" or "the Bush administration," we include many people that the President never talks to or hears much about, and assume that some intermediary carries their insights to him and his wishes to them. This is a very large assumption, given the circles and rivalries of White House politics and the pressures of time and events. This convention has elements of convenience and psychological comfort also. Still, for this investigation, presidential policy includes White House or administration policy as long as we hold to the assumption that some direct and reasonably accurate communication between the President and his appointees has occurred. Since we cannot know the course of the decision process, any communication during or after the policy is formed is counted as presidential policy. Thus a president might give a speech defending a policy he had not known about until the speech was written. It becomes clear that any such working definition of presidential policy making will probably overestimate the amount of the President's activity.

We might then expect presidents to be active and personally involved in a highly selected set of issues: on matters involving military action abroad and those of personal and political importance to them. Presidents have their personal interests and projects, certainly, as the many presidential biographies point out. We think of Kennedy and the nuclear test ban treaty, or Reagan and Nicaragua. We also expect presidents to take action in their capacity as Commander-in-Chief, and in such matters as relations with the Soviet Union or other issues prominently featured at the time. There is a political agenda, too, that should get the President's attention. Just as economic manipulations can be made to accord with the biennial national election cycle,[35] so events and announcements in foreign policy can be timed with the same cycle and with fluctuations in public approval. One study, for example, shows that hard-line stands and peace initiatives with the Soviet Union occurred with different frequency before and after presidential elections. Other studies point out that uses of force abroad follow downturns in the economy at home much more frequently than can be expected by chance.[36]

This does not necessarily mean that presidents make the "most important" policy, leaving the details and routine to subordinates or congressional committees. Events can be set in motion and key policies defined long before they reach the President's desk, as we know from the various studies of decision making on Vietnam.[37] Front-page news, presented by journalistic definition as the most important events of the day, typically includes statements by administration officials. The converse is also true: what the White House says is most important is treated that way in news media reporting. While advisers would try to ensure that presidents were briefed on the most important problems, we cannot assume that is always the case.

Presidential policy making should then be most likely on a highly select range of issues, leaving a large part of policy outside the Oval Office. Indeed, the following chapter will show just how selective it is.

These are actually quite familiar arguments about the President and Congress, supported by a considerable institutional literature. They have not been applied to foreign policy studies, however. Combining congressional and presidential expectations, we would expect stability or inactivity, not conflict, to be the norm. If this is the case, the current debate masks the real problem that much of the nation's foreign policy might continue by its own momentum, unwatched by any elected representatives, a policy making by default .

DESIGN OF THE STUDY

This book provides the first accounting of congressional activity in a range of foreign policy areas, compares it with the President's role, and asks how it does, and does not, change across time. A picture emerges sharply at odds with the approved wisdom and unflattering to both elected branches. Therefore it is important to emphasize at the outset that this *is* a first study and to lay out the major arguments and materials to be used.

The popular commentary assumes that there has been a *change* and increase in congressional assertiveness since the 1970s and makes the broader characterization that Congress is now active and aggressive. It takes presidential activity for granted: hence the meeting of two active and aggressive branches creates the potential for "struggle." The book presents a variety of evidence, however, which does not support this assumption of struggle. This is the clearest empirical contribution of the investigation. The purported increase in assertiveness is not seen in the working agenda of chapter 2, in the cases of trade, intelligence, and arms sales of chapter 3, in support of the President in the uses of force (chapter 4), or in foreign aid authorizations or conference-committee compromises (chapters 5 and 6). Indeed, Congress's growing difficulties with budget making and the conference procedure suggest, if anything, a *decrease* in influence in some areas in recent years.

The second assumption—about some absolute level of assertiveness and activity—is of course harder to address. Nevertheless, an argument is developed from the same body of evidence that neither the President nor Congress is as busy as it might seem. In some foreign policy areas Congress has always been active across the thirty years of the study; in some areas the President is active. Each branch picks its issues carefully and sparely with a large remainder of issues left untended. The results—far from a struggle—create an illusion of activity that may be in the interests of both branches to maintain. This thesis is supported in part by a look at the small number of issues appearing on the working agenda from year to year (chapter 2), at the recurring problems of trade and intelligence policy (chapter 3), and at the imaginative ways Congress finds to seem active when no real compromise can be achieved (chapter 6). These latter include passing symbolic and nonbinding resolutions, calling for more information on issues it cannot make decisions on, and passing restrictions on authorizations that do not in fact restrict. The thesis is perhaps made clearest in the detailed discussion of the Nicaraguan case (chapter 7), where we find both President and Congress hotly contesting their prerogatives in one small area of policy in one tiny country of the world.

In the process we can compile a list of devices that carry on the illusion of activity: the selection of highly visible contests, especially by the President; the restrictions with their escape clauses; the demand for presidential reports. Indeed, the growth in reporting requirements reveals one of the most intriguing patterns to emerge from the study: how oversight is used to substitute for, rather than to extend, congressional action. When the new Congress cannot legislate, it asks for a report. So, increased oversight, designed to strengthen executive accountability, becomes a device to avoid legislative accountability. Everyone keeps busy. Congress writes in its reporting requirement and the executive, amid complaints of "micromanagement," routinely submits its reports.

A few features of the evidence should be made clear. People have looked at the congressional role in isolation and by examples at one point in time. This book will focus instead on cases spanning thirty years, from 1961 through 1991—before and after the

Vietnam War, with Democrats and Republicans in the White House, from the time of John Kennedy to George Bush. If there is a longitudinal trend at work, it should be observable here.

The evidence also allows us to identify a *universe of cases,* the comprehensive set of actions we wish to generalize about. Studies of American foreign policy to date have not said what the universe of cases might be.[38] Writers who talk about change while looking at only one point in time do not use a universe of cases, nor do those who select their examples from some unspecified larger set of cases. Needless to say, generalizations are hazardous when the universe is not known.

One universe of cases consists of "legislated" foreign policy, as debated by either the House or the Senate and subjected to a recorded vote. We can thus devise one measure of a "working agenda" for the congressional institution and isolate a smaller number of issues of "major legislation" (see chapter 2). This measure gives a sense of the diversity of policy being enacted as well as the stability of the agenda across time. Indeed, the agenda is much smaller than readers might suspect: approximately six to eight major pieces of legislation come before one of the chambers each year. These cases can be thought of as potential agenda, for President and Congress, at any one point in time. Congress might pay attention to arms sales, for example, in any one session or it might not. Activity, therefore, can be seen by the appearance of an issue on the actual working agenda, of either the President or Congress. Hence this activity can be compared between the branches, across time, and for different policy areas.

A second universe of cases consists of major military action engaged in by the United States. Since Congress itself compiles this record (see chapter 4), it has the advantages of being officially recognized and widely available. It should also be important to see Congress's own response to cases the institution identifies as significant uses of U.S. force abroad.

A third universe of cases consists of foreign assistance authorizations, with the documents compared across time and with presidential draft bills where available. (See chapters 5 and 6.) These authorizations comprise about thirty cases in the time period and issue primarily from the two foreign affairs committees. It is true that these two committees work closely with the leadership and with the money committees (Budget and Appropriations) in the annual appropriations process. Nevertheless, the two authorizing committees are considered the main source for substantive policy change. Traditionally, the authorizing stage has been used by the committees as an opportunity to review and debate the full range of foreign policy: hence the cases not only provide detail in one substantive area but a look at congressional activity more broadly. They give insight into presidential activity also, since, like Congress, presidents have used the foreign assistance program as a kind of multipurpose instrument of policy making.

A final feature of the evidence should also be noted. It offers a diversity of material, spanning the main areas of congressional research: floor voting, committee and leadership decisions, oversight, and conference-committee determinations. Overviews of the agenda and authorization decisions are supplemented by detailed discussions of particular policies. Conventional wisdom dies hard, if at all: hence those who might not be persuaded by one kind of evidence have several alternatives to choose from.

We can thus undertake a closer look at the nation's foreign policy, or at least that portion of it formally enacted and open to review. Supplemental evidence, as shown in the appendixes, is provided from hearings, from presidential positions on legislation, special messages to Congress and other activities, and speeches to the American public on foreign policy issues. Certainly, the evidence cannot systematically investigate informal activity. It must therefore exclude much of the negotiations conducted behind doors, covert activity in which the President is involved, leaking of White House positions to news sources. Nor does it include informal congressional activity—interviews, talk-show appearances, private negotiations. Unfortunately, no record is available to measure such activity across time, and some of it, by definition, could not be measured. It may be, then, that the formal record understates both presidential and congressional policy making. Or, again, it may understate a particular *illusion* of activity, as the events surrounding the Nicaraguan case suggest. All of the covert activity, interviews, secret negotiations, and the rest dealt with only one particular policy problem.

Since the two branches do not appear locked in a mythic struggle for power, both President and Congress must begin to ask what they are and should be doing. The public must learn to recognize the various devices of illusion and begin to separate substance from spectacle. So, a final chapter summarizes the patterns identified, draws the implications for "democratic" foreign policy making, and sets forth the prescriptions indicated and contraindicated by the study. Indeed, many of the familiar prescriptions offered by both presidential advocates and congressional reformers are contraindicated by these results. This should not be surprising. We have been chasing an illusion which is part of the problem we need to correct.

2

❖ ❖ ❖

THE
LEGISLATIVE
AGENDA

FOREIGN POLICY to many people means the military action that makes the front page. Beyond this dramatic use of force, however, lies a vast area of policy making. Government officials write treaties and trade agreements, spend billions on economic and military assistance, help shape international monetary policy, authorize the sale of arms abroad. The major decisions, taken primarily by legislation, affect the posture of the United States and its relations with the other nations of the world. Examples occasionally reach public attention—a controversial treaty, a question of sanctions, an investigation of illegal arms sales. Yet, for the most part the dimensions and character of this vast terrain remain uncharted. Before we can debate the role of Congress in foreign policy, we need to know what activities we are speaking about.

Once we sort out the mushrooming of trivial and symbolic business that has grown in recent years, we see Congress active across the time span on major policy questions and willing to oppose the President. Yet, in any one year only a few issues receive this serious congressional attention. Moreover, presidential attention varies greatly, leaving a majority of issues unwatched by either President or Congress. Thus a two-part illusion needs unraveling. On a range of foreign policy issues, neither President nor Congress is as busy as it might seem.

Exaggerated views of presidential power can dismiss these policies as unimportant. Presidents, after all, are able to spend discretionary funds or conduct secret negotiations independently of, and even in opposition to, the legislated policy. But while presidents can do these things, a more balanced assessment suggests that they do them at their peril, risking relations with Congress and jeopardizing their entire program. Institutional norms bring Republicans and Democrats together against assaults on the congressional prerogative; and a policy frustrated at one point will return to haunt the White House—in appropriations, authorizations, amendments to other legislation, or a congressional investigation. Certainly, Richard Nixon was in trouble in Congress well before the Watergate hearings for what was called backdoor spending. Ronald Reagan's second-term success rate in Congress, lowest of all the modern presidents,[1] was clearly not helped by the Iran-contra revelations. Foreign policy legislation, we will see, is sufficiently controversial that presidents cannot take it for granted that their own programs will prevail. They put their reputation at stake when they take positions on these bills, winning some and losing others. Interest groups, foreign and domestic, also appear to treat these policies seriously, given the amount of effort and money they spend influencing the outcome. Following these cues, we should assume the policies are important and need to be understood.

What *is* the foreign policy agenda as far as legislation is concerned? This apparently simple phrase is notoriously difficult to handle. Considered broadly, an agenda can be called the list of subjects or problems to which government officials, and people outside of government closely associated with those officials, are paying some serious attention at any given time.[2] However, even if this near-infinite array of subjects could be identified, it makes little sense in Congress where so much of the business—the bills submitted and the speeches made—has more to do with constituents and groups than with the passage of legislation. About one bill in ten succeeds in becoming law,[3] and the fate of most is known when they are first introduced. For the presidency, too, we need to separate those issues handled somewhere in the executive branch from those that the President must pay some personal attention to. Hence a narrower definition of a *working agenda* appears more useful for both branches.

For the President, the agenda includes those subjects the

President himself has discussed publicly—in speeches or messages to Congress. It also includes the congressional roll calls on which the White House formally records the President's position. These roll calls have traditionally been used to measure presidential activity and success in Congress. For Congress, we can take the agenda to be those subjects to which members of Congress, faced with a decision in the Senate or House, must pay serious attention. To be part of this working agenda, a bill must be formally before the Congress, with the members required to take a public position pro or con.[4] We thus distinguish the working agenda on the one hand from all legislation submitted, much of which has no chance of passage, and on the other hand from the set of bills actually enacted into law. We can further check these various agenda items, for the President and for Congress, against what commentators have described as the various accomplishments and legislative battles of the time. Together, these various measures should help us compare presidential and congressional agendas, look for change across time, and see the combined effect of activity between the branches.

CONGRESS'S WORKING AGENDA

The congressional agenda includes all bills and resolutions subject to at least one recorded vote (teller or roll call) in either the House or Senate that deal with the following subjects: relations, whether diplomatic or hostile, between the United States and other nations, war powers and intelligence activities, the prerogatives of President and Congress in foreign policy, membership or contribution to international organizations, and U.S. commitments and operations abroad. Excluded are appropriations bills making no substantive changes in foreign policy, defense procurement decisions that do not directly impact on foreign nations or organizations (a B-1 bomber or Trident submarine), immigration policy and treatment of foreign nationals within the United States, travel of committee members abroad. While the line between foreign and domestic policy is always hazy, the attempt is to be as inclusive as possible.

Despite this inclusiveness, we will see an agenda surprisingly small and stable across time. On the surface Congress is hard at work and increasingly active across the years. Beneath this superficial activity, however, we find few cases of substantive legislation and very few cases of new legislation. The patterns are similar in the House and Senate across the years.

The delineation of the agenda proceeds in two steps: first by isolating all bills which meet the criterion of floor decision in one chamber; and second by pruning from this list the various trivial resolutions and routine bills to obtain a list of major proposed legislation.

All Bills on the Agenda

A first mapping of the House foreign policy agenda is shown in table 2.1. The first column shows the average yearly number of bills subjected to a recorded vote for each administration from Kennedy to Bush. On the surface, the House appears to have increased its activity across time. The rate climbs from thirteen bills on the average in the Kennedy years to more than twenty in the early 1970s, reaching a high point of thirty-two in the Carter administration and falling back somewhat in the Reagan and Bush administrations.[5]

Is this the increasingly active Congress that the conventional

Table 2.1
The House Agenda

	Average Number Per Year			
	Bills	Bills Minus Resolutions	Funding Bills	Substantive Legislation
Kennedy	13	10	4	6
Johnson	16	14	6	8
Nixon	20	15	8	7
Ford	27	19	9	10
Carter	32	20	10	10
Reagan	26	13	6	7
Bush*	23	12	7	5

NOTE: The table lists all bills subjected to at least one recorded vote. Funding bills include authorizations and appropriations. Substantive legislation are the bills remaining when the resolutions and the funding bills are removed.

*The averages are based on the first three years of the Bush administration.

wisdom leads us to expect? As the second column of the table shows, much of this activity is attributable to resolutions, those statements of the "sense of Congress" which usually have no binding legislative authority. With the resolutions removed, the time curve looks very different: swelling from some ten bills as an annual average in the 1960s to more than twenty in the 1970s and then falling back again almost to its initial level. The same curve is seen for substantive legislation, in the final column of the table. These are the few bills remaining when the resolutions and the appropriations and authorizing legislation are removed. Beginning with six to eight cases of substantive legislation a year, the number reaches about ten in the 1970s, and then falls back to seven cases on the average in the more recent years, down to a new low point of five in the Bush administration. The most recent congresses are clearly no more active than those in the 1960s except for the matter of passing resolutions.

By this more refined picture, the increase in congressional activity is closely congruent with the decade of the 1970s. It becomes noticeable in about 1972 and has subsided by 1981,[6] although the substantive caseload is at no point sizable. Indeed, the last congress of the Carter administration (1979–80) shows almost twice as many bills as the first congress of the Reagan years (1981–82).

The resolutions which have so swelled the congressional workload deserve a closer look. In the decade of the 1960s these were in large part devoted to major issues. At White House request, Congress declared itself in favor of sanctions against Castro's Cuba. It disapproved Soviet action in Berlin, and twice gave the President authority to call up reserve troops during the Berlin crisis. The resolutions were not all crisis-related: the House also voted in support of restrictions on the importing of honey bees. Nevertheless, most of the resolutions were important enough for the President to take a position on. Kennedy, for example, took positions on seven of the eight House resolutions passed during his years in office, and won the vote he wanted on all of them.

In subsequent years, the number of purely symbolic resolutions increased sharply. Among the statements, the House condemned the Aldo Moro assassination, criticized the Soviet mail delivery, and asked repeatedly that Andrei Sakharov be released. It declared itself against international kidnapping, deplored the memory of Armenian genocide, and twice urged that the hostages in Iran should be released. The 1980s set a new record. In one year Congress praised the Philippines for lifting martial law, congratulated Habib for his efforts in Lebanon, and proclaimed Raul Wallenberg a U.S. citizen. In another year resolutions called for a safe environment for the Salvador elections, spoke out for two Russian refugee families, congratulated Thailand on its bicentennial, and proclaimed "Afghanistan Day" and "Dutch American Friendship Day." (One killjoy voted against this.) The change across the years can be seen in how important the White House considered these statements. In the 1960s presidents took positions on more than half the resolutions. By the 1980s the ratio was one in ten.

The substantive cases, in the final column of table 2.1, also should be looked at closely. Most of the major legislation shaping American foreign policy is in place by the end of the Kennedy years—the foreign assistance program, the Peace Corps, the Export-Import Bank, other international development programs. The Food for Peace program, passed in 1964, is expanded two years later to Food for Freedom, with its changed emphasis from surplus commodities to commercial exports. A major arms sale bill is written in 1968. While some major legislation is passed in the next twenty years—trade acts, war powers, the ending of the draft, an omnibus drug bill—most of the bills either *extend* the earlier legislation, often making country-specific changes, or devote themselves to very narrow topics: textile imports, quotas for duty-free rum, emergency relief for India, disaster assistance for Bangladesh, a new tuna agreement. At minimum, we can say that substantive legislation has not increased across time. In fact, it appears to have decreased substantially.

It is true that Congress can and does work hard on one or two pieces of legislation a year. Activity is not a matter of quantity of output alone. Also, as we will see later, most of the real changes in policy take place through the authorizing and appropriations processes, and these bills remain fairly constant in number across time. Nevertheless, the table helps to show that surface impressions can be misleading.

So, in the first three years of the Bush administration half of the legislation facing the House dealt with sense of Congress resolutions. Even the record low for substantive legislation is somewhat inflated by symbolic issues evoked by the Gulf War. Three of the substantive bills in 1991 concerned the awarding of medals for conduct in the war—one for the troops, one for Colin Powell,

Table 2.2
The Senate Agenda

	Average Number Per Year			
	Bills	Bills Minus Resolutions	Funding Bills	Substantive Legislation
Kennedy	10	8	4	4
Johnson	10	8	3	5
Nixon	14	12	7	5
Ford	18	11	5	6
Carter	19	13	6	7
Reagan	18	8	4	4
Bush*	15	8	5	3

NOTE: The table follows the definitions of table 2.1. A series of minor treaties, enacted together by one vote, is counted as one piece of substantive legislation.

*The averages are based on the first three years of the Bush administration.

Chairman of the Joint Chiefs, and one for General Norman Schwarzkopf. Needless to say, the votes were not controversial. Counting all resolutions, funding bills, and substantive legislation together, fourteen of the twenty-four House votes in 1991 dealt with the Gulf War.

The Senate agenda set forth in table 2.2 shows the same pattern, with a temporary increase in foreign policy bills accounted for mainly by resolutions. Omitting the resolutions, activity in the 1980s is the same as in the 1960s, about eight bills a year. Substantive legislation, shown in the final column of the table, increases slightly in the Ford-Carter period and then falls back under Reagan and Bush to a low point of four and then three bills a year.

While the Senate is more restrained than the House in its use of resolutions, the senior chamber has its share of bumper years. From an average of two resolutions in the 1960s, the Senate jumps to ten resolutions in 1980 and a high of *twenty-six* resolutions in 1987. A few are important and controversial: for example, votes on the Iran-contra investigation or the question of presidential compliance with the War Powers Act. Most of the resolutions, however, announce broad consensual statements and are typically passed by unanimous votes. Among the record-high twenty-six resolutions, the Senate expressed its support for the Philippine government of Corazon Aquino, disapproved of the collapse of elections in Haiti, supported democracy in South Korea, disapproved of the violation of human rights in the Soviet Union, and spoke against the Soviet presence in Afghanistan.[7]

The increased activity is similar in the House and the Senate. It appears limited to a particular point in time and follows the overall increase in the congressional workload.[8] The change is not specific to foreign policy, nor does it last—beyond the incidence of resolutions—into the 1980s. Indeed, the inflation of resolutions obscures what appears to be a downward trend in substantive bills in the most recent period. It also helps to mask how few pieces of foreign policy legislation are actually before the Congress.

Major Legislation

Even this fairly small agenda can be refined further to look for legislation that is widely held to be important or controversial or both. We can thus omit routine extensions of programs, commodity-specific trade and tariff legislation, and country-specific changes in foreign assistance where these do not involve major issues of the day. What remains are all new or revised legislation subject to controversy, the annual foreign and military assistance funding, major treaties, as well as any other bills closely associated with the President's program.[9]

As one can see in the summary table that follows, by this definition a very small number of bills are on the working agenda—about four or five bills each year. (A list of the cases is given in appendix A.) Moreover, the number has not changed substantially from the 1960s through the 1980s:

Years	Author/Approp.		All Other		Total	
	#	Average Per Year	#	Average Per Year	#	Average Per Year
1961–70	26	2.6	20	2.0	46	4.6
1971–80	25	2.5	29	2.9	54	5.4
1981–90	33	3.3	15	1.5	48	4.8

The number of cases remains fairly consistent across time, with a slight bulge in activity in the 1970s. One shift is evident: a much larger proportion of legislation in the most recent periods occurs through the appropriations and authorization processes. Funding bills, becoming ever more difficult for Congress to manage, have increased, while substantive legislation has decreased. This shift, and its implications, will be discussed at a later point.

Mayhew's Classification of "Important" Legislation

We can compare the agenda with David Mayhew's classification of important legislation: i.e., major bills actually passed into law.[10] For this universe of cases Mayhew draws on annual journalistic assessments of important bills passed, supplementing these with scholarly sources and other retrospective evaluations where possible. Mayhew includes both domestic and foreign policy cases, although he admits that some legislation, such as foreign aid and defense bills, would be missed when passed as part of larger routine programs. Also excluded would be important provisions included in the omnibus budget legislation of the 1980s. The Boland provisions on Nicaragua or the Cooper-Church restriction on Vietnam, for example, would not be included.[11] Since much of foreign policy legislation as we will see is passed as part of the authorization process, it is not surprising that Mayhew's list emphasizes domestic over foreign policy. The list includes 267 pieces of important legislation in the period from 1947 through 1988 or about thirteen for each two-year congress. Of the thirteen, 1.3 enactments on the average deal with foreign policy.

While Mayhew's list is very different from the agenda in this study, it, too, shows no change in activity over time. In the period of this study, from 1961 through 1988, a Kennedy congress leads in important foreign policy legislation, with a Nixon and a Reagan congress tied for second place. In 1961–62 Congress passed the Alliance for Progress, the Peace Corps bill, a trade expansion act, and a major foreign aid bill. In 1973–74 Congress passed the War Powers Act, a trade act, and a revision of foreign assistance. In 1987–88 Congress passed a trade bill, the INF treaty with the Soviet Union, and a bill concerning Japanese-American reparations from World War II. The other congresses in the time period either passed one piece of legislation or none.[12] Thus particular congresses in the sixties, in the seventies, and in the eighties might be called equally active in passing important foreign policy bills.

THE PRESIDENT'S AGENDA

The legislative agenda, of course, will be influenced by the President's program. Some presidents have more ambitious legislative programs than others, and some are more willing than others to take actions to shepherd their programs through. Students of the presidency point out the great variation across presidents in matters of style, interest, personality, legislative skill. These differences will be increased by the political context the presidents must work within: their political party, the number of same-party members in the Congress, the support in the public opinion polls. In other words, one cannot say that the President sets a legislative agenda without asking which president and on which subject. Presidents vary in their priorities, in their personal lobbying activity, and in success.

Overall, Democratic presidents in the modern period, facing same-party congresses, have taken more positions on legislation than their Republican counterparts. The difference holds for the House and Senate and for foreign as well as domestic policy.[13] At the extreme, on the House roll calls considered here, Carter takes more than double the number of positions that Nixon takes in his first term.

The success rate of presidents on roll calls in Congress also varies with party control.[14] In the House presidents who belong to the same party as the majority in Congress show average success rates in the middle seventies while opposite-party presidents (who are all Republicans) average in the low sixties. In other words, they win 60 or 70 percent of the roll calls on which they take a position. The same division is seen in the more supportive Senate. The same-party presidents average close to 80 percent success, while the opposite-party presidents average in the middle 60s. No trend is evident. Carter shows the same success rate as Johnson in House roll calls, while Reagan wins more in the Senate in his first term than former Senate majority leader Johnson won: 84 percent compared to Johnson's 72 percent.[15]

Presidents vary also in the kind of priorities they set—the signals they send to Congress and others about what is personally important to them.[16] An indication of these priorities is given by the public acts presidents take directly: speeches to the nation on foreign policy, and major messages to Congress requesting legislation.[17] There are limits with this measure, of course, as there are with any attempts to measure an agenda. It cannot tell us what is happening behind the scenes and what the presidents are really worrying about. Nor does it tap the kind of priorities reflected in administration budget requests. Nevertheless, these public acts can be more revealing of presidential activity than the overall roll call measures used so widely. They reveal what the presidents are willing to spend their attention on and tie their reputation to. Speeches or direct and formal requests to Congress are not cost-free. They show, for example, that Kennedy was willing to give three nationally televised addresses dealing with the controversial nuclear test ban treaty, and that Reagan spoke on Nicaragua and related subjects almost exclusively over the course of three years. A summary of these particular individual acts is shown in table 2.3.

Presidents send about two to three messages to Congress a year and speak rarely to the nation on these issues, at the most about once a year. Kennedy and Carter rank relatively high on both dimensions. Johnson is high in legislation and low in speak-

Table 2.3
Presidential Activity in Legislated Foreign Policy: Number of Actions per Year

President and Years	Messages to Congress	Nationally Televised Addresses
Kennedy (3)	3.0	1.0
Johnson (4)	3.3	0
Nixon I (4)	4.3	0
Nixon II (1.5)	3.3	.8
Ford (2.5)	1.6	0
Carter (4)	3.0	1.0
Reagan I (4)	1.8	1.3
Reagan II (4)	1.8	1.0

NOTE: Excludes speeches and messages relating to hostilities abroad or the use of force by the United States. Johnson is counted from the time of his first election. The activities are compiled from the *Public Papers of the Presidents*, various volumes, Kennedy through Reagan.

ing, while Reagan is the reverse. Ford is low in both messages and speaking. Omitted from the table are the speeches on international hostility and the use of force by the United States. Kennedy gives four speeches on these subjects, while Reagan gives four also, in his first term. Nixon gives *eleven* speeches in his first term on the war in Southeast Asia. Johnson, in contrast, between 1965 and 1968 gives one.

The public might be more familiar with presidents speaking on international crises, but it does hear from time to time about the nation's legislative needs. Kennedy talked about the nuclear test ban treaty. Nixon proposed his Vietnamization program and terms for peace in Vietnam. Carter talked about treaties and international agreements: the Panama Canal, the Camp David treaty, implications of the Vienna Summit, and SALT II. Reagan spoke about his Star Wars defense program and on arms-limitation agreements with the Soviet Union. He spoke several times on aid to Nicaragua.

The messages to Congress show a somewhat larger agenda. Kennedy sent annual messages on foreign aid as well as requests for trade agreements and the test ban treaty. Johnson also sent annual messages on foreign aid, requests for additional assistance to Southeast Asia, and messages in support of Kennedy's Peace Corps. He requested special funding in preparation for a Latin American summit meeting. These messages, of course, comprise a small percentage of the domestic agenda that Johnson was writing to Congress about. In 1967, for example, when he sent four foreign policy messages, he sent eleven on specific domestic programs: natural resources, space, crime, youth, the elderly, veterans, consumers, education and health, community work programs, urban and rural poverty, and equal justice.

Nixon sent several messages on foreign aid, a draft-reform bill, and a major trade bill. Ford asked for supplementary assistance for Vietnam and Cambodia and an administration-sponsored reform of the intelligence agencies. Carter sent messages on all his treaties and asked for special foreign assistance. While Reagan sent a trade-bill request and messages on the arms-limitation agreements, he concentrated on Central America: the Caribbean Basin Initiative, special aid to Central America, and several separate requests on aid to Nicaragua. Overall, on legislated foreign policy, the presidential agenda looks narrow indeed.

THE AGENDA ACROSS TIME

We can now see how this very limited number of issues, raised by President or Congress or both, work together to shape the agenda across time. Kennedy sought an expanded foreign assistance program which would have a higher ratio of economic to military aid than had been provided in the Eisenhower years. He proposed a Peace Corps, a cadre of young American volunteers who would put their resources and skills to work in poorer nations. The Peace Corps, first advanced by the candidate in the 1960 election campaign,[18] became one of his first proposals to Congress upon taking office. Another idea from the campaign was to strengthen ties between the U.S. and the other nations of the Western Hemisphere: there would be an Alliance for Progress and U.S. funds that would support developing Latin American nations. The Alliance was mentioned in the inaugural address and officially launched in March of 1961. Kennedy convened the ambassadors from the Latin American nations to hear his ten-point plan and followed the speech with a special message to Congress requesting funds.[19]

These three programs—foreign assistance, the Peace Corps, and the Alliance—would continue to have priority throughout Kennedy's years in office. He also sought to make initiatives to Communist bloc countries in Eastern Europe. In the last year of his administration, he initiated, negotiated with the Soviets, and brought before the Congress, a nuclear test ban treaty.

Congress, however, was not a passive partner in these expanded foreign policy initiatives. With some members deeply suspicious of international programs, and especially foreign spending programs, Congress negotiated with Kennedy dollar by dollar and step by step. Kennedy got his Peace Corps and initial Alliance funds. The Foreign Assistance Act of 1961 followed the outlines of Kennedy's draft bill, although Congress adjusted the funding, added restrictions, and required annual authorizations against the President's request. At the same time, Congress reorganized the Arms Control Agency and rewrote an agriculture assistance bill. It said that American foreign policy would not include aid to Poland or easing of trade barriers with the nations of Eastern Europe. It passed foreign aid restrictions in 1962 and 1963, cutting the overall request each year by 18 percent.

The normal liaison with the Congress became more urgent in 1963 with the negotiations for a test ban treaty with the Russians. While one Kennedy team negotiated with the Soviets, another took on the equally formidable task of convincing the United States Senate. The White House lobbied the Senate carefully, briefing key committee members at all steps along the way, with Kennedy himself on the phone to individual senators. The White House also prompted the formation of a "Citizens Committee for a Nuclear Test Ban," and the President twice addressed the nation, arguing for the importance of the treaty.[20] While Kennedy won the two-thirds vote he needed for the treaty, the victory was at a high cost of presidential effort and attention.

Johnson, too, appears active and successful in relation to many of the other presidents. Nevertheless, many of his foreign policy requests simply continued Kennedy programs. Johnson's priorities, of course, lay more with the passing of domestic legislation. Pressured by this agenda as well as by the war in Vietnam, Johnson understandably had little time left for other foreign policy legislation: his messages to Congress on foreign policy are a very small fraction of his total legislative requests. Indeed, his clearest legislative success in foreign policy would become his gravest burden: the 1964 congressional resolution supporting the SEATO nations, otherwise known as the Tonkin Gulf Resolution. Speeches to the nation suggest no other priorities: Johnson is the lowest ranking of the modern presidents in all speeches to the nation and in foreign policy speeches as well.

His success rate, too, should be looked at carefully. Congress was growing increasingly unhappy with the foreign aid program during the Johnson years. Some members worried that foreign aid lay the groundwork for future defense commitments; others felt the nation had become overcommitted generally in such programs.[21] Foreign aid, in any case, became an important focus of the congressional agenda. While administration requests were passed with only minor cuts in 1965 and 1966, Johnson, ever attuned to congressional grumbling, had pared his requests to the minimum, reducing them each year from the preceding levels. In 1966 Johnson asked for a separation of the economic and military assistance bills and for multiyear authorizations. Congress kept the two bills together and gave a one-year authorization. The programs picked up new congressional restrictions from year to year, and further limits on the President's discretionary authority.

They were cut further in 1967 and deeply cut—by 29 percent—in 1968. The authorizing committees would cut the requests, and then the appropriating committees would cut them further.

Johnson did try to get from Congress a statement of increased economic support to bring with him to the Latin American summit meeting in Punta del Este, Uruguay, in 1967. The House passed a mild resolution of support, but the Senate Foreign Relations Committee, increasingly disturbed by the war in Vietnam, was less willing to help the White House. The statement prepared by the committee was so weak as to be termed "worse than useless" by the administration.[22] Johnson went to the summit without congressional endorsement.

At the same time, Congress was busy conducting major hearings on the Vietnam War, on U.S. arms sales, on the nation's role in the United Nations and in NATO. The arms sales hearings, held in the Senate Foreign Relations Committee, made public the scope of the U.S. arms sales program, pointing out that the United States had helped to arm both sides in the Arab-Israeli war of 1967. The hearings led to restrictions added to several bills, and a new arms sales program was passed in 1968. In this period Congress also wrote, with the help of the various relevant departments, an expanded agriculture-assistance program. Johnson took a position supporting the bills, but there is no evidence of any other presidential involvement.

Johnson did win, against major Senate opposition and by a very narrow vote, a consular treaty with the Soviet Union, which outlined procedures for the operation of consulates in each country if and when such consulates were established. After two years of congressional opposition, he also won some loosening of trade barriers with Soviet bloc nations, a program for which Kennedy had fought in vain. The House blocked the Johnson policy with a vote on an Export-Import Bank bill; the Senate weakened the restriction; and the conference weakened it still further. A House vote to reject the conference report failed only by a very narrow margin. Since House members do not normally challenge their conference reports, the congressional action hardly signaled an open door for the Johnson administration on East-West trade.

This conflict in the 1960s is worth attention. Congress was hardly being acquiescent when it made Kennedy fight for his special programs or embarrassed LBJ at Punta del Este. Nor was the Congress concerning itself with minor or trivial matters during this time. Issues included the nation's conduct of a war, its role in the NATO alliance, relations with the Soviet Union and the nations of Eastern Europe, the commitment to foreign assistance, and the impact of arms sales in the Middle East and Latin America. Indeed, this congressional record in the middle to late 1960s will not be easily matched in the later years.

While the Nixon years would bring more dramatic conflicts in foreign policy, it can be argued they were differences of degree rather than kind. Unlike Kennedy and Johnson, Nixon faced an opposing-party congress and a heightened public opposition to the war in Vietnam. By his second term the Watergate scandal would bring the White House to a new low of public support. The same congress that made decisions in the earlier years could thus be expected to be more critical of presidential policies under these circumstances, arguing that it was merely reflecting public opinion in the process.

It is interesting that most of the foreign policy Nixon is known for—whether in Vietnam or in China or in the Soviet Union— minimized the need for congressional support. Nixon picked his issues carefully: draft-reform legislation, the Vietnamization program, a proposal for foreign aid reform, a trade bill. He took the fewest positions on controversial legislation of all the modern presidents. The White House, for example, did not record its position on the repeal of the Tonkin Gulf Resolution or limits on troops in Cambodia and Laos. The few positions Nixon took on roll calls came largely on broadly consensual votes.

In Congress, most of the major funding legislation from 1969 to 1973 was debated in the context of the war in Southeast Asia. This, along with the broader issue of presidential war powers, was becoming the congressional agenda. Most of the legislation, too, was accompanied by some restrictive action in at least one chamber. Administration programs were held up months to a year as Congress debated the war and reviewed the future of U.S. commitments abroad, the foreign aid program generally, and the need for limits to presidential discretion. Foreign aid, military sales, even defense procurement and the Peace Corps staggered back to the White House after their congressional battering with funds slashed, restrictions added, and new reporting requirements.

So in 1969, with no major controversial legislation proposed by the White House, Congress cut defense procurement and the Peace Corps, while the Senate passed a resolution affirming the congressional role in making national commitments. In 1970, again with only routine administration requests, Congress repealed the Tonkin Gulf Resolution, restricted the use of American troops in Cambodia and Laos, and warned the President in passing a supplemental foreign aid authorization (cut below requested levels) that it must be notified before aid of any kind could be sent to Cambodia. By 1972 it added restrictions to the foreign military sales authorization, against objections by the White House, and told the State Department that it must see the texts of all international agreements. State had opposed the provision, but withdrew its opposition in the face of near-unanimous Senate approval. Congress took a close look at authorizations for Radio Free Europe and Radio Liberty, programs funded covertly for years by the Central Intelligence Agency. In 1973 Congress broadened its restrictions on a supplemental appropriations bill, banning combat activity "in or over or off the shores of" Cambodia, Laos, and North and South Vietnam. Congress also passed the War Powers Act.

All this action occurred in response to routine and minimal White House requests. In some of the few legislative successes during this time, the draft-reform legislation was passed and the Salt treaty was successfully negotiated. Still, the treaty had been submitted and pending since the Johnson administration, and compromises were necessary to secure the necessary two-thirds Senate vote. The Nixon administration did work to put together a trade-reform policy. However by the time the trade bill had been debated twenty months in Congress, the Trade Reform Act was rechristened the Trade Act. This was appropriate, since much new legislation had been written into the bill and most of the reforms had disappeared.[23]

Some people point out that congressional opposition to the war was weak and late, and that for all its activity, Congress never actually cut off funds for the war until the peace talks were under way. While it demanded to see executive agreements, it demurred from giving itself power to overturn the agreements. Strong action by one chamber was weakened in the second chamber and eliminated in conference, in a pattern we will see more of later. Nevertheless, it is probably easier to argue that Congress did enough to make its message clear and helped to hasten the administration's winding down of the war. Certainly, on *legislated* foreign policy, Congress was the more assertive of the two branches.

The pattern changed again in the years after Vietnam and Watergate, giving a classic illustration of compromise between President and Congress. These compromises continued even though the various presidents differed greatly in activity and success. The scope also narrows—in the Ford and Reagan presidencies and in the congresses of the period. It appears that both President and Congress are picking their issues carefully.

Of all the presidents Ford had the least supportive conditions to develop a foreign policy agenda. He was a nonelected president, with a strong Democratic majority arrayed against him in Congress, and only twenty-nine months in his term. Given these conditions, it is not surprising that he ranks as the least active and successful of the presidents. Yet, he managed to hold threatened reforms of the intelligence agencies to a minimum, at a time when the public was hearing about agency abuses. He won a major arms sale package, although Congress fought for two years on the question of military assistance to Turkey. After a compromise in 1974, the White House lobbied strongly for the package, which resulted in a partially lifted ban in 1975. An administration-proposed refugee-assistance bill for South Vietnam was passed, although Congress set a ceiling on its funds and rejected the military aid component. Congress also set broad presidential reporting requirements.

At the same time, Congress could claim it was being vigorous and effective too. It was investigating the intelligence agencies, watching the arms sales, and being extremely interested in any aid to Vietnam. The restrictions were not merely a matter of congressional budgetary tinkering. Congress had come to believe, since a Senate Foreign Relations Committee study in the 1960s, that foreign aid was a wedge in the door that led to later military commitments. In the wake of the Vietnam War, Congress was saying never again.

While Kennedy had struggles along with his successes, Ford had successes in the midst of the conflicts and limitations of his term. Indeed, within a few years after the crises of Watergate and Vietnam, arms sales, intelligence policy, and the use of force were primarily back under executive direction. Congress, for its part, would pick its issues: the sale of arms to one country, limitations on aid to Vietnam (now that the war and the controversy were over), committees to receive intelligence reports. Congress could continue to appear vigilant, but the scope was narrowing from the time of the Nixon administration. This, too, was a compromise that both branches appeared willing to pay.

Compromise continued in the Carter years, despite a sharply accelerated White House agenda. In the breadth of the requests demanded from the White House, the Carter administration is most comparable to the Kennedy years. Indeed, many have criticized Carter for trying too much, for being overcommitted in both foreign and domestic agendas.[24] Foreign policy was debated between Congress and the White House on Latin America (aid to Nicaragua, the Panama Canal); the Middle East (arms sales, aid to Israel and Egypt); Africa (human rights violations, the importing of Rhodesian chrome); the Soviet Union (a Salt II treaty); and Communist China. Carter apparently wanted both the SALT II treaty and the Panama treaties in his first year in office, against the advice of some who thought the President should postpone the controversial canal treaties to a second term.[25]

On the positive side of the scorecard, Carter got the necessary Israeli-Egyptian aid from Congress that allowed him the major foreign policy victory of his administration, the Camp David accords. He won his arms sales proposals and a modest foreign aid reorganization bill. The Israeli-Egyptian aid—the "price" of the peace treaty—was no small legislative matter, totaling $4.8 billion of grants, arms credits, and direct military assistance, in the first year alone.

Senate William Proxmire and a few others pointed out that supplying military assistance to two ancient foes might not be the best way to secure peace in the Middle East. "The notion that we must provide military assistance to [these] nations," Proxmire stated, "is precisely what has led us down this long and bloody and reprehensible road of providing the weapons of death and destruction in the name of peace." Yet, Carter himself and his aides lobbied vigorously in Congress during and immediately after the Camp David meetings.[26] The treaty was signed and announced to the world on March 26, 1979. In April Carter formally asked Congress for the necessary initial appropriations, and by July the administration was beginning the series of promised arms deliveries. This was not only a personal victory for Carter, but a major commitment of U.S. policy in the years ahead, and a large chunk of the military assistance funds. Even in the budget austerity of the Reagan years, the Camp David bill was still being paid. If we are looking for illustrations of an "acquiescent" Congress, one of the best examples is found in 1979. Carter, quite rightly, gained credit for his statesmanship in arranging the Camp David accords, but Congress was quick to give him what he needed to do so.

In more mixed results, Carter achieved the Panama Canal treaties only after accepting restrictive amendments requiring additional negotiations with Panama; and he won some heavily restricted aid to Nicaragua. Although Carter asked for rapid action, Congress delayed seven months. On the negative side, Carter did not get his Salt II treaty, which was finally withdrawn in 1980 before the ratification vote. And, while the administration pursued detente with Communist China, the Congress wrote separate legislation for the Taiwan government. Carter was forced to sign the bill.

Unlike Carter, Reagan was more selective in picking targets of opportunity in Congress. The result is an uneven record of White House attention to legislation across the eight years. The uneven record is underscored by the irony that Reagan's two most dramatic successes in Congress appear to have opposite policy objectives. He began his term with calls for a major rearmament, primarily in relation to the Soviet Union. In speeches in the campaign, the inaugural, and the first economic message to Congress, Reagan called on the nation to correct "a decade of neglect."[27] The budget proposals alone, largely accepted in Congress, produced a 19 percent increase in the military aid component of foreign assistance between the years 1981 and 1984. The same policy directed a greatly expanded arms sale policy. Reagan then ended his term with the signing of the INF treaty, limiting intermediate- and short-range nuclear force missiles by the United States and the Soviet Union. In the spirit of *glasnost,* the treaty had little difficulty in Congress, especially since many congressional Democrats had been calling for arms limitation since 1982. People found out that the Cold War was over when the nation's new armaments were in place.

Other White House proposals did not fare as well. The Caribbean Basin Initiative, encountering opposition in Congress, was passed in part and rejected in part. The plan for Radio Marti (to broadcast to Cuba) was delayed two years and then compromised. Military aid to El Salvador was compromised in 1983, the Reagan administration asking for no restrictions and the Congress wanting to cut off the funds. When Congress remained unhappy with the continuing human rights violations, it cut the military aid request by 40 percent. Some administration arms sales proposals were passed (AWACs for the Saudis: AWACs, or the Airborne Warning and Control System, are radar command planes), while others were postponed (arms for Jordan). Still others were withdrawn (missiles for the Saudis and Jordan) in the face of sure congressional opposition.

The arms sales provide a good illustration of executive-legislative compromise in the Reagan years. On the first successful AWACs sale, the White House joined in all the lobbying that was going on, by personally lobbying individual members. Some observers called it horse trading: a hospital for one, a coal-power plant for another, a U.S. Attorney appointment for someone else. The White House efforts to influence Congress and public opinion went on for five months, in what House Speaker Thomas (Tip) O'Neill called "an awesome display of power."[28] The bill finally passed in the Senate by three votes. Later in the term, a different kind of trading went on. Faced with stiffer congressional opposition—to the Saudis and to any policies coming from the White House—the Reagan administration traded down: in 1986, it took out the F-15s and the M-1s to keep the Sidewinder and Harpoon missiles in the bill; in 1986 it dropped several more weapons to get a few replacement F-15s through.

Support for the *contra* fighters opposing the Sandanista regime in Nicaragua was clearly one of the highest priorities of the President, given the number of speeches he personally devoted to it, and the other actions of the administration, including the illegal ones. Reagan called the contras "the moral equal of our Founding Fathers" and donned his T-shirt reading "I'm a contra, too." Administration officials appeared in print and on the airwaves asking members of Congress whose side—in the fight between communism and freedom—they were on. [29] Nevertheless, military aid for the contras was fought in Congress year by year and vote by vote. While it was never clear what Congress might do on the *next* contra vote, the end result was that Reagan did not get the support he asked for.

Observers have described the "sparring" in the early years in which "the Administration and . . . Capitol Hill tried to outmaneuver each other and wound up making compromises that merely postponed decisions on the basic issues."[30] By the second term, however, conflict between Reagan and the Democratic Congress, spurred on by the revelations in the Iran-contra scandal, was out in the open. The White House responded by withdrawing some of the more controversial policies and compromising others. In 1985, faced with the threat that Congress would pass sanctions against South Africa, the Reagan administration reluctantly imposed its own sanctions. The fight in Congress was seen as forcing Reagan's hand. By 1986, still unhappy with Reagan's apartheid policy, Congress passed another sanctions bill. When the White House vetoed that bill, Congress successfully overrode the veto, the first successful occurrence of an override on foreign policy since the War Powers Act of 1973.

For another example, a normally routine State Department authorization became the focus in 1987 of a whole range of issues troubling the Congress, including, but by no means limited to, embassy security leaks in the Soviet Union and the fact that an Assistant Secretary of State had lied to Congress on Iran-contra. Eighty-six amendments were added to the bill. State got an authorization, of course, but with major substantive restrictions. State also had to prepare more than 170 position papers for the bill to be ready for conference.[31]

Like Nixon, Reagan cut his legislative agenda in the second term to preserve at least some congressional success. But at the same time, Congress was trying to hold the line on issues—aid to the contras, antiapartheid sanctions, El Salvador, arms sales. Even the INF treaty, preceded by strong support in Congress for arms limitations, owed at least as much to Congress as to the White House for its success. As late as 1987, frustrated with the lack of White House action, Congress threatened to put SALT II type constraints in every available budget measure.[32] In short, Reagan came late to the consensus that was already building in Congress and the public. It would be difficult to say who won and who lost in the Reagan years in the struggle between the branches.

All of this sparring was accompanied by a large amount of public activity and posturing. The sanctions bill alone occupied both branches for much of 1985 and 1986, and provides a nice illustration of the activity in these years. Amidst public and media outcries against the apartheid policies of the South African government and the repressive measures used by that government in putting down rebellion, members of Congress began to push for a stronger antiapartheid policy. These members criticized the Reagan administration for its policy of "constructive engagement," a policy which attempted to promote changes through diplomatic channels while maintaining good relations with the repressive government. Frustrated by the lack of response of the White House and aware of the public outcry, both chambers of Congress passed sanctions against the South African government. A conference committee met to reconcile the differences in the two bills, and, despite threats of a presidential veto, constructed a compromise which should be able to pass both houses. This, then, was to be a congressional policy initiative.

The White House, however, engaged in activity of its own. First it used the threat of presidential veto against the sanctions bill. When that did not appear to be sufficiently prohibitive, it announced its own sanctions policy, much weaker than the proposed congressional bill. The White House also lobbied the Republican Senate leadership and other Republican senators to support the administration's sanctions, a lobbying effort that would in fact be successful. All this represented time and the expending of enormous political currency on the part of the Reagan administration.

The scene then shifted back to the congressional activity and the Senate's response to the conference committee report. Although conference reports are almost always accepted by the respective chambers, this report became subject to filibustering, parliamentary maneuvers, and a whole set of dramatic and bizarre actions before it was finally laid to rest and allowed to die at the end of the session. When the Democratic leadership tried to break the filibuster by an ingenious parliamentary maneuver, the Republican leadership countered by noting that the conference report had "disappeared" from the Senate chamber. It had in fact been removed by Richard Lugar (R., Ind.), chairman of the Foreign Relations Committee and himself a member of the conference who had written the report. The Democrats protested vocally and at length, but the end result was the agreement to avoid further filibusters and let the report die. All of these antics of course were given extensive media coverage.

Congress would pass another sanctions bill in the following year and manage to override a presidential veto. In the meantime, the supporters of sanctions consoled themselves that they had forced the President's hand. It is hard to fault either branch for its vigor and energy on this issue, but when all the activity was over, a one-time limited sanctions bill was the result.

Ironically the most recent administration shows some of the clearest signs of a *conventional* pattern, of presidential influence and congressional support. George Bush won the controversial vote on the use of force against Iraq. He also won his choice of CIA director Robert Gates, and a close vote on extending fast-track trade procedures. He held the line against those in Congress who wanted to sanction China for human rights abuses, following the uprising in Tiananmen Square. He secured more leeway for presidents in conducting covert activities without informing Congress. He successfully vetoed a bill on textile quotas. While he signed what was considered by some to be a routine State Department authorization, he announced that he might "ignore" at least nine of its provisions, which he said interfered with his constitutional powers to conduct diplomacy.[33] Provisions included sanctions on China, requiring congressional observers at the next European arms negotiation, and a prohibition that the U.S. not negotiate with any PLO known terrorists.

Bush even managed to block one of the usually consensual symbolic resolutions. A proposal for Armenian Genocide Day, commemorating the 1.5 million Armenians killed under the Ottoman Empire in the years 1915–23, was put forward by Republican leader Robert Dole of Kansas. When Turkey, a key NATO ally of the United States, vigorously protested to the Bush administration, the White House began to lobby *against* the resolution. The Senate vote, pitting the Republican Minority Leader against the Republican White House, gave a narrow victory to the administration: 48 for to 51 against the bill and the Armenians.

While Bush did not manage to get through Congress the controversial trade treaty with Mexico, his record remains impressive. Certainly one finds few signs of a Congress usurping presidential power during the Bush years.

PATTERNS OF POLICY MAKING

From these several views of the working agenda in foreign policy, a picture begins to emerge. Certainly, there is no obvious trend apparent across the years in congressional activity or in challenges to the President. The expanded agenda of the 1970s is cut back in the following decade, and substantially so in areas outside of the authorization and appropriations processes. Democratic presidents win more roll calls overall, combining measures of activity and success, than the Republican presidents do. Yet, none of the presidents won all that they asked for, when one looks closely at the major agenda items. Most suffered at least one major defeat and enjoyed one victory. Even Kennedy, who managed to get several new policies through the Congress, had his share of compromises and failures. He did not get all the Latin American aid he wanted; he did not get more than annual authorizations; and he did not get his opening to Eastern Europe. Congress visibly opposed White House policies during the Johnson and Nixon years, and it was at least as formidable, if less visible, an opponent in Reagan's second term, forcing the White House to prune and cut back controversial requests. Congress acquiesced in some of Kennedy's proposals and in Carter's Camp David peace treaty. It opposed Nixon's shift from economic to military assistance and it supported Reagan's further shift to a military assistance budget in his first term. If this is "meddling" in foreign policy, Congress has consistently meddled throughout the period, on at least a few issues each year.

Indeed, it appears to be the *presidents* who are varying their activity more than the Congress, giving attention to legislated foreign policy depending on their own agendas and other priorities of the time. Kennedy and Carter propose a number of new programs, Nixon and Reagan select a few issues, Johnson sends over routine requests. Congress, on the other hand, appears fairly consistent in activity, at least when compared with the differences across presidents. In most years—with the exception of the Nixon era and its exceptional events—Congress picks its activity carefully. Certainly it appears active when contrasted with the cases of military intervention that will be seen later.

Seen in this light, we find no shift from a conventional to a reform pattern of policy making, as some popular wisdom leads us to expect. Congressional activity does not appear to be a response to the reforms of the 1970s or any post-Vietnam and post-Watergate malaise. Indeed, the Bush presidency shows how influential a president of the 1990s can be. Overall, both President and Congress pick their issues and pick the times they wish to engage each other. The particular issues vary, but the amount of activity in Congress—and the amount of engagement—has hardly increased across the years.

These are the overall patterns, however. Just as there is less activity than meets the eye, there may be less opposition and struggle, too, beneath the visible surface. Indeed, it is striking how small and selective the legislative agenda is. Presidents pick two or three issues to concentrate their attention on. Congress appears to do the same, even though it has advantages of organization—in a division of labor and committee and subcommittee system—over a single head of state. This means that while any one policy (foreign assistance, for example) is debated in one year, another (trade or arms sales) is not. While President and Congress fight over U.S. policy toward Nicaragua, many other countries and areas of the world go untended. Issues of nuclear proliferation and human rights are debated in a few congresses; for the rest of the time they are left undebated.

The conflict is sufficient to support the notion of a struggle between the branches. Some debate is always occurring, for Turkey or for Nicaragua or for another issue that the President or Congress select. Thus reassured that our elected officials must be making foreign policy, we do not ask about all the other issues that do not appear.

3

✦ ✦ ✦

A Closer Look

C ONGRESS APPEARS ACTIVE, though selective, across time on
a range of foreign policy issues. In some cases it accepts
the invitation to struggle with the President and in some
cases it declines the invitation. Presidents, even more clearly, are
selecting their cases, choosing when to push Congress and when
to lie low. So, while each year two or three issues carry on the impression that these democratic representatives are engaged in
struggle, the results do not add up. There are too many cases remaining where no activity occurs.

We can see this more clearly by looking at three major foreign
policy issues—intelligence, trade, and arms sales—asking when
they appear on the working agenda and what results follow. The
working agenda, defined as those bills that Congress as an institution is paying serious attention to, consists of bills subjected to at
least one vote in either the House or the Senate. These issue areas
are important enough, with consequence for the nation and the
well-being of many other nations, for us to assume that our democratic representatives are deliberating them. Each shows a different pattern overall, *when it appears on the agenda.* It is off the
agenda, however, more than it is on it. And even when President
and Congress do get involved, they do so only in very particular
ways.

INTELLIGENCE

The question of governing the intelligence agencies raises issues
central to democratic government, balancing needs of secrecy
in the pursuit of national goals with needs for responsibility to

elected officials. The central policy issue emerging in the modern era has turned on the mechanisms by which covert activity could be overseen without compromising the activity itself. While we will look at intelligence oversight overall, the primary focus is on the Central Intelligence Agency, where controversy has centered when it occurs at all.

By law of Congress, the intelligence agencies report to the National Security Council and the President, Congress retaining the power to oversee and to determine the budget through its power of the purse.[1] By and large, however, Congress has preferred not to know what the intelligence agencies are doing. Following the *conventional* pattern, Congress supports executive requests.

Who is this "executive," however, that Congress is supporting? Presidents, by nature of their position, cannot know too much about what the agencies are doing. They must achieve plausible deniability, the ability to deny responsibility for covert activity being carried out by the government.[2] It is true that they have to be able to use the agencies to secure major objectives, but they cannot watch too closely or they would lose deniability. The term, and the practice, is a standard part of the conduct of foreign policy, not limited to the United States. Certainly, presidents have their own projects, whether legal or illegal, that they can work for with the agencies. But who is watching all of the other projects? Secretary of State Dean Rusk, who served Presidents Kennedy and Johnson, admitted that he knew little of what the Central Intelligence Agency was doing and had never seen a CIA budget. Of the thousands of covert-action projects engaged in through the end of the 1960s, only some six hundred were reviewed by a National Security Council body.[3] If, as former CIA director Richard Hughes testified to the Church Committee, "we're hired out to keep those things out of the Oval Office,"[4] then the CIA is watching itself. Since both President and Congress are lobbied by the intelligence agencies and the larger defense bureaucracy, they have further incentives not to look too closely at the bureaucratic requests.

Three distinct periods of congressional policy toward intelligence can be identified in the post–World War II period. In the first period, extending to about 1974, Congress followed a hands-off policy of passive support. Oversight was in the hands of the Armed Services committees, whose members were selected in large part from supporters of a stronger defense. All "headline hunters" or those considered "irresponsible" were kept off the CIA subcommittee, by a series of committee chairs. The subcommittees met only two or three times a year to hear briefings from the CIA director and staff. Former legislative liaison people with the agency were told to answer all of Congress's questions. However, the members asked few questions. As Clark Clifford has noted, "Congress chose not to be involved and preferred to be uninformed." The same committee members who asked rhetorically, "Who are we to say No to the military?" defined their role in intelligence as one of passive support. According to Clifford, "The president was the commander in chief and the chief formulator of foreign policy, and the Congress preferred to defer to executive leadership in intelligence matters."[5]

Needless to say, intelligence rarely emerged from its subcommittees to become part of the working agenda. The committee system, backed up by institutional norms of specialization, agreed with the presidential policy of hands-off support. The committees were strong enough in this period even to stand up against other congressional leaders. In an attempt to break up the love match between the subcommittees and the agencies, Senate leader Mike Mansfield and Senate Foreign Relations Committee chair J. William Fulbright tried to mobilize support for the formation of separate oversight committees. The resolution was defeated by the Senate 61–28 in 1966, the Senate voting to return it to the Armed Services Committee, thus killing the bill. The vote makes clear that the committees' support for the agencies reflected a much broader Senate opinion. It would be almost ten years before the idea was tried again.

In the second period, from 1974 to 1980, Congress initiated moderate, although restrained, oversight. The Central Intelligence Agency had come in for its own unfavorable coverage in the course of the Watergate hearings. In addition, in the aftermath of Vietnam and Watergate, Congress, like the public, had become more generally distrustful of the executive branch. So, in December 1974 when the *New York Times* published a front-page article by Seymour Hersh charging that the CIA, in direct violation of its charter, had been engaged in massive domestic intelligence as well as other illegal activities, Congress moved to investigate the agency. Hersh's story, based on access he had been given to CIA documents, spoke of surveillance and bugging of American students and journalists, experiments with mind-control drugs carried out against unwitting subjects, a mail-intercept program, cooperation with police departments and other government agencies, connections with the Watergate affair, and assassination attempts.[6]

Amidst the rising public furor, both Senate and House conducted investigations, and followed these in 1976 and 1977 with the establishment of permanent select intelligence committees. Like standing committees, these committees had power to recommend legislation. However, the fact that they were select committees meant that their membership would be appointed by the party leadership, Republican and Democratic, in the Senate and the House.

Ironically, at the same time Congress moved to act on the issue, the same reform spirit that was prompting the activity undercut the power of Congress to act. Unlike standing committees, the special committees appointed for the purpose would have no prestige from seniority and no support from specialization norms. They would need to rely on the individual prestige of the members selected and the ability of members suddenly thrown together to develop working rules and relationships. To some extent, the Senate committee under Senator Frank Church succeeded in doing this, but the House committee did not. The first House committee was disbanded, and the second was repudiated by the House, when its report was suppressed and its own members investigated for leaking intelligence information.[7]

The extent of activity in this second period should not be exaggerated. The investigations were careful to stay with past events and not to stray from a few narrowly targeted areas of questioning. For example, much of the domestic activities was investigated only up to the mid-1960s. No one asked what the agency might have been doing *since*. The House took the extraordinary action of voting down its own investigatory committee, the Pike Committee, voting 246 to 124 not to make the committee report public. When the report was subsequently leaked to the *Village Voice*, the House voted to conduct an investigation of the leaking. The Ethics Committee moved to conduct its first formal investigation in its nine years of existence, requesting $350,000 to discover the source of the leaks. The entire Pike Committee investigation had cost only $120,000 more than Ethics now wanted to spend to investigate the investigators.[8] Overall, there was more support to investigate the leakers on the committee than to investigate the intelligence abuses that the committee had been formed to review.

Major legislation, setting up the machinery for future oversight, was added to a foreign aid bill, in the form of the Hughes-Ryan amendment. Hughes-Ryan also sought to reaffirm, from the original 1947 act, what the CIA could and could not do. Yet, Hughes-Ryan was supposed to be preliminary. The new permanent select committees were supposed to be drafting an intelligence charter—legislation that would attempt to frame some areas of law and responsibility to govern the agencies. The committees, however, had little support from within Congress or from the White House. Senate efforts to write a formal charter governing intelligence activity failed in 1978 and again in 1980. Considered too long and complex, the 1978 draft ran into opposition from within the Carter White House, and never reached the floor. A shorter compromise draft in 1980 also met up with a White House divided on the issue, and in the resulting deadlock, the bill died. Even with this failure, the Senate had progressed farther along the legislative road than had the House.[9] The House committee, chaired by Tip O'Neill's friend and roommate Edward Boland, concentrated on budget oversight and was seen by many as an advocate of the agencies.[10]

In the third period, from 1980 to the present, Congress took a step back toward the pre-1974 situation. Public dismay over intelligence abuses had subsided. A harder-line position on defense became increasingly popular with the hostage crisis in Iran and the Soviet invasion of Afghanistan. Carter used the Soviet invasion (and his own upcoming election) to call publicly for a relaxation of the restrictions on the CIA, which, he said, were hamstringing the agency's activity and, by implication, the nation's defense policy. An administration-backed Intelligence Oversight Act of 1980 was passed along with the intelligence authorization. The act repealed Hughes-Ryan and put an end to the Senate's attempt to develop an intelligence charter.

The new act reduced from eight to two the number of committees entitled to receive notification of covert actions. These two would be the permanent select committees. The act also allowed the President more discretion in when he needed to notify the committees. If prior notice of an action was not given, the President would have to report the operation "in a timely fashion" and "provide a statement of the reasons for not giving prior notice."

Finally, the act specified that even when and if the committees did receive notification, they could not disapprove of the covert actions. In this case as in so many others, Congress is not *losing* a struggle for influence: it is Congress that is defining what it can and cannot do.

Paralleling this change in the climate of opinion, the Reagan administration in 1981 issued new executive orders (EO 12333 and EO 12334) designed to strengthen intelligence operations. It raised expectations for the operations, assigning the agencies the responsibility to satisfy—not merely respond to—government needs. Whereas a Carter 1978 executive order had required agencies to "adhere" to the laws and to claims of privacy and civil liberties, the Reagan order asked the agencies to act in a manner "consistent" with the laws. In line with the greater liberalization for the agencies, the orders decreased the personal involvement of the President in overseeing policy. Under the Carter order, for example, the President established standards and criteria for when counterintelligence must be approved by the National Security Council. This was eliminated by the Reagan order.[11]

The new mood in the 1980s can also be seen at work in the development of the select committees in Congress. For staff, the two oversight committees drew heavily on analysts from the intelligence community. Contacts grew closer and friendlier as people began to move in both directions from committee staffs to intelligence analyst jobs.[12] Barry Goldwater, for example, chair of the Senate committee for a period in the 1980s, appointed a staff director who had been a former high-ranking CIA officer and president of the Association of Former Intelligence Officers, which led one observer to remark that the CIA had gained one of its more notable penetrations. In words remarkably reminiscent of quotes from the 1960s, the Senate chair observed, "There are many bits of [intelligence] information that I would just as soon not know."[13] Certainly, as committees and agencies began working together, Congress gained more information, but it also gained a clearer understanding of the agencies' point of view. "It's not exactly a Faustian bargain," one member of the Senate committee explained. "But if we wish to have access, we are bound."[14]

Under the eye of the new committees, Reagan-appointed Director William Casey rehired most of the eight hundred agents let go by former director Stansfield Turner during the housecleaning of the 1970s. Casey was known and respected by members in

Congress and had worked with them for years. The staff exchanges between the committees and the agencies strengthened the reciprocal support. From 1980, when the committees first became responsible for intelligence authorizations, to 1986, the CIA budget was estimated to have doubled and the budget for the entire intelligence community to have tripled.[15]

Again, the surface gives a misleading impression. The two oversight committees are hard at work and are manned by expert professional staffs. Contact between the committees and the agencies has dramatically increased over the earlier period. The committees receive some five thousand reports each year from the CIA alone and about a thousand oral briefings. This contrasts with about one hundred briefings a year in the mid-1970s. Certainly there are individuals on both the House and the Senate committees who try to keep a watchful eye on intelligence. They may work behind the scenes, work on projects of their own particular interests and in their own particular ways. Nevertheless, the information they receive does not keep pace with the work. "We are like mushrooms," Norman Mineta once remarked about the CIA briefings. "They keep us in the dark and feed us a lot of manure."[16]

One student of congressional oversight, Loch Johnson, analyzed the interest of the various members of the House Intelligence Committee. While he found only four of the thirteen members characterized by high interest and activity, his description of these four reminds us how devoted individual members of Congress can be:[17]

> Congressman A wading through thick briefing books on the CIA, writing detailed comments in the margins; Congressman B spending long afternoons in the isolated committee rooms, tracing the Agency budget line by line; Congressman C, seemingly frozen to his chair, sitting through each hour of lengthy CIA briefings, patiently asking for clarifications; Congressman D, the committee gadfly, pouring out a stream of provocative questions during closed hearing, driving CIA officials to the point of exasperation; all four coming by the committee rooms regularly to discuss intelligence developments with the staff.

Of course, at least four equally devoted members could probably be found on most committees in any decade of the post–World War II era.

Certainly also in the one case where congressional policy differed from administration policy—aid to the Nicaraguan contras —the committees conducted investigations. Even, then, however, the investigations were framed narrowly and pursued only up to a point. A later chapter will trace in detail a pattern of executive activity and committee response through the Nicaraguan contra affairs. Briefly, it can be called the deceive-and-forgive syndrome. When the committees discovered funds were being sought elsewhere to evade the congressional prohibition, they were outraged. They received an admission that they had been deceived and an apology. When they later found out that the Nicaraguan harbors had been mined without their consultation, they were again outraged. Again they received an apology. They would later discover, during the Iran-contra hearings, that they were still being lied to about the diversion of funds and other activities. *All this time the committee was actively conducting hearings and being briefed.*

The same pattern of activity carried on to the Bush administration when the committees conducted very visible and public hearings of Robert Gates, for the post of CIA director. Gates had been deputy director at the CIA during the 1986 events, and was believed to have lied to Congress according to some witnesses who would later come forward. Several committee members expressed the same concern. While the hearings created suspense and public drama, it was known in advance that the nomination would go through. It did.

Watching the committees through these events, the casual observer might see an assertive Congress, investigating executive abuses, scrutinizing the President's nominee. On a closer look the committees appear more protectors of the agencies than overseers of it, developing a pattern that is found in other committees with other clienteles. What looks like increased *activity* on the part of Congress is not increased assertiveness. The committees are much better informed than the Armed Services members of the 1960s, but like them, they tend to support how the intelligence bureaucracy is doing its job.

If Congress has not gone full circle on intelligence, it has traced a definite curve back to its earlier acquiescent posture. This same curve is seen in Loch Johnson's study of intelligence oversight from the Era of Benign Neglect to the Era of Skepticism to the Era of Uneasy Partisanship.[18] Only briefly throughout the time period did the subject appear on the working agenda: in the years from 1974 to 1977 with the public revelations of CIA abuses; in 1980 with the harder-line position on defense shared by President and Congress; and peripherally, and in a limited way, in the investigations of activity in Nicaragua. In each of those cases, Congress responded to a broader public sentiment, in investigating scandals or shifting its position on defense.

This is not the typical pattern, however. Indeed, only one year after Congress concluded its Iran-contra investigations and made its recommendations, it failed to pass any of these same recommendations when the opportunity arose. According to the votes on the intelligence authorization bill of 1988, the President would not need to notify Congress in each instance of covert activity, nor would he be more restricted in selling arms to "terrorist" nations, such as Iran. The urgency had faded, and the President responsible for the Iran-contra affair was about to leave office.[19] The provisions, supported in large part by Democrats, ran into unified Republican opposition in the House, and were dropped from the final bill.

Disappointed backers of the restrictions rationalized the outcome, speaking of the "deterrent value" of the investigations and the fact that Oliver North and John Poindexter were forced to leave office. "It's going to be a long time," Representative Lee Hamilton remarked, "before a national security adviser says 'The buck stops with me.'"[20] Yet, we can ask why it should be a long time if neither President nor Congress wants the buck to stop with *them*. In the large majority of congresses, the conduct of intelligence is a matter only for its supportive committees. Since the agencies must still protect the President, and keep things out of the Oval Office, much of the time intelligence policy is made only by intelligence officials. The one opportunity to make policy, pursued in the Senate at the end of the 1970s, was not supported in the White House or the House.

Notice that the presidents throughout, despite different political circumstances, have been largely supportive of the agencies and opposed to new congressional restrictions. This was true in the early period when Kennedy, Johnson, and Nixon worked closely with the Central Intelligence Agency for their own projects, many of which they did not want Congress to oversee.[21] But it was also true in the middle period, particularly in the Ford administration. When the intelligence abuses first broke, Ford moved quickly to contain the investigation. He appointed his own

Rockefeller Commission to try to deflect the impact of the congressional investigation. He limited the commission's mandate, allowed only a portion of its findings to be made public, and immediately moved to put into place some of its less sweeping recommendations. At the same time, he held the line against requests by the Senate's investigating committee.[22] Carter's actions in this as in other matters were more ambivalent. His vice-president, Walter Mondale, a strong believer in intelligence oversight, was given free rein to work with the Congress on the proposed charter. Other White House advisers, however, were urging Carter in the opposite direction. When world events overtook the intelligence debate—the Iranian revolution, the Soviet invasion of Afghanistan—Carter then took actions more like those of the other presidents to strengthen the agencies.

Reagan and Bush, too, took actions to strengthen the agencies against congressional oversight and criticism. The Reagan administration followed the Carter initiative with directives erasing even more of the 1970s restrictions. Bush, like Reagan, lobbied Congress for an easing of restrictions, and in 1990 pocket-vetoed an intelligence authorization bill which tried to establish clearer reporting procedures, an issue that many of the committee members had been working on for years. Knowing that a Bush veto threatened, conference committee members, in consultation with the White House, sought to weaken the restrictions in the proposed bill. Even after the bill was weakened, however, Bush vetoed it. In 1991 an even further compromised bill was finally passed.

One of the key issues in the dispute concerned what "timely" meant in notifying Congress of covert activities. Bush had promised to notify the intelligence committees of covert activities in "a timely fashion" in most cases, but did not want to be restricted as to what timely would mean: i.e., how many days *after* a covert event. The remainder of the cases, when Bush would not inform the committees, would be based on his authority under the Constitution, the President said. A second issue concerned whether Congress would be notified if the U.S. government asked *others* to conduct covert activity, others being either foreign nations or private citizens. Bush argued that the provision infringed his own constitutional powers to regulate diplomacy.

Thus by the end of the 1990–91 dispute Congress found itself with few means to oversee covert activities. It would presumably not be notified if the U.S. government asked someone else to conduct a covert operation nor would it be notified of any covert activity at all until the President decided the timeliness was right. The loosening of restrictions from the Carter and Reagan years remained. Bush's appointment of Robert Gates as CIA director, an appointment blocked in the Reagan years because of Gates's implications in the Iran-contra events, was confirmed. There the matter of intelligence oversight stood at the end of Bush's term in office.

Presidents are active, then, in one way in making intelligence policy, in that they have taken clear stands to protect the agencies against congressional restrictions. Certainly the Bush administration had to work for two years to get policy on covert activity more to its liking. The activity, however, has had the result of giving the agencies freer reign to choose and oversee their own operations.

TRADE POLICY

On the surface, trade policy might seem the opposite of intelligence. It is highly visible and laden with import for domestic economies. It is the kind of policy, like so many in the domestic arena, where lobbying flourishes. Both President and Congress, then, might be expected to be active, responding to pressure from their constituencies at home and interests abroad. While many might like to think that presidents represent the interests of the nation while Congress represents the local economies, it is worth pointing out that presidents of both parties have domestic constituencies, too. Banking, finance, labor, steel, oil, manufacturing, agriculture—all these have deep interests in the nation's trade policy. Indeed, as presidents gained more discretion in matters of trade, they attracted more pressure from domestic groups.

With both President and Congress pressured to be active, we might expect a *reform* pattern of policy making overall. This pattern does appear on the surface. In contrast to intelligence, matters of trade make the working agenda year after year: oil import quotas, coffee agreements, sugar, textiles, tuna fish, to mention a few. Much of the substantive legislation discussed in chapter 2 consists of specific trade policies, exemptions, and quota adjustments, for a commodity or industry.[23] Larger trade issues recur at least once in each administration, with an ensuing struggle between President and Congress as to whose preferences will prevail.

The surface activity is not surprising. Trade and tariffs have occupied a place of importance in American politics since shortly after the Civil War. They were major issues in many presidential and congressional elections, and continued to occupy time once the officials were elected to office. According to the Constitution, Congress has the power to lay and collect taxes, duties, imposts, and excises. After the Depression, however, Congress was persuaded by Franklin Roosevelt and the severe repercussions of high tariffs to delegate some of its authority to the President to negotiate trade agreements with other nations. The Trade Agreements Act of 1934, passed over the nearly unanimous opposition of Republicans, made this grant of authority, which would need to be extended and renegotiated by later presidents. Thus the stage was set for what would become periodic skirmishes between President and Congress.

A *default* pattern could also be expected, however. Trade issues pose conflicts between domestic interests: tariffs prompt retaliation; prices for raw materials affect manufacturing and labor; quotas for one product affect the market for another. As a representative legislature, Congress may feel unable to resolve these conflicts, deferring them to other decision-making bodies. The pressures on presidents are even more intense. Presidents are supposed to represent all Americans, or at least those in their nominating and electoral coalitions. As they say in their inaugural speeches, they are the president of business and labor, farmers and consumers, the rich and the poor. Taking stands on trade issues does not fit well with the inaugural rhetoric, to say the least. It risks loss of support from key groups and, by undercutting the symbolism of the office, from the public at large. Both President and Congress, then, might seek to routinize and displace the resolution of trade issues from elected officials to bureaucratic appointees.

Indeed, a large and complicated bureaucratic machinery now exists to deliberate, negotiate, adjudicate, and implement trade matters. Trade is handled in an office headed by a cabinet-level official, the office of U.S. Trade Representative, and by people in the departments of Treasury, Commerce, and State, and in independent regulatory agencies. Additional agencies have been established to coordinate policy among the various bureaucratic units, while efforts to centralize have met resistance in Congress and within the agencies themselves. This raises the question of how much trade policy is presidential policy. As a senator who had also served as a trade representative explained to his colleagues, *"Given the reality that it is not the president who ultimately will make all trade decisions,* it does make a difference which cabinet officer has primary responsibility in a given area."[24]

At a more immediate political level, one finds the same ambiguity about who in the executive branch Congress is deferring to. While the president is given discretion to resolve industry complaints under an escape clause provision, such complaints engender an impressive bureaucratic response. Following an inquiry by the U.S. International Trade Commission, an independent regulatory agency, presidents have sixty days to make a response. During this time they are advised by at least two agencies—the Trade Policy Staff Committee and the Trade Policy Review Group—as well as by the cabinet-level Trade Policy Committee or another cabinet-level council.[25] This machinery not only protects the Congress from the responsibility of a decision, it protects the president as well.

A counterargument, therefore, suggests that much of trade policy will be handled by bureaucratic agencies. President and Congress should enter this arena of conflict infrequently and on issues of their own choosing.

Dancing Apart: Periodic Skirmishes and Last Minute Negotiations

Trade issues do make the legislative agenda, often pitting one branch against the other in dramatic and highly visible ways. Typically, also, each president has faced one such dramatic contest in his administration. Kennedy made liberalizing trade initiatives one of the key points of his foreign policy program, asking for unprecedented authority to negotiate with Common Market nations for reciprocal tariff concessions. Kennedy gained important bipartisan support from business groups, from former president Eisenhower, and other Republican supporters of free trade. He made speeches to Congress and to manufacturing groups around the country. While the House passed the bill with a solid majority, he faced a battle in the Senate, which would be decided by three dramatic roll-call votes. First, a vote to restore restrictive provisions was passed, to the dismay of the Democratic leadership and the White House. Then the Senate leadership rallied and persuaded enough abstainers to vote against the restrictions, thus overturning the earlier provisions. Finally, Kennedy won the key vote on passage by the narrowest of margins, 38–40. He thus won the Trade Expansion Act of 1962, in which he got substantially everything that he asked for, but only after an extended congressional battle.

The trade battle recurred in 1967 when it came time to renew the discretionary authority. By this time protectionist interests had gained strength in Congress, partly in reaction to the Kennedy Round of negotiations. President Johnson, enmeshed in a war and in trouble at the polls, was no longer in a strong bargaining position with the legislature. Not only was the request for an extension denied—it never emerged from the Ways and Means Committee—but the administration had to spend all its efforts to stop new protectionist measures. Separate bills and amendments on meat, cotton, lead and zinc, low-wage imports, and naval construction, many of them proposed by Democrats, had to be separately targeted and defeated.

The battle was joined once more in the Nixon administration. Nixon, like Johnson, asked for renewed discretionary authority, and his bill, too, never escaped from Ways and Means. A new bill, written by the committee and passed by the House, also did not get enacted. Strongly protectionist in content, with proposed quotas for textiles, oil, and shoes, as well as for other products, it won an accolade from the *New York Times* as "the worst piece of trade legislation in 40 years."[26] The bill stimulated controversy not only from the *Times* and the Nixon White House, it also brought opposition from industries who felt their products would be hurt in retaliation. When the House-passed bill reached the Senate, opponents filibustered until the provisions were taken out and sent back to the Finance Committee, where they were never heard from again.

While the Democratic party succeeded in stopping the Nixon bill, it did not offer an alternative that could pass in two chambers. In fact, it would be inaccurate to say that there was a Democratic position, or a Republican one for that matter, beyond the Nixon request for expanded executive authority. Nixon, like Johnson, failed in gaining the presidential discretion he asked for. Nevertheless, he was successful, along with freer-trade supporters in Congress, in stopping more protectionist measures from becoming law. The issue engendered a series of very dramatic events—

presidential speeches, an uproar over proposed legislation, a filibuster—but when the smoke had been cleared away, no new legislation had occurred.

The skirmishes continued every three to four years. Ford was successful where Nixon was not in gaining increased presidential negotiating authority in the Trade Act of 1974. The bill, stopped in the Senate because of Soviet emigration policy, required Henry Kissinger to negotiate a separate understanding with the Senate as well as with the Soviets. The Soviet government soon broke the informal agreement, but only after the Senate had voted the authority to Ford. Soviet emigration policy, of course, had little to do with the central problems of trade legislation. However, the public debate between President and Congress was focused on this issue more than on what trade legislation was or was not supposed to do.

In one of the most recent engagements, Bush won a two-year extension of the fast-track procedure for trade negotiations. First passed in 1974, the fast-track procedure gives Congress only sixty days *after an agreement has already been negotiated* to vote the agreement up or down. Since a negative vote at this last minute would raise severe diplomatic embarrassments to say the least, the fast track is understood in both the executive and Congress as a restriction on congressional input in the process. Despite Bush's high level of success in most foreign policy legislation, the fast-track extension was opposed by labor and environment groups, many of whom feared a prospective trade treaty with Mexico. The Bush White House met with environment groups and carried on intensive lobbying in Congress. The result after very close votes in both the House and Senate was that the fast-track procedure passed.

The skirmishes not only recurred, they began to fall into recognizable types. Reagan's first round with Congress was reminiscent of the Johnson and Nixon struggles. Reagan was denied expanded authority in 1984, while Congress wrote a clean bill in committee. Then came the threat of presidential veto and desperate last-minute negotiations. Working against the clock of adjournment, conference committee members negotiated point by point with the White House, modifying or eliminating those provisions the White House most strongly opposed. The result was a congressional bill, modest in scope, that the White House said it could live with. Widespread press coverage of the dramatic countdown allowed people to forget the substantive issues and the question of what was or was not being compromised.

Reagan's second round, reminiscent of the Ford administration and representing the second type, focused debate on a peripheral issue. The 1988 bill was huge in scope and in the number of detailed provisions. It had been three years in the making in Congress and subject to lobbying by specific groups every step of the way. But the Reagan White House threatened a veto because of a plant-closing notice incorporated in the bill. Public awareness of the trade debate was thus centered on the plant-closing requirement. Once the plant-closing notice was detached from the trade bill and passed on its own by veto-proof majorities, the enormous trade bill was quietly passed into law.

There are exceptions to these patterns of course. One of the best examples of presidential victories over Congress in trade conflicts comes, ironically, from one of the most recent administrations. Following the uprising and massacre in Tiananmen Square, many members of Congress wished to "review" China's most-favored-nation status in trade with the United States. The bill gathered support from other members concerned with human rights abuses generally and from those who opposed lower tariffs for Chinese goods imported into the United States. Bush, however, who had personally taken care to maintain good relations with the Chinese government at the time of the uprising,[27] threatened to veto this attempt at sanctions. Congress backed down from the veto threat and the bill was never passed. The Bush administration policy on trade with China stood.

Two other cases stand out as exceptions, showing how *Congress* can legislate when it wants to. Working under streamlined congressional procedures designed for the purpose, Congress gave Carter expanded authority in the 1979 bill, and passed legislation to reduce nontariff barriers to world trade. The legislation brought U.S. laws in conformity with agreements reached by the major industrial nations in the just-completed Tokyo Round of multilateral trade negotiations. Typically trade bills were derailed by a barrage of amendments, as members tried to exempt particular local industries. In this case, procedures allowed the two specialist committees—Ways and Means and Finance—to bring the bill to the floor under rules that forbade amendments. Carter, too, had worked closely with Congress throughout the process, along with his special trade representative Robert S. Strauss. During the negotiations the bill had been tailored to prevent opposition from such industries as textiles and steel. Here, the President had worked with two prestigious committees of Congress, as well as with the Democratic and Republican leadership, to pass legislation that the U.S. had already agreed to in principle. It is no wonder, with all the cooperation and streamlining, that the bill passed with few dissenting votes.

The second case, producing a very different product, occurred in 1988. Angered by the lack of White House initiatives in the face of growing trade deficits and currency imbalances, Republicans and Democrats joined together to author the trade bill. The bill, three years in the making, worked its way through multiple committees and a 200-person conference committee. Protectionist in nature, the bill had something for everyone: the traditional legislative Christmas tree. The Reagan administration, it should be noted, did not interfere with this bill beyond targeting the plant-closing issue. Once that issue was solved, the leaders of both parties agreed to restrict floor amendments and the bill was acted on with little controversy in either chamber.

Clearly no increasing activity is seen by Congress in trade policy. Even in the exceptional cases, Congress acted once to support the President, and once in lieu of any White House action. The more fundamental question is what the pattern of periodic skirmishes means.

These routine dramatic episodes appear less a battle between the branches than what one writer has called an "intricate political minuet."[28] During and between the times the public battles are fought, with their threats of veto, dramatic votes, and final desperate negotiations, a large array of bureaucratic and judicial agencies make policy. By delegating power to these agencies, Congress and President deflect political heat. They avoid the twin terrors of appearing too protectionist on the one hand, thus incurring future economic retribution, and too unresponsive on the other hand to the plight of specific domestic industries.

Everyone involved gains. The agencies strengthen their hands in disputes and negotiation by warning of an upcoming congressional furor. Congress expresses its anger in speeches and resolutions and a fight with the President. It shows itself mindful of constituency interests, while being protected from itself in the matter of passing restrictive legislation. It cries out against unfair trading practices, and then sighs when it can do little to change the policy.[29] The President maintains his "flexibility," i.e., the delegation of power to the agencies and courts, while seeming to hold the line in a statesmanlike fashion against an overprotectionist Congress.

Seen in this light, it is notable that in three of the cases described above, the President did not succeed in getting the new initiatives he wanted, but neither did Congress succeed in passing new legislation. Both branches were active, but nothing was done. Even some of the new legislation can be seen as maintenance of the uneasy status quo. New restrictions are added that merely make the bureaucratic and judicial caseload heavier. President and Congress play good cop, bad cop, in the words of one writer. Both hold the line for a time against each other, and throw up their hands in despair that they could not do more.[30]

Behind the periodic public debates, policy making goes forward. The Reagan White House used its discretion in 1982 to adjust import quotas on sugar, and in 1983 on steel and textiles. Both were responses to behind the scenes congressional pressure. Some said the sugar relief was a favor to Southern Democrats in the House who had supported Reagan in his 1981 budget venture.[31] These are commodities that are often the subject of controversy in the legislated trade bills, of course. The controversial provisions are removed by the conference, else people would call Congress protectionist. They then reappear in the form of a White House ruling, often at the request of members of Congress, when the bill is no longer in the public eye. In both the Carter and Reagan administrations, key trade negotiations with Japan went forward while a trade bill was being debated between President and Congress. The trade bill, with its threats of vetoes and overrides, provided the dramatic background against which the negotiations occurred. As one writer summarizes,

> The game is complex and is played at several levels: sometimes congressional threats are real; sometimes they are merely to frighten reluctant administrations into action; and sometimes an administration asks to be frightened so that it can then point to the danger of congressional action as a negotiating tool.[32]

In other cases the legislation does make changes that are so small and technical as to go unnoticed by most observers. The 1984 bill responded to an earlier unfavorable ruling against the shoe industry, changing the criteria slightly in the hope of future relief. The bill also redefined grape growers, under pressure from that industry, allowing them to file complaints with the wine makers.[33] It changed the definition of what a foreign "shipment" was since the old definition was harmful to a domestic industry, allowing combined shipments to count as unfair under certain conditions. These provisions, however, go unnoticed in the midst of all the dramatic effects.

U.S. trade policy has changed across the years, along with changes in trade policy worldwide. The shift away from tariffs and multilateralism brought about decisions understood and acquiesced in by both the White House and the Congress. These decisions have continued in the 1980s and beyond. Yet, the legislation itself has typically failed to address, debate, or announce these changes. One analyst speaks of the congressional "hypocrisy of demanding action while continuing to write laws containing . . . loopholes that ensure no action."[34] In a few cases Congress has shown that it could legislate if it wants to, most notably in the very different bills of 1979 and 1988. Both occurred when the leadership was willing to take responsibility and streamline procedures to keep destructive amendments from the floor. Yet, the 1988 bill shows its own kind of blame avoidance. The multicommittee bill, culminating in a conference committee of two hundred members, allowed scores of members to claim some credit, while targeting no one with failure. It was passed in a context where members publicly admitted it would not address the nation's trade deficit or related economic problems in any serious way. "It's a plus," Finance chair Lloyd Bentsen stated, although he agreed it would not change the deficit substantially. And critic Daniel Evans, Republican of Washington, observed, "The best thing that can be said about this trade bill is that it is probably too late, if it was ever necessary."[35]

Dancing Together: The U.S.-Canada Free-Trade Agreement

A somewhat different pattern—with fewer skirmishes—is seen in the U.S.-Canada trade agreement of 1988. Here the dance of legislation did result in a dramatic new initiative; yet the President and Congress kept a slow and even pace with each other. By the 1980s both the White House and Congress had come to realize that some regional trade agreements might be in the U.S. interest, paralleling other regional economic arrangements that were coming into being around the world. A free-trade agreement with Canada appeared the easiest first step, given the long-standing friendship between the two countries and the close ideological and cultural ties. From a political perspective, however, neither President nor Congress wished to take the lead too obviously, thus antagonizing domestic interests opposed to such an agreement. On the other hand, neither wished to place itself *against* an idea which appeared in the United States' best interest. The result was a long period of nonaction, during which both President and Congress remained open to action and took some basic facilitative steps.

The confusing signals from the White House can be traced across Ronald Reagan's eight years in office. Reagan had campaigned in 1980 on a platform which included opening international markets to competition. This campaign pledge, of course, did not necessarily signal any new direction: many presidential candidates had campaigned on the broad issue of trade liberalization before. By 1983, however, after U.S. efforts for another round of international trade negotiations had failed, the idea gained currency that the administration might seek agreements with individual countries as a prelude, or alternative, to more global agreements. In this context, a Canadian proposal to begin a series of limited trade discussions met with a positive response, and the United States Trade Representative was commissioned to begin the talks. The talks soon foundered, and no further progress was made in Reagan's first term.

The second term began auspiciously with a summit between Reagan and Canadian Prime Minister Brian Mulroney. Yet, the WhiteHouse appeared to give little priority to the negotiations in the following two years. The new U.S. Trade Representative, appointed to fill the vacancy created by the retiring Trade Representative, was seen as a relative outsider in Washington, without access to the President and with no experience on Capitol Hill. The particular negotiator for the talks with Canada, Peter Murphy, was not appointed until February of 1986. Murphy was young (thirty-seven) and also did not have access to Reagan. Canadian officials considered both appointments disturbing signals of the relative lack of interest on the part of the Americans in reaching any new accords.[36] Much more disturbing was the news, as the first negotiating round was getting under way, that the President had just signed a five-year 35 percent duty on imports of Cana-

dian wood products. The action brought a letter of protest from
the Canadian prime minister to the United States and retaliatory
tariffs on U.S. goods.

Congress, meanwhile, was waiting to be persuaded by the
President. The 1986 vote on fast-track authority, which would be
necessary for any future agreement, ran into serious opposition in
the Senate. Senators complained that they had not heard from the
White House on the issue; the trade representatives complained
that neither the White House nor the Congress was giving the
matter any concern.[37] A serious tax-reform bill was being written
in Congress; the White House was fighting the war in Nicaragua.
Canada, along with other aspects of U.S. trade policy, was the task
of about one hundred overworked professionals in the Trade
Representative's office. At the last moment, the White House did
engage in lobbying in Congress, complete with top-level staff
meetings and visits to Capitol Hill. A senator switched his position, and the attempt to block the fast-track authority failed.

While the negotiations continued, so did the low priority
given them by American elected officials. The nation was negotiating a nuclear weapons treaty with the Russians. The revelations of Iran-contra took Washington by storm. Finally, as the
fast-track authority was due to expire, the Canadians had had
enough. In September of 1987, with no visible progress in sight,
the Canadian negotiator walked out of the meeting. Conferring
with the Prime Minister, he announced a suspension of negotiations to the world's press. This did get the attention of President
and Congress. Treasury Secretary James Baker, a close friend of
the President, became actively involved. A group of members
from the Senate Finance Committee met hastily to see how to re-
vive the failed negotiations. A congressional plan that had been
previously put forward was offered as the new U.S. position. The
negotiators reconvened with the new proposal, this time in the
presence of Secretary James Baker, and a tentative agreement was
reached. It was delivered to Capitol Hill literally minutes before
midnight on October 3, 1987, when the fast-track authority was
due to expire.

Who was making foreign policy in the case of the U.S.-
Canada free-trade agreement? Clearly the President and Congress each played a role, although one carefully calibrated to
match what the other was doing. On the White House side, Reagan
had met with the Prime Minister and later sent his vice-president

and Treasury secretary on a visit. Treasury Secretary Baker would play a central part in the final successful negotiations. Reagan also briefly lobbied the Congress for fast-track authority when Congress, in effect, asked to be lobbied. On Congress's side, it did move on the fast-track legislation and played a key role in saving the negotiations at the last moment. The draft legislation, prepared by Representative Samuel Gibbons of Florida, became a key document at the negotiating table. In this case the dance did result in new legislation, while keeping the midnight drama and cliff-hanging suspense that we had come to expect.

The regular skirmishes in trade policy go on, giving the impression that both President and Congress have been active. This pattern persists from 1961 to 1988. Congress agreed to presidential requests in the Kennedy, Ford, and Carter administrations. It rebuffed requests of Johnson, Nixon, and Reagan. It did work with the Reagan administration in passing the U.S.-Canada free-trade agreement in 1988. Certainly one cannot argue that Congress has become more aggressive in trade policy across the years: indeed, it has seemed more willing to delegate responsibility to executive officials. Through the same period, however, one cannot say that presidents have become more active either. Faced with the difficult political problem of making trade policy while avoiding the antagonism of key domestic constituencies, presidents have delegated responsibility, too.

Judging by the ongoing debate in Congress, the speeches of presidential candidates, and the veto messages issuing from the White House, no one is happy with the nation's trade policy. But beneath the surface activity in either Congress or the White House, little is done.

Arms Sales

Arms sales policy shows a third pattern, a kind of mixture of the *conventional* and *reform* models. Contrary to its handling of intelligence policy, Congress has kept an eye on this government program. It has appeared on the working agenda in the 1960s, 1970s, and 1980s and slightly more than once every three years. As opposed to the pattern of trade policy, however, Congress has been more willing—after a battle—to accede to presidential requests. The battles catch the headlines, but we need to look beneath the surface here as well.

The arms sales program began as a relatively small portion of the military assistance program. Arms in the 1950s and 1960s were only one part of the nation's strategy to strengthen allied countries against Communist expansion. Hence nations qualifying for economic and military assistance of any kind could also purchase arms if they had the cash. Congress and the White House debated the level and kind of military assistance, but the regulation of arms sales was of minor concern. Even when the Kennedy administration sought to persuade NATO nations to spend more on U.S. arms, to compensate for the growing balance of payments problem caused by the stationing of so many U.S. forces abroad, the policy was debated largely in terms of the military assistance program.

The dramatic change in arms sales policy began with the Nixon administration. After the experience of Vietnam, Nixon sought to shift some of the nation's defense responsibilities to Third World countries in a policy that became known as the Nixon Doctrine. At the same time, the OPEC oil price rise of 1974 meant that several Middle East nations would have the price for U.S. arms. The Nixon White House thus lifted restraints on selling of sophisticated weapons and encouraged U.S. firms to solicit sales from the oil-producing nations. This initiative resulted in a sharp rise in military sales to the Third World. Total sales to the Third World rose from $1.4 billion in fiscal 1971 to $10.4 billion in 1974 and $15.8 billion in 1975. Sales to the Persian Gulf nations alone showed a five-year increase of 2500 percent.[38]

Congress, meanwhile, was learning its own lessons from Vietnam. One was primary—that a United States "presence" in a foreign nation could be a direct precursor of military conflict. This perception plus the mushrooming arms sales led a Senate Foreign Relations Committee study to conclude that the arms sales program was "out of control" and in need of new legislation. Congress passed an amendment to the 1974 foreign assistance bill voting itself the power to veto major sales, and in 1976 it passed the Arms Export Control Act. The act sought to provide comprehensive new legislation for the policy area and to establish procedures for congressional veto and review. In effect, Congress separated out arms sale policy for special attention from the routine military assistance program. It served notice that arms sales in the future would receive its own careful review.

Nevertheless the act, like the War Powers Act passed in the same climate of opinion, was easier to enact than to follow. In the same year that it was passed, and following its passage, Congress chose not to use its new legislative tools. When President Ford submitted to Congress $6 billion worth of weapons contracts for eleven nations, the proposal was initially blocked by the Senate Foreign Relations Committee. (Under the terms of the 1976 act, Congress had thirty days to halt the sales.) While the committee was generally agreed that it should take some restraining action, it was divided on how many sales should be blocked. One senator submitted thirty-seven resolutions of disapproval covering all eleven of the nations. The committee eventually decided to make the symbolic statement of targeting one sale, that of 650 Maverick air-to-ground missiles to Saudi Arabia. However, Secretary of State Henry Kissinger appeared before the committee warning that the veto could damage "our basic relationships with Saudi Arabia and the prospect of stability and moderation in the Middle East."[39] After hearing Kissinger's testimony, the committee took no further action in blocking the sale.

Two years earlier Congress had objected to the sale of fourteen Hawk missile batteries to Jordan. The objection had forced the Ford administration to compromise in the negotiations, angering the king of Jordan but winning congressional consent. Now after the new tough legislation had earned its headlines, Congress declined to stop the eleven-nation sale.

This pattern—a selective targeting of a particular arms sale followed by conflict and eventual consent—would hold through the post-Vietnam period. Ford, Carter, and Reagan faced very different conditions of party support in Congress; yet, the congressional reaction persisted despite variations in same- or opposite-party control. So, when Carter submitted the controversial proposal to sell AWACs to Iran in his first year in office, Congress at first refused. Some members worried that the sophisticated weaponry could fall into the hands of the Russians; others were concerned that the weapons would need U.S. personnel in Iran for supervision and training, creating a new U.S. presence in the Middle East. Carter resubmitted the proposal three months later, with some of the sophisticated weaponry removed, and the sale was allowed to go through.

This was 1977. In 1978 the Carter administration submitted an even more controversial deal: the sale of $4.8 billion worth of military aircraft to Israel, Saudi Arabia, and Egypt. Egypt was being offered the aircraft for the first time. After a lengthy debate, Carter won approval by a close Senate vote, with a majority of Republicans, and less than half of his own party, supporting Carter and the sale. House opposition to the sale had been strong, but since both houses need to agree to the concurrent resolution of disapproval, the Senate vote was sufficient to allow the sale to go forward. Many called this an impressive foreign policy victory for the President,[40] but it had its pyrrhic qualities. The Mideast sale dominated relations with Congress in early 1978, splitting the President's party and showing that a majority would vote against him.

In 1980 the conflict recurred. More and more voices in Congress warned that the United States appeared to be arming the Middle East, through outright sales and loans. Nevertheless, tanks with special infrared night-vision mechanisms were sold to Jordan, $550 million in loans to Egypt were earmarked for weapon sales, following from the Camp David agreements, and weapons were sold to Saudi Arabia to go with its previously purchased war planes. In each case after the debate and the grumbling were over, Congress let the sale go through.

This acquiescence is all the more intriguing since Carter was the one president who had publicly indicated his worries with arms sales. Carter was the first to raise the issue in a presidential campaign, warning of the "nation's role as the world's leading arms salesman," and promising to work to reduce the commerce in arms.[41] He followed his campaign promise with statements in his first year in office and a set of directives for a policy of arms restraint. Despite the sincere efforts of the Carter administration in devising the guidelines and defending them against critics, it soon became clear that the actual arms transactions were proceeding as usual. The Congressional Reference Service noted no fundamental shift in U.S. export policy under the new guidelines,[42] and the overall level of exports continued to rise. This ambivalence in the Carter administration, however, did not prompt a stronger congressional reaction. Both President and Congress *said* they were worried about arms sales policy, but continued to enact the policies in place before. In 1977 and 1978, immediately before the Iranian revolution, U.S. arms sales to Iran totaled $5.7

billion and $2.6 billion for the year; arms to Saudi Arabia totaled $6.4 billion in 1979 and $5.2 billion in 1980.[43]

Throughout the Ford-Carter years Congress had been less willing to sell arms abroad than the presidents were. It showed itself willing to question individual sales, at about the rate of one a year. In most cases, however, when the drama was over, Congress gave in to the executive request. This pattern continued in the Reagan years despite a White House shift to an expanded arms sale program. Reagan officials affirmed that there was nothing "inherently evil or morally reprehensible" about arms sales and went on to introduce several new features, extending sales into areas hitherto restricted.[44] Whereas the Carter policy had restricted the most sophisticated weapons, in the fear of escalating a Third World arms race, the Reagan administration took out this restriction. While the Carter administration had at least formally opposed sales to nations violating human rights, Reagan explained, "I don't think that you can turn away from some country because here and there they do not agree with our concept of human rights."[45] Administration requests for sales to Argentina, Chile, and Guatemala followed from this point of view.

The AWACs sale in Reagan's first year in office illustrates the congressional continuity on the issue. The sale of five AWAC planes to Saudi Arabia was considered a key point in the administration's Mideast policy. Reagan personally lobbied members on the issue. While the sale was opposed in the House, the Republican Senate supported it by a narrow four-vote margin. Indeed, the issue was similar in its suspense and its outcome to the Mideast sales controversy in Carter's second year.

Once the congressional veto was declared unconstitutional, Congress returned to the pattern of debating arms sales as part of the military assistance budget. This kept a perfect record. Since the first passage of legislation in 1974, Congress had never used its veto successfully to stop an arms sale, although the threat of a veto had forced presidents to renegotiate some of the terms. With the veto weapon removed in 1983, Congress continued to challenge individual arms transactions in about the same rate and with the same effects as before.

Certainly, one can argue that Congress has acted as a brake on this policy, forcing presidents to choose their major arms sales with care. If they do not, their secretaries of state will need to be dispatched to plead with Congress, close votes on the floor will need the efforts of White House lobbyists, special negotiations with foreign nations will have to be made. But one can ask why Congress did not push harder, especially during the Carter years when the President himself was worried about this policy.

At least part of the answer lies with the locus and timing of the decisions. As Senator Frank Church complained, after the unsuccessful attempt to stop an arms deal in 1976, "U.S. companies get out and promote the sales . . . by the time they come to this panel, it's practically a *fait accompli*. The contracts are already negotiated, the pressures are there."[46] The "pressures" stem from a process of interaction between U.S. firms producing weapons, Defense Department agencies who work closely with these producers, and foreign nations themselves.

By law, thus by the agreement of President and Congress, tens of thousands of arms transactions are automatically processed each year by the relevant agencies in Defense and State. Only the exceptional case is brought to the presidential level: because it involves selling sophisticated weapons to Third World countries, or because the country has been cited for human rights violations, or because the sale is too large to be treated any other way. An extensive prehistory, however, precedes this point. U.S. firms, increasingly encouraged to promote their wares since the time of the Nixon administration, engage in a number of promotional activities with foreign nations, as well as lobbying the relevant U.S. agencies. If the foreign nations are interested, they also lobby the agencies, and the process of negotiation begins. So, by the time the request has reached the presidential level, a substantial momentum has built for a particular sale. It has even been tentatively negotiated—all that remains is for the President and Congress to sign on. Hence it is easy to see why presidents often plead with Congress that to turn down a sale might harm relations with a Third World country. The sale is virtually ready to be made. At this point Congress is placed in an unenviable position: it risks harming U.S. foreign relations by an insult at the eleventh hour; it is forced to challenge the President on a foreign policy question; and it is forced to say no to the defense agencies and the American producers.

Yet if this shadow government of agencies and clienteles determines the outcomes of arms policy, forcing presidents and Congress to eleventh-hour assent, it is only because it has been given this power through the passing of laws. Presumably if Congress wanted to play a larger role in arms control, it could alter the timing of some of these decisions.

The congressional record on arms sales can be usefully compared with congressional activity on broader arms limitation issues, especially treaties about nuclear arms control. This latter area is one in which Congress appears very actively involved, according to many observers. Barry Blechman, for example, cites activity in the Carter-Reagan years as evidence of the newly assertive Congress. He cites its role in SALT II negotiations in both administrations: the support for the nuclear freeze movement in the House; the demand for Senate arms control observers.[47]

These issues attracted considerable public attention and concern; so perhaps it is not surprising to find Congress more interested too, in comparison to its attitude toward the less visible and more technical arms sales issues. These visible issues do not recur on an annual basis. They can be addressed periodically and sporadically, like the high points of the intelligence debates or the various rounds of trade negotiations. Congress, in short, then has the incentive and the time to mobilize and can have an impact that is not immediately undercut in the following year or two. In this way, arms limitation treaties are more like the dramatic trade negotiations we have seen in this chapter than like issues of arms sales. Still, it is worth pointing out that a keen interest in major arms treaties is by no means a new role for Congress. In the Kennedy years it kept a very close eye on negotiations for the proposed nuclear test ban treaty with the Russians. Before the treaty was ratified, by a narrow two-thirds majority, three separate committees as well as a phalanx of individual senators had to be consulted with and satisfied. In the 1960s as in the 1980s presidents had to work closely with Congress to secure their support.

The Partnership

These three policy areas appear different on the surface. They have come into being at different times and show different patterns of domestic support. Yet beneath the surface they show a President and Congress willing to delegate authority and postpone decisions. In intelligence, Congress supported the agencies in the 1960s as in the 1980s. In arms control, it legislated a procedure whose timing precludes its own participation: in its rare objections it risks undercutting long and delicate negotiations. Even in trade policy Congress has shown an increased willingness to bind itself, through fast-track procedures, to the results of others' decisions. This is hardly an aggrandizing Congress. Yet, it is not the President who benefits from this deference, but the professionals: in intelligence, in the defense agencies, in the Office of the Trade Representative. So, policy grows by agency decision and judicial finding, and the maze of trade legislation becomes decipherable only by technical experts. The arms sales agreements reaching the President's desk and the Congress are almost *faits accomplis*. And so the periodic contests between the branches are not debates about policy as much as face-offs on very specific issues, often peripheral to the legislation in question. These periodic battles give the impression that something is happening, but the primary decisions have been made elsewhere.

A few cases of presidential initiative stand out. Kennedy was instrumental in engineering a freer trade policy. Nixon encouraged an expanded arms sales, breaking the program apart from military assistance and facilitating U.S. corporations' efforts to sell their goods in the Third World. With Reagan, the arms sales program took another large step forward. Carter, Reagan, and Bush were active in the intelligence oversight disputes, although the activity was directed to returning the program to its earlier, less restricted condition. This is less initiative than the return of a program to an earlier status quo. A major attempt at an initiative came with the Carter guidelines for arms sales restrictions; however, the guidelines were never accepted, even within the administration, and were contradicted in the actual requests the White House brought before the Congress.

Congress, for its part, showed some initiative, too, although it was heavily concentrated in the years from 1974 to 1979. Congress wrote legislation for arms export control in 1974 and 1976; it set up restrictions for intelligence activity and developed its own oversight committees. While one may criticize the intelligence committees for accepting their own kind of Faustian bargains, the work of individual members deserves acknowledgment and respect. Congress also worked with the administration on a major trade bill in 1979 and was able to conclude, again in conjunction with the White House, the important new free-trade agreement with Canada. These acts changed the existing policy. In contrast, the congressional activity culminating in the Trade Act of 1988 made few changes once it emerged from its multiple committees and 200-person conference.

At the same time, there was a growing consensus within the Congress, especially on trade and arms sales, that the current policy was poor. Why could not Congress do more? Clearly an aroused public opinion is a factor facilitating congressional activity. Public attitudes help to explain why Congress could write the legislation of the middle 1970s, why it was moved to investigate intelligence abuses, and why it was moved to stop when the climate of opinion had changed. Yet many people continued to work for an intelligence charter and worked hard for trade reform even when these issues attracted little public attention. The former atrophied in the Senate and the latter was transformed into a typical legislative Christmas tree with trimmings for all the members who took part.

Ironically, the same climate of opinion that brought the new legislation undercut the ability to continue to legislate. The power of committees was undermined, with the weakening of norms of seniority and specialization; while the resulting decentralization, rather than strengthening the party leaders, forced them to find new support from the rank and file members. It is no wonder, then, that weak committees, without the protection of seniority or support from the specialization, were unable to write successful charter legislation for the intelligence agencies. It is also no wonder that these permanent select committees, without support from within the institution, would need to develop reciprocally supportive arrangements with the agencies they were supposed to oversee. It is notable that when Congress knew it had to pass new legislation, as in the trade bill of 1979, it worked through Ways and Means and Finance, two of the most traditionally powerful committees.

In proposing ways to rationalize and regulate arms control policy, one writer suggests the creation of special congressional oversight committees modeled on the intelligence committees, "endowed with the authority to review pending transfers while they are still in the planning stage."[48] It is likely, however, that using the same model of weak, specially appointed committees, will only achieve the same result. Congress might like to oversee arms sales the way some members would like to oversee intelligence, but on what will the committee depend for support? Congress's *power* to pass new legislation was rooted in the traditional committee system. If it now has the *will* to make policy, it finds its power lacking. Congress has still to find ways to bring its power and its will together.

Yet, it is clear from the preceding account that strong committees and a concerned public are not sufficient. Presidents have not appeared very eager to propose legislative solutions either. For the most part both presidents and Congress have chosen symbolic battles over real debate. How break apart and recombine this curious partnership? One plausible institutional mechanism is the political party. Parties provide the only route within Congress to counter individual interests and gain majority votes. The party leadership traditionally supported the committees and the norms and were in turn supported by them.[49] But parties also offer the one bridge across the separation of powers structuring both cooperation and debate: cooperation between the branches, often within one party; study within congressional party committees to help maintain an institutional perspective; and debate between the parties. Parties provided the streamlining in the few cases in this chapter when Congress moved to change policy: in initiating the intelligence investigations; in writing an arms export act; and in negotiating new trade legislation. The shadow of party was also visible in those cases where some members tried to act, but were ultimately unsuccessful. The Democratic party had the initiative on intelligence, but weak committees, steered by the Democratic leadership, combined with ambivalence in a Democratic White House brought the initiative to an end. Both parties in Congress were unhappy with trade legislation in the 1980s and willing to write a bill, but unwilling to take the lead to make it more than the aggregated product of their many members. The impact of party leadership will be seen more clearly later by the decisions taken, and not taken, in the committee stage.

Many people urge better collaboration between the branches as a solution to some foreign policy problems.[50] But they do not specify why President and Congress should want a different collaboration to occur nor do they specify the institutional mechanisms that would assist it. At present the elected officials are antagonists in the symbolic battles and partners in the real battle of avoiding tough issues. There is a kind of partnership, and collaboration, now.

4

* * *

THE USE OF
FORCE

UNLIKE OTHER ISSUES of foreign policy, force typically
unifies the nation against a common foe. The events are
visible, dramatic, evocative of patriotic emotion. The
President addresses the nation. The flags and yellow ribbons of
the Gulf War decorate every storefront. Students, rescued after
the successful invasion of Grenada, kiss the American ground.
Controversy will resume if the wars continue and appear unsuccessful, but for the moment there is a respite from normal political
routines. It is not surprising, then, that of the various kinds of
foreign policy, the use of force shows the clearest *conventional* pattern: presidents are active and Congress accedes to what the presidents request. On these occasions both Congress and the public
rally around the President and the flag.

Despite arguments to the contrary by many writers, this pattern can be seen in operation from the post–World War II period
to the present day. To show this continuity, this chapter first traces
the typical pattern and the exceptions. It looks past the flourish-
ing debate and discussion of the War Powers Act to actual practice. Finally, it considers other congressional responses to the use
of force and discusses the implications. The subject area, we will
see, is different in qualitative and quantitative terms in its treatment in Congress from other matters of foreign policy. This difference, moreover, has remained across the years.

In contrast to the preceding chapter, we take presidential activity as a given. It is true that presidents may not have seen an
event emerging or been briefed on necessary military facts. The

crisis in Cyprus, for example, where U.S. naval forces were sent on July 22, 1974, was probably not at the center of the President's attention. Another crisis had been occurring which would bring his resignation within two weeks. Nevertheless, as Commander in Chief presidents sign the orders—they are by definition active and involved. Typically they do much more, addressing the nation when the troops are deployed and engaging in news conferences and other briefings. While we still wish to see the kinds of actions presidents take, we concentrate on the congressional response.

The cases to be used are based on the listing provided by the Congressional Research Service of the Library of Congress. According to CRS, instances of the use of force include all deployment of forces abroad in situations of conflict or potential conflict "to protect U.S. citizens or promote U.S. interests." It does not include covert activity or stationing of special forces, participation in occupation forces, or what it calls "base agreements or routine military assistance or training operations." (For the list, see appendix B.) It thus excludes the Berlin crises in the Kennedy years (occupation forces), the Bay of Pigs invasion during Kennedy's term (technically not U.S. personnel), the advisers remaining in Korea after the Korean War, and all use of special forces. While the list understates the actual military force the United States is deploying at any point in time, it does succeed in capturing some of the most visible of these operations. It has the additional advantage, besides keeping up to date, of being a *congressional* list, thus the events Congress should be most clearly aware of.[1]

According to this list, there have been thirty-three separate occasions from 1961 through 1988 when the United States has engaged in the use of force abroad, or slightly more than one a year. The Vietnam War is counted as one use of force. While Vietnam, fought primarily in the 1960s, brought by far the greatest number of American casualties, it is interesting to see that the separate uses of force have increased across time, with seven in the 1960s, ten in the 1970s, and sixteen in the 1980s through 1988. (Four additional uses of force are listed for 1989.) Including the Bay of Pigs and the two Berlin crises in the Kennedy years makes the 1960s and the 1970s comparable; hence the clearest increase has been in the most recent years. Overall President Reagan instituted the largest number of instances, with sixteen events in eight years. Ford was second, with six events in two and a half years. The numbers alone suggest that the use of force has become a continuing part of American foreign policy. How do the President and Congress share these decisions?

THE TYPICAL PATTERN AND THE EXCEPTIONS

The typical pattern can be described as follows. When presidents have gone before Congress to ask for a resolution or other support, they have received what they asked for—with speed, little debate, and virtual unanimity. This occurred in the crisis in Formosa in 1955, in the Middle East in 1957, and in Berlin in 1962, to mention some early examples. This was also the case with the Tonkin Gulf Resolution, which initiated the wider involvement in Vietnam. After attacks on U.S. destroyers patrolling the Tonkin Gulf, President Johnson asked for a resolution expressing the nation's determination to support freedom and protect peace in Southeast Asia. Congress responded with the Tonkin Gulf Resolution, supporting "all necessary measures" the President might take to prevent further aggression. Later, Congress would try to distance itself from this resolution, by repealing it twice.

Further, when presidents have reported on *prior* actions taken without congressional authorization, they received support for what was already done. This was the case with President Truman's decision to join United Nations forces in the Korean War and President Kennedy's decision to impose a quarantine on Soviet vessels entering Cuba during the Cuban Missile Crisis. Truman did consult with a few congressional leaders in the two parties and the key committees—fourteen members in all. The "consultation," however, involved responding to language already drafted for the U.N. resolution, and occurred at the same time that the news of the decision was released to the press.[2] Congress was hardly being consulted and certainly was not asked for its advice. Kennedy consulted with no congressional leaders, even though his decision was reached after a week of deliberation with a number of advisers, some twenty individuals in all. These included people with little formal connection to the event (the Secretary of the Treasury), the British Ambassador, and a few private citizens.[3] After the decision was arrived at and a speech written, Kennedy briefed congressional leaders at 5:00 P.M. and at 7:00 P.M. addressed the nation. While a few members of Congress murmured that they would have liked to have been consulted in advance, these murmurings were lost amidst the strong chorus of assent.

We know from public opinion studies that the public rallies around the President in time of international crisis.[4] Public support in the polls rises no matter what the President has done. Therefore these cases of congressional acquiescence are supported by underlying public attitudes. Congress is reflecting—and participating in—the public's support.

Congress became increasingly active as the Vietnam War attracted more and more public consternation. In early 1965 following the Tonkin Gulf Resolution, 60 percent of the public thought it was not a mistake to send troops to Vietnam and only 25 percent thought it was a mistake. The gap progressively narrowed until in early 1967 the lines of the graph crossed: more people—about 45 percent—thought it was a mistake than thought it was not. By 1968—and the upcoming presidential election—one-half of the public thought it was a mistake; Johnson's popularity was low enough to convince him not to run for another term.[5] It is interesting to watch the course of congressional action follow the lines of the graph. The Senate Foreign Relations Committee began hearings on the war in 1968. Legislation and repeal of the Tonkin Gulf Resolution followed in 1970.[6] The debate in Congress reached full scale with the Nixon administration's move into Cambodia in the spring of 1970. So, the Senate passed legislation restricting funds for U.S. involvement in Vietnam and setting a timetable for withdrawal. It also amended a foreign aid bill to limit future action in Cambodia. The House began hearings on the President's war powers and Congress repealed the Tonkin Gulf Resolution twice.

While public opinion spurred on the congressional action, the parties were also important, providing the main structure for debate and opposition. The hearings in the Senate Foreign Relations Committee, led by the Democratic chair J. William Fulbright, gained more support among Senate Democrats once their own party was out of the White House. (Fulbright had so offended Johnson when he began the hearings that this old friend was dropped from the White House invitation list.) With Republicans in office after the 1968 election, Democrats were freed from the inhibition and embarrassment of opposing the actions of their own party's president. The votes on the floor, too, followed a party structuring. Antiwar voting in the key Ninety-First Congress (1969–70) showed clear party lines, with more than two-thirds of the Democrats opposing and more than two-thirds of the Republicans supporting the administration's handling of the war. On key Senate roll calls, the percentage of antiwar votes was as follows:

Democrats   78% antiwar votes
Republicans 31% antiwar votes

Some defection from party lines is not surprising. Many Southern Democrats supported the Nixon administration policy, and several of the more liberal Republicans opposed it: Edward Brooke of Massachusetts, Mark Hatfield of Oregon, Jacob Javits of New York, among others. By and large, these defectors on both sides of the aisle were reflecting the dominant opinion in their constituencies. Nevertheless, each side clearly commanded a large majority of its supporting party. So, in this exception to the normal pattern of congressional acquiescence, two facts stand out. First, public opinion did not support the war or the Cambodian bombing, and thus deviated from the typical pattern of support for the President. Second, divided party control between Congress and the White House facilitated the forming of an opposition along party lines. Party became the structure through which debate and opposition in Congress occurred.

Congressional reaction culminating in the War Powers Act of 1973 showed the same two factors as important. The act was passed in a Democratic Congress with a Republican president; with a president whose credibility and public support had been dealt a severe blow by the Watergate scandal; and at a time when the public was still mindful of Vietnam. So, the War Powers Act, viewed as a striking exception to the past acquiescence of Congress, was passed under highly exceptional circumstances of its own. Whether it would be enforced at a future time—with same-party control, with a more popular president, and with Vietnam a matter of history—posed a very big question.

ANOTHER LOOK AT THE WAR POWERS ACT

The act restricts a president's independent authority to employ forces on a sustained basis to a sixty-day period (with a short extension possible), within which time Congress must vote either to validate or to invalidate the action. Both President and Congress have responsibilities under the act: the President must *report* to Congress within forty-eight hours of the time armed forces are introduced (section 4); and Congress must *act* within sixty days, or the extended thirty-day period, of the time the forces are introduced, whether or not the President reported them (section 5). Presidents are also supposed to *consult* with Congress "in every possible instance" before the use of force is employed (section 3). Each of these activities—consulting, reporting, and congressional action—forms a heading in the legislative act. While the War Powers Act has been subject to volumes of writing, primarily by legal scholars—as to its legality, its vagueness, its loopholes, its intent—few have looked closely at the result of the legislation.[7] Passed by extraordinary majorities in both chambers over a Nixon veto, the act on paper suggests a strong reassertion of congressional war-making powers. What has it produced in fact?

How has the presidential reporting worked? The War Powers Act had its first test in 1975, under the Ford administration, in two events: the sudden crisis evacuation from Vietnam and the capturing of the American merchant ship *Mayaguez* by Cambodian Communist troops. In the *Mayaguez* affair, Ford ordered the combined forces of the marines, navy, and air force to the area, reporting to Congress slightly more than two days later. Ford reported after the forty-eight-hour limit and after the ship had been retaken and the American forces withdrawn. Ford did not report when the troops were used to assist in the Vietnam evacuation. Carter did not follow the act in the Zaire airlift of 1978, although he did in the unsuccessful helicopter rescue attempt of the Iranian hostages in 1980. Reagan followed the act in the Grenada military action and in the air strike on Libya, but did not follow it in the actions in El Salvador or in the first deployment of troops in Lebanon. Presidents, it appears, are deciding when they will report and when they will not.

Overall through 1988 presidents reported to Congress in fifteen cases, although some reports were made after the hostilities had begun or even after the forces were withdrawn. On ten occasions, according to the Congressional Research Service, presidents did not report. These included the Cyprus crisis in 1974, the evacuations in Korea and Zaire, the shooting down of Libyan jets over the Gulf of Sidra, and the increase of military personnel in Panama, El Salvador, and the Persian Gulf.[8]

It is also important to see that on only one occasion has a president reported under the section that triggers the sixty-day clock. Ford did in *Mayaguez*—although the clock stopped at the same point it began, since the affair was over. The usual pattern has been for a president to make a report noting that it is "consistent with the War Powers Resolution," but citing no particular provision. Presidents are also careful to point out that the action was taken in line with their own constitutional powers as Commander in Chief: they are granting the War Powers Act no special constitutional grounding.

How has the consulting worked? Typically presidents have informed Congress after the decision is made, and at times, even after the proposed action has been taken. This was the case with Ford's reporting on *Mayaguez* and with Carter's attempted helicopter rescue of the hostages. Both held meetings with congressional leaders after the events had occurred. In the case of Grenada, President Reagan held a meeting with some members of Congress two hours after he had signed the order for the landing the next morning. As Speaker Tip O'Neill pointed out, "We weren't asked for advice."[9] In the air strike on Libya, Reagan informed the leaders that the airplanes had already been dispatched on their mission. The leaders were convened at 4:00 P.M., while the planes would begin bombing at 7:00 P.M. The time frame, it is interesting to see, is almost identical to that used by Kennedy in the Cuban Missile Crisis. Kennedy briefed the leaders at 5:00 P.M. and announced the embargo at 7:00 P.M. in a speech to the nation.

In the use of cruise missiles against Iraqi intelligence headquarters in June 1993, Clinton informed a few members of Congress before the strike. He formally notified Congress two days after the attack in a note "consistent with the War Powers Act." Kennedy, Reagan, Clinton: the similarities are more striking than the differences across thirty years of the use of force.

People have complained that the consultation provision was vague. It did not define clearly enough what consultation meant, when it should occur, or who in Congress should be consulted. Yet, by any definition, what the presidents are doing is not consulting, since the time to offer advice is over. The marines had already landed (on the wrong island) to rescue the good ship *Mayaguez*. The bombing mission for Libya was already in the air. In the case of the failed hostage rescue mission, Carter administration officials explained in hearings before the Senate Foreign

Relations Committee that early communication with members of Congress might have jeopardized the secrecy of the mission.[10] But this is precisely one of the issues that the War Powers legislation tried to address: that is, how to balance the needs of military security against the need for responsible consultation with elected officials. Members also asked why consulting some eight members of Congress would jeopardize security in view of the one hundred or so officials already apprised of the operation. The War Powers Act says that presidents should consult with Congress "in every possible instance," the members pursued. Who will determine whether the instance is possible or not? The official could only respond that the President had made that determination.

One of the more popular pieces of advice heard recently is that President and Congress should collaborate more—that presidents should consult with Congress before a situation is virtually too late to change.[11] The advice, while certainly nice and wholesome-sounding, does not go far in suggesting a solution. In the case of the War Powers Act, Congress has made the consultation mandatory, and yet the same lack of consultation persists.

In several cases presidents have not acknowledged that an event has occurred: hence there would be no consultation or reporting. The Reagan administration set up exercises in the Caribbean and Central America, involving several thousand combat troops stationed in Honduras and maneuvers of the U.S. fleet. Since these were called training exercises, the War Powers Act was not deemed relevant. Both Carter and Reagan sent military advisers to El Salvador, again claiming that the War Powers Act did not apply. According to the White House arguments, the advisers were not being introduced into a situation of imminent hostility, even though some of the advisers were subsequently killed. At the time Reagan made this argument about El Salvador, the troops were stationed in headquarters within zones of conflict, were flying reconnaissance missions over battlefields, and were fired at on at least eight separate occasions.[12]

What has Congress done when it has been informed? On only one occasion—in Lebanon in 1983—did Congress invoke the provision of the act that triggers the sixty-day clock. Even this action followed an agreement with the White House that the troops could remain in Lebanon for eighteen months. In many cases, of course, the issue was moot, since the event was over before the clock could begin. Congress's hesitancy in enforcing its own act is underscored by its plaintive demands from time to time that the presidents should be the ones who start the clock. Why won't presidents invoke the provision, Senator Joseph Biden, Jr., of the Foreign Relations Committee asked. "Can any of you think of any time . . . where a President has taken the action of committing U.S. forces anywhere that the Congress has not, if asked immediately after the action was taken, that the Congress has not supported it?"[13] In effect, Biden was asking the White House to take responsibility instead of the Congress, guaranteeing that Congress would follow with its support.

This means that the cases of use of force since the War Powers Act was passed should be remarkably similar to those before. Ford in *Mayaguez*, Carter in the hostage rescue attempt, Reagan in Grenada and the strike on Libya, Bush in Panama: all have acted the same, and have received the same response, as Kennedy and Johnson some years before. Following the typical pattern, presidents report on decisions made or on actions already taken and receive support from Congress for what they did. One could switch presidents and cases, have Johnson try the air strike and Reagan pass the Tonkin Gulf Resolution, with no difference in predicted results. Kennedy's decision to go ahead with the Bay of Pigs invasion, Ford's action in rescuing *Mayaguez*, and Carter's decision to try the helicopter rescue are strikingly similar in several respects, not least of which is the virtually nonexistent role of Congress. Kennedy did include one congressional member, J. William Fulbright of the Senate Foreign Relations Committee, in a group considering the proposed strike. The other two presidents did not include any member of Congress.

Some members of Congress have brought suits to the courts to try to begin the clock mechanism, but the courts have passed it back to the Congress. This was the case in the Persian Gulf crisis of 1987. In early 1987 the Reagan administration significantly increased U.S. naval forces in the Persian Gulf, adopting the decision to reflag Kuwaiti oil tankers and escort them through the Gulf. ("Reflagging" means registering the ship in the name of an American company, and thus flying the American flag.) At this time in the Iran-Iraq war, the American action was seen as helping Iraq in protecting its oil supply from Kuwait. The question in Congress, then, was whether the U.S. forces were in a situation of imminent hostilities, and thus whether the War Powers Act should be invoked. The Reagan administration, however, made no report to Congress until thirty-seven sailors were killed by an Iraqi aircraft missile. This was May. It was not until September that the administration filed a report "consistent with" the War Powers Act. By this time 111 members of Congress had filed a suit in federal district court to trigger the sixty-day clock.

Congressional action against the administration was divided between those who wanted to invoke the War Powers Act themselves and those who preferred the judicial route. Individuals argued and debated, but no concerted strategy emerged. Also, no party or committee leadership emerged. The Senate Democratic leadership would not get involved, since some of the leaders supported the administration policy: for example Majority Leader Robert Byrd and Armed Services Committee chair Sam Nunn. In the House, the petition to the courts took away most of the push toward floor action. Indeed, the court observed, quite accurately, that the dispute seemed to be with the plaintiffs' fellow legislators. By the time an appeals court heard the case, in October 1988, the Iran-Iraq cease-fire was in existence and the case was dismissed on grounds of mootness.

Throughout this period the courts' position has been clear. Suits concerning Grenada, Nicaragua, and the Persian Gulf, brought by several members of Congress during the Reagan administration, all resulted in the same advice: if Congress wants to confront the executive, it must do so by legislation and should not expect to be rescued by the courts. In the Bush administration the suits continued and the advice was the same. In two decisions concerning the sending of troops to Saudi Arabia, U.S. district courts rejected the legal claims. The President had not refused to accept a statutory restriction, the court observed. Only then, might the issue be justiciable.[14] In the words of Justice Lewis Powell in a case from the Carter administration, if Congress "chooses not to confront the President, it is not our task to do so."[15] The courts saw no assertive Congress in these years, to say the least.

It is true that Congress was less supportive of presidential action in the case of Lebanon than in many of the others, but ultimately it took no action of its own. By the theory of the War Powers Act, Congress should act within sixty days of the outbreak of hostilities. However, ninety days after the thirty-seven sailors were killed, Congress was just beginning to go to the courts, deciding in effect that it could not invoke the War Powers Act on its own. Some two dozen members of Congress also protested the action in El Salvador, by filing a suit in federal court that was later dismissed. Congress also opposed the policy by budgetary action, as we will see in a later chapter. It is notable, however, that it did not seek redress through its own war powers legislation. In an analysis of the act in the Reagan administration, one political scientist concludes that "the political power of Congress to constrain the president through . . . enforcement of the War Powers Resolution is severely limited if it is not dead altogether."[16] We might add: if it had ever been alive.

The actual practice of the War Powers Act can be summarized for all uses of force from the time of its passage through the end of the Reagan administration:

	Yes	No
Presidents Report to Congress	15	10
Presidents Report and Start Clock	1	24
Congress Starts Clock	0	25
Congress Starts an 18-Month Clock	1	24

The situation is as follows: presidents are not invoking the sixty-day provision, and Congress is not invoking it either; nor will the courts do it for them. Neither the consulting nor the reporting nor the invoking of congressional action is following the stated purpose of the legislation. What is the War Powers Act doing?

For one answer, the War Powers Act appears to be providing a symbol of congressional assertiveness as required in a postreform and post-Vietnam era. It would probably be impossible after Vietnam, Watergate, and Congress's own reforms to go back to the more complacent style of the 1960s: press and public would be swift with their dismay. On the other hand, the exceptional conditions that helped pass the legislation did not continue: hence the act could be passed at one point in time, but not enforced at another point. Senator Biden was right in one way in his comments on the sixty-day provision: under typical circumstances public and Congress support the President when, as Commander in Chief, he calls for the use of force abroad. They would support him in the 1980s as they would support him in the 1960s. Seen in this light, the act and much of the continuing debate about it is a means of carrying on the necessary symbol of assertiveness, when the reality must be otherwise.

Yet, a fuller answer implicates the President, too, in this symbol making. The act has allowed both President and Congress to carry on military policy in times of heightened consciousness after Vietnam, giving the impression that they are jealously guarding the nation's foreign policy and watching each other. The trade policy reviewed in the preceding chapter was likened to a minuet between the branches: the debates on the use of force seem more like a mock fencing match, with dramatic thrusts and parries, but no real outcomes. Congress avoids the difficult position of challenging the Commander-in-Chief in a time of military tension. Presidents, on the other hand, gain a kind of tacit consent, of potentially great value in the post-Vietnam period. Since the War Powers Act is on the books, there is implicit support for a president's policy if the act is *not* invoked by Congress.

Meanwhile, the debate goes on as to whether the War Powers Act is a good thing or a bad thing, and as to how it might be clarified or amended. After *Mayaguez,* members of Congress complimented themselves on how well the War Powers Act had worked even though there was no consultation and a report submitted only when the event was over. One member called it a "semi-historic occasion." He added, "I think it should give every citizen some comfort to know that in the future this awesome power to make war will be exercised both by the Congress and by the President."[17] After the hostage rescue attempt, a Senate hearing inquiring into various matters, including the lack of consultation, concluded that the consultation requirements needed to be "clarified."[18] There had been no consultation at all, however—it was scarcely a matter of confusion. Even after the questions raised in the Reagan administration concerning the lack of presidential compliance, House Foreign Affairs Committee chair Dante Fascell observed in 1988 that "we are in far better shape today than we were before 1973."[19]

Despite the testimonials, many members of Congress feel that there is something wrong with the legislation. Various amendments have been proposed, some to clarify the consultation requirement, others to strengthen or weaken the legislation or to repeal it altogether.[20] Few raise the possibility that Congress has been acting in much the same way, whether or not the act is on the books. The bills are dutifully reported to the relevant committees for study, and debate on the war powers legislation goes on.

It is true, as some people argue, that the existence of the act may influence presidents as they make their decisions. Given the increased number of cases in recent years, it has hardly acted as a deterrent on military action. Possibly, though, it leads to shorter wars—Grenada, Panama, the Libyan air strike—thus minimizing the need to consult, to report, or to worry about congressional reaction. It is also true that the threat of opposition from Congress can be an influence in determining the timing and amount of force used. It was widely felt, for example, that the Reagan administration limited the advisers in El Salvador to a small enough number (fifty-five) to minimize congressional opposition. Nevertheless, it is hard to avoid the conclusion that the War Powers Act, like the cases seen in the preceding chapters, gives the impression of more assertiveness and activity in Congress than may actually be the case.

OTHER CONGRESSIONAL ACTION

The Gulf War Debate

We can compare the presidential and congressional reaction in a superficially different situation—the 1991 Persian Gulf War. Here were the members earnestly explaining why they would vote a particular way. There was suspense and drama: the outcome was expected to be close. On the surface, then, this debate appeared an even stronger assertion of Congress's constitutional powers than attempts to invoke the War Powers Act.

It is important to see at the outset that both President and Congress faced a difficult political decision. In December of 1990 public opinion was divided and falling slightly among those who supported an aggressive policy in the Gulf. About 60 percent of the public thought U.S. lives were too high a price to pay in the conflict. There was substantial public pessimism generally about how well the country was doing.[21] Bush also faced divided opinion in Congress and among foreign policy experts. Some felt the timing was wrong and that use of force should have been employed earlier; others wanted to pursue sanctions and opposed any force at the time. But the kind of action contemplated by the administration—heavy aerial bombardment and the commitment of ground troops—meant that *the question of war powers could not be evaded.* There could be no gradual escalation as in Vietnam. Nor could the action be short enough, like the air strike on Libya, for the President to be able to report that a war had occurred once the war was over. Somehow Bush would need Congress's consultation and assent.

Congress, for its part, had no united position to take: there could be no institutional position on the war. Most Republicans supported the President, and a majority of Democrats opposed him, with some defections among the Southern Democrats. The Democrats, however, could look for no strong public support against the war, as they could in the party-line votes on Cambodia and Vietnam some twenty years before. Following the typical pattern when the Commander-in-Chief asks for support in military action abroad, somehow Congress would need to give Bush the resolution of support that he asked for.

Thus the very visible congressional debate on the war gave both branches the solution they needed. Congress appeared active: it was debating whether the United States should go to war. All the members could give their speeches to be heard in the home districts. Yet, it was generally understood before the debate that the President would get the votes he needed. Members of Congress predicted it in advance on television interviews. Several senators, including Minority Leader Robert Dole, made reference in the course of their speeches to what the final vote would be. As Dole remarked, "I think we know where the votes are. If we do not, we ought to get some new counters. . . . But I think it is important that we state our views."[22] The vote occurred as predicted. In the Senate, where the closest vote took place, the parties split, with the Republicans supporting the resolution 42 to 2 and the Democrats opposing it 45 to 10. Seven Southern Democrats and three Northern Democrats voted with the Republicans, giving Bush the 52 to 47 margin. Congress got to debate the war and the President got his resolution. Needless to say, it was in the interests of both branches not to mention the War Powers Act.

While people praised Congress for being so responsible, few raised a basic question. Congress has the power to declare war, according to the Constitution. Why did it not declare it? When Speaker of the House Thomas Foley was asked this question on a news interview, he responded that the resolution was the "moral equivalent" of a declaration. Yet, Congress (and the Democratic leadership, of which Foley was the head) had chosen to take a moral equivalent rather than the constitutional provision. Congress could seem active and assertive, in line with its post-Vietnam image. At the same time it could follow the typical pattern of giving the President the support he asked for. The 1964 Tonkin Gulf Resolution and the 1991 Use of Force Resolution were different in that one vote was nearly unanimous and one divided along party lines. They were similar, however, in the form the action took: a president's speech to rally the nation, followed by a congressional vote, not on war powers but on the President's request. They were both moral equivalents—in 1964 and in 1991. They were similar also in their outcome, in that Congress agreed to the President's policy.

Was the Gulf War debate a historic occasion, as each speaker in Congress took pains to point out? Wars themselves are historic certainly, but the debate merely ratified, or legitimized, a decision which had already been taken in the White House. But did not Congress assert its power to declare war? Is not this the new aggressive Congress in action? The answer is no for three reasons: first, Congress had had this power since 1789; second, it only asserted a kind of "moral equivalent" of this power; and third, it debated an issue which had already been decided. The debate made the legislature *seem* to use a power it did not actually wish to exercise.

Constitutional scholar Louis Fisher, who agrees on the minimal role Congress has played in the use of force, concludes one analysis with the words: "Congress has the constitutional power. It needs also the institutional courage and constitutional understanding to share with the president the momentous decision to send U.S. forces into combat."[23] In the Gulf War debate, Congress did not share a decision—it supported the president's decision. It did not give evidence of its constitutional understanding as to the power to declare war. What it did do was give the appearance of an institutional courage that it did not actually possess.

Hearings and Floor Speaking

Congress engages in other action besides a direct response to executive decisions. In committee, in its debates, and in work on budgetary authorizations, it can influence policy and make its opinions known. But does it do so in the cases of force? And how has this activity changed across time?

Floor speaking, in fact, occurs only on selected issues, and has decreased over time. (See appendix B1.) Of all the recorded uses of force, about half of the cases did not show substantial floor speaking in either chamber. Only eight cases showed any substantial speaking in both chambers. Neither chamber was particularly more or less vocal than the other.

The cases attracting the most amount of speaking are not surprising. Forty-four members of the House and about half of the Senate spoke on Cambodia in 1970. Eighty-two House members took to the floor on Grenada, and large numbers of both House and Senate spoke on the Vietnam evacuations. What is more striking is the number of cases where Congress appears virtually silent. No speeches were made on the floor after the events in Laos, 1962; Lebanon, 1976; Zaire, 1978; Egypt, 1983; Chad, 1983; the Persian Gulf in 1984; and Panama in 1988. (Members could *not* speak after the events in Libya in 1981, since Congress was not in session.)

Judging by these results, Congress certainly does not feel obligated to speak when U.S. troops are deployed abroad. Nor has the speaking increased with the reforms and resulting decentralization of the mid-1970s. Indeed, the largest percent of cases where little or no speaking occurs is found in the most recent decade. More than half of the uses of force in the 1980s provoked no substantial floor speaking.

Nor is this speaking necessarily critical of the President or part of any real debate. Eleven of the House members speaking on *Mayaguez* rose under the one-minute rule to praise what Ford had done.[24]

I am very proud of our country and our President today. When the chips were down, we did not shirk our responsibility in a time of crisis. (Jack Edwards, R., Ill.)

In one convincing action, the President has reaffirmed our willingness to fight for our commitments and reenforced the freedom of international sealines for all nations of the world. (William Broomfield, R., Mich.)

Mr. Ford acted with deliberation, yet with boldness and firmness in freeing the ship and protecting the crewmembers. His actions should be clear evidence to all in the world that this Nation is prepared to protect its citizens and its property. . . . As one of the authors of the War Powers Act, I was deeply pleased to see that Mr. Ford complied fully with the act by keeping Congress completely aware of all actions. (B. F. Fisk, D., Cal.)

Clement Zablocki, Democrat of Wisconsin and chair of the International Relations Committee, also spoke briefly in support of Ford's action, commenting that the "worth of the war powers has once again been demonstrated." In this particular day's session, Elizabeth Holtzman, Democrat of New York, was the lone speaker who criticized the action as illegal, raised the question of unnecessary casualties, and pointed out that diplomatic efforts had been underway.

On other occasions, of course, as in the October 1983 debates on Lebanon and Grenada, people spoke at greater length on different sides of the issue. The leadership in both House and Senate made time available for floor speaking. Speeches ranged from short patriotic statements in support of the Grenada action to several speeches raising questions on the need for the action and the issues of consultation and press censorship. The debate in the House ran about five to one against the administration, and the House ultimately invoked the War Powers Act. The "war," however, was over quickly, and the White House kept control of the news coverage.[25] The House resolution was blocked in the Republican Senate, and allowed to die after the favorable public response to events. As House Democratic Speaker Tip O'Neill confessed, you had to get off the steamroller before it ran over you.[26]

The record of hearings shows more activity on the part of Congress. Only one in four of the cases of force brought no hearings in their wake. (See appendix B2.) This activity, however, has not increased across the years: it was highest in the 1970s and has been down sharply since:

	Average Hearings Per Case	Average Number of Pages Per Case
1960s	1.6	16
1970s	5.3	29
1980s	1.8	21

Hearings serve many different purposes, of course. They can support the President, as many of these hearings do, asking for briefing by administration officials with few hard questions along the way. The hearings on the *Mayaguez* and Libya are examples. They can deal with issues peripheral to the actual use of force—the monetary cost of an exercise or the security of an embassy.

Only a few of these hearings show the committees engaged in serious questions on the event itself. The Congo in the 1960s, Cambodia in the 1970s, and Honduras in the 1980s are perhaps the best examples.

Yet the hearings announce to the White House, as well as to the officials who must testify on the Hill, that certain things are on Congress's mind. In the extreme cases, such as the reflagging of Kuwaiti vessels, they may alter administration policy or signal that compromise is necessary. Three committees held hearings once the 1987 Persian Gulf operation resulted in American casualties. An Armed Services Committee panel kept the Secretary of Defense on the witness stand through one hundred pages of questions. A Foreign Relations panel also held hearings, as did the Merchant Marine Committee, which critiqued the administration policy of reflagging ships.

Even in the more routine cases, hearings establish a record that will be useful in budgetary decisions, an area in which Congress has much more confidence in its own judgment. Thus the Senate Foreign Relations Committee, under Senator Church, asked administration witnesses to explain why Congress was not consulted after the attempted Iranian hostage mission in 1980. The State Department witness gave his own testimony at length. He brought with him additional reports and was asked for more. The questioning went beyond the consulting, in fact, to the technical preparation for the mission. This same theme was being pursued by the House Appropriations Committee:

> It appears that Defense failed [to support U.S. foreign policy] in this instance. The mission failed. We must explore whether or not the failure is symptomatic of serious problems in the Defense Department or is an isolated failure.[27]

No one in the White House or Pentagon is missing the point.

Certainly Congress is taking the events seriously enough to schedule a hearing in most instances. Yet, if the hearings have an effect on policy, it is primarily in this indirect way, cueing executive branch officials as to what matters the members are concerned with and establishing their own record for later use. Educated watchers of the news might ask the same questions: when did the troops first arrive? how long do you think they must stay? what do you expect the outcome to be? In most cases the committee members are monitoring events—they are not deciding them.

At least, the hearings do not give the impression that Congress is laying claim to a more active policy-making role.

Congress's strongest action in foreign policy, seen in the following chapter, takes place through its power of the purse. Only rarely, however, is this power used to dispute military decisions of the Commander-in-Chief. In the 1960s Congress argued for a stronger military action in Cuba; in the 1969–73 period, it sought to cut back the troops in Southeast Asia; in 1976 it prohibited military action in Angola; and in the 1980s it sought to limit military activity in Central America. Congress has been divided itself on these issues and has sought primarily to indicate when executive policies do not have widespread support.

Presidents have countervailing power, however, with the growth of secret funding in effect since World War II.[28] At this time Congress established unvouchered (secret) funds for the White House, the Defense Department, the Bureau of Narcotics and Dangerous Drugs, the Secret Service, the Bureau of Customs, and other agencies. The CIA budget is secret, with funds included in a number of department budgets. So when public funding was denied the President for activities in Honduras, the Defense Department used its funds to continue maneuvers and to train and equip Honduran forces. According to estimates, close to one thousand U.S. military personnel were stationed in the country with thousands more on ships off the coast—all without congressional authorization.[29] Defense Department and CIA funds were also employed to support the contras in Nicaragua. It is important to see that Congress, which established the secret funding, remains aware of its existence even as it publicly limits the authorization. The CIA budget is secret because Congress has agreed not to look at it. At times, therefore, the dispute is less one between executive and legislature than between public and secret budgets.

IMPLICATIONS

The congressional record on uses of force can be compared to the cases in the preceding chapters. While presidents are more active in these events than they are in other foreign policy areas, Congress is less active. The uses of force have been frequent—more than one a year on the average—but they only rarely make the congressional agenda in votes on the House or Senate floor. Even more rarely do they find Congress opposing the executive decision.

Only seven of these events made the working agenda in twenty-seven years, if we look for action within one year of the time the event occurred. Two of the seven—Cuba and Tonkin Gulf—were virtually unanimous resolutions of support asked for by the administration. A third, a House resolution on the Dominican Republic crisis, was also supportive. The House voted 312 to 52 to support Johnson's actions in the crisis after a Senate committee had held nine days of critical hearings. In two other cases, the Vietnam evacuation and the Sinai peacekeeping force, Congress gave the President more limited authorization than was requested. A vote on the reflagging of the tankers represented a compromise with the administration. Only in the seventh case, the House vote invoking the War Powers Act on Grenada, did Congress directly counter administration policy. (A vote on invoking the act in Lebanon would occur more than a year after the forces were in place.)

Much of the time, in the 1980s as in the 1960s, Congress supports the President in the use of force abroad. Decision making since the War Powers Act appears remarkably like the decision making before, in consulting, reporting, and congressional response. Other activities, too, such as floor speaking and committee hearings, show no increased congressional role.

Seen from this perspective, the War Powers Act seems most important as a symbolic statement of congressional concern, a way of saying to the nation that its elected representatives care about this kind of policy. It allows both President and Congress to appear more responsible in the most recent era: they have "learned the lessons of Vietnam." At the same time it allows them to maintain the traditional pattern whereby Congress supports a presidential decision. Meanwhile, public debate on the act carries on the illusion, suggesting that Congress has used this power or will do so at any time. People speak about "tightening the War Powers Act" or clarifying the reporting requirements, as if a change in wording would change the attitudes of the elected officials.

On occasion, the War Powers Act has served to allow behind-the-scenes bargaining, perhaps limiting troop levels in El Salvador and the U.S. contribution to the Lebanese peacekeeping force. It can also affect the kind of force the presidents choose. However, it is important to see that this symbol has become reality in only one case since passage—the negotiated extension of the use of force in Lebanon, finally passed by Congress more than a year after the troops were deployed. Since that time the United States has used force on several occasions, and fought a major war, without finding the War Powers Act important in these decisions. It is possible therefore that the symbol is losing whatever power it had.

There are also similarities to the cases seen previously. We see the same swelling of activity in the immediate post-Vietnam era and the subsequent decline. The questioning of war powers, like that of intelligence abuses, was concentrated in a short period of time and followed an expression of wider public concern. Congress, responding to that concern, took exceptional actions that it would not maintain in more normal times. So, the Hughes-Ryan intelligence restrictions would be repealed and the War Powers Act would not be enforced. The congressional response is similar also in focusing attention on a few very visible symbolic activities: "tightening" the War Powers Act, aid to the Nicaraguan contras, the Gulf War debate. Like the veto fights and filibusters seen previously, these keep the public's attention on the few selected conflicts the two branches choose to engage in.

The decision to use force is the most serious issue a nation must face, with results directly affecting its own security and the lives of its citizens. In the post–World War II period the United States has made decisions on force in the White House. In effect this has been the current American solution to the question of how democracies can make war. At times Congress is treated like a slightly more privileged public: it is informed, often a few hours in advance, and asked for its support. At other times even this nod to the Constitution is withheld. It is one thing if American citizens see this situation and support it. It is quite another matter if they believe instead that the decisions are made through a broader representative process. The highly publicized debates and battle over war powers help to carry on this erroneous belief.

5

✦ ✦ ✦

CONGRESS AT WORK

B EYOND THE SURFACE of foreign policy, many people in Congress have been hard at work. They work on the foreign aid bill, primarily within the two foreign policy committees, and without the interviews or front-page stories that attend their more public-relations minded colleagues. Year after year this work goes forward, permitting a detailed and extensive review of the major issues of the time. Certainly any examination of Congress's role in foreign policy must acknowledge this activity and ask about its change across the years.

This is no congressional backwater that the members are relegated to. Quite the contrary, foreign aid bills have been used traditionally to critique and make changes in the whole range of U.S. foreign policy: war policy; alliances, both bilateral and multilateral; the stability of governments; as well as foreign economic development. Policy toward Communist China, Eastern Europe, the Middle East, Panama, Nicaragua has been debated, and often influenced, through the foreign assistance authorization bill. Most of the arms sale policy discussed previously was enacted as part of the foreign assistance bill and its military-related programs. The bill legislates such subjects as military sales and leases, the stationing of technical and military advisers abroad, peacekeeping operations, and funds furnished for the purpose of constructing or maintaining nuclear facilities. Indeed, as Robert Pastor comments, "The foreign aid bill can be considered the principal vehicle by which [Congress] attempts to influence and make U.S. foreign policy."[1] Examples of the kind of policy debated during the authorization review make clear that Congress is not looking at foreign assistance narrowly. So the foreign affairs committees warned repeatedly in the 1950s that the United States should not recognize the Communist government of China. In the 1960s the Battle Act reflected congressional disapproval of assistance to Communist bloc nations. The authorization process was used to debate the Vietnam War, the Cooper-Church amendment being one (unsuccessful) provision added to a foreign assistance bill. The landmark Hughes-Ryan amendment of 1974, in which Congress attempted to set restrictions on intelligence agencies, was passed as part of the annual foreign assistance bill. Jimmy Carter was warned through two authorization debates that Congress had problems with a Panama Canal treaty, and Ronald Reagan was told that military assistance would not be given to governments engaging in terrorism and that no aid, beyond humanitarian assistance, would be given to the Nicaraguan contras. Put simply, the Reagan White House had to look to other nations for cash since the Congress would not provide it.

Perhaps the clearest illustration of the authorizing committees' importance is seen in the historic Camp David accords. When a United States president met with the heads of state of two foreign nations, Israel and Egypt, why were there special telephone lines at Carter's side that went to the House Foreign Affairs Committee? The "price" for this treaty of peace was that the two archfoes would be given military assistance by the United States, and Carter had to be sure that the committee would agree to the terms. While the committee members did not pose with the President for the celebratory handshakes at the completion of the meetings, the decisions made across those telephone lines would continue to have impact through the 1980s. It seems fair to say that every major issue of American foreign policy has been raised at some point in the authorization debates. They are indeed a microcosm of the range of foreign policy debated between the President and Congress.

Why foreign aid should be a kind of microcosm for the nation's foreign policy is readily understandable. First, it suits the congressional character, always at its most skilled and comfortable with using budgetary decisions as a means of policy control. The foreign aid budget, growing from $5 billion to about $17 billion in the postwar years, offers a resource, like many resources in domestic policy, that can be divided, adjusted, and compromised almost without limit.[2] Influence over different regions and different kinds of policy could be divided among the experts in the committees and subcommittees. By eliminating aid to one nation or attaching restrictions to another, *all within the customary legislative process,* Congress makes policy for these nations, often overriding the requests of the executive branch.

Second, the multipurpose nature of the aid program has made it a key to the nation's foreign policy in the executive as well as the legislature. As foreign assistance came to substitute for older forms of traditional diplomacy, it became a major foreign policy weapon—to be used in maintaining balances of power, bargaining with allies and Third World nations, and all the political strategy of the Cold War. It is perhaps not surprising that a nation which relied on its resources for winning wars would rely on them in other kinds of international activity as well. If it did not have the centuries-long experience in diplomacy of the European nations or the chess-like strategies of its Russian opponents, it had something that all nations respected—its wealth. At the same time, it could stand before the world as a humanitarian and generous nation, a role that Americans have liked to see themselves as taking. As McGeorge Bundy was to observe in 1975, speaking before a subcommittee of the Senate Foreign Relations Committee, "In many ways the multi-purpose grab bag which is our current foreign assistance program accurately reflects the many and varied purposes of the Executive Branch, the Congress and of public opinion itself."[3]

Foreign aid became an all-purpose weapon which, for a small fraction of the defense budget, could serve many different purposes simultaneously. While the goal of fighting communism is widely agreed to have been the chief purpose of the foreign aid program to date, other economic and political goals could be advanced simultaneously and had their supporters in the executive and Congress.[4] Political scientist Hans Morgenthau once listed six different purposes that foreign assistance could fulfill, although several of these appear overlapping. It could provide subsistence to some nations, economic development to others, and serve humanitarian purposes. It could also be used militarily, help American prestige in the world, and be used as a bribe in diplomacy.[5] Morgenthau did not mention the economic usefulness to the donor countries in such matters as trade and foreign investment. With such a multipurpose program at hand, it is not surprising that both executive and legislature recognized the power of the purse in foreign policy making. For many nations it became the most tangible—and the most important—form of U.S. policy. For all nations it signaled symbolically and materially the shifts in American foreign policy and the country's posture in the world.

We can look at this foreign policy microcosm in both the presidency and Congress by focusing on the annual authorization bills for economic and military assistance, from Kennedy to Reagan. The bills are sometimes combined and sometimes enacted separately, and in several years no authorization is passed, the government continuing its foreign assistance policy through supplemental and continuing legislation. Overall there are twenty-two separate authorization bills passed. (See appendix C.)

While the authorization process is not the only arena for foreign assistance policy in Congress, it is a particularly central one. It is carried out primarily by the members of the two foreign policy committees—the Senate Foreign Relations Committee and the House Foreign Affairs Committee—in close consultation with the leadership and the money committees. Given the continuing, although weakened, norms of specialization in Congress, it is the members of the two authorizing committees who are considered the main congressional experts in foreign policy, exclusive of defense, and the main source for substantive legislation. Committee members use the foreign aid bill to discuss whatever areas of foreign policy they choose. So while both authorizing and appropriations committees have regularly cut the President's requests, appropriations lets the authorizing committees make most of the substantive changes, and the cuts tend to parallel each other across the years. The authorizing committees cut the bill and make their substantive changes, and the appropriations committees cut the bill further. The conference committee stage, to reconcile differences between the House and Senate drafts, adds a critical input of the leadership to these substantive decisions. Hence if we are seeking a congressional role, we would expect to see it most clearly in these authorization decisions.[6] By comparing the presidential request bill with the public law that emerges from Congress, we can see over time the extent to which each branch makes changes in the policy.[7]

Unlike the cases in the preceding chapters, we cannot be sure that presidents see the draft bill or discuss any of its provisions with their advisers. In this case arguments that Congress should not meddle in foreign assistance policy usually do mean that they should not meddle with the State Department or other agencies which are routinely reviewing the bill and sending it to the White House for the President's signature. Nevertheless, presidents do take broad positions on what they want by way of economic and military assistance, often designating particular provisions of special interest. In terms of prestige it is "the President's bill" that can be amended, cut, or revised in Congress, and the President's foreign policy objectives which may be challenged by congressional revisions. We can, therefore, assess the role of Congress in this particular kind of foreign policy compared to the President's role as long as we understand that the presidential role may already be overstated.

The comparison between the branches is important for two reasons. It will show how much Congress does in this particular kind of policy, separating the illusion of activity from the actual legislative impact. But by showing Congress at its most hardworking, it will also begin to reveal where problems lie. Just as the massive congressional workload that was seen in chapter 2 hid a very small substantive output, here, too, a great deal of work does not translate into legislation. The result is a foreign aid policy, disliked and debated in both branches, that remains the same across time.

THE SHORT UNHAPPY HISTORY OF FOREIGN AID POLICY

"Christmas is almost upon us, and foreign aid is before the House." So began the Republican minority report in the House in 1969. "The gift list in this bill was not hastily drawn up," the report continued. "Those the Executive overlooked or slighted the Committee took care of."[8] Indeed, from its inception in the Truman years, foreign aid has aroused skepticism in Congress. It cannot easily be translated into constituency jobs or real estate or any of the traditional divisions of domestic politics. Indeed, in constituency terms it is seen as the reverse—as taxes, or giveaway programs, and foreign ones at that. American citizens educated in the need for military preparedness were not similarly persuaded about the importance of aid for national security. Consequently, there has been little constituency support for aid programs and no sizable vested congressional support. Since the end of the 1940s Congress has lagged behind the executive on aid, as presidents of both parties have complained. Its general policy has been less aid, for less time, tied to more restraints, and with more signs of "appreciation" from the recipient nations.

In this foreign policy area Congress typically has *not* acquiesced to the executive branch. Debates on foreign aid have been marked by as much controversy and defeats for the President, we will see, as have many domestic programs. The famous response "Who are we to say no to the military?" used by committee members to rationalize support for defense spending is not heard in the foreign aid debates. Congress apparently knows who it is and is willing to say no quite frequently. The congressional skepticism has meant that presidents, at least in the past, have had to bargain for whatever foreign assistance they get and give to Congress a share of the policy making. It is this bargaining position we need to watch in foreign assistance policy across the years.

The White House record on foreign assistance has been less consistent. Truman and Kennedy made foreign aid programs a major part of their foreign policy agendas. In the Marshall Plan and postwar aid to Greece and Turkey, Truman first sold the notion of aid to Congress as a weapon in the fight against communism. Kennedy added new proposals and a greatly expanded aid program to Third World nations. While all presidents have wanted the use of aid funds, free of congressional restriction, for their foreign policy goals, several have given the programs lower priority than they were given in the Truman and Kennedy years. Nixon and Reagan fought for a greater share of the funds to be allocated for military assistance, and other presidents fought for particular objectives. Thus the aid program has limped along, facing opposition in Congress and variable support in the executive branch.[9]

This is not to say there has been congressional unanimity on the subject. It is important to see that the divisions in Congress have followed party lines throughout much of the four decades, independently of the particular issues, the presidents in office, or the ideological alignments of the time. While a majority of Republicans did join with Democrats to support the Marshall Plan and its extensions, they opposed the mutual security program of the early 1950s and gave mixed support to the requests of Eisenhower, a president of their own party. Eisenhower's victories depended on the Democrats and on compromises in the program to win some Republican votes. By the Kennedy years the partisan divisions were even clearer. All of the key roll calls on foreign assistance in the Senate and House were party votes, where a majority of one party opposed a majority of the other.[10] Kennedy would lose or win depending on the issue and how many partisans could be persuaded to change sides.

Despite the fluidity of alignments that marked the post-Vietnam years, the partisan divisions continued. Taking all the controversial aid roll calls from the Ford to the Reagan administrations, we find that three-fourths are party votes, with the majorities of the two parties opposed. Party majorities took opposite stands on such issues as military aid to Turkey and Central America, assistance to El Salvador, Panama, and the OPEC nations, and restrictions on aid to nations violating human rights. They divided also on increasing or reducing aid to the International Monetary Fund, the Asian Development Bank, and the African Development Fund. In the Reagan years all of the controversial roll calls on aid to the Nicaraguan contras were party votes.

Overall, presidents would win about two-thirds of the foreign assistance roll calls on which they took a position, for about the same success rate as votes on domestic policy.[11] Congress is clearly not giving presidents any special consideration on this policy. Its opposition, moreover, has been facilitated by the parties in Congress and formed along party lines.

While the interbranch battles continued, there was growing dissatisfaction with the aid program within and outside of Congress that transcended party divisions. As early as 1965 Congress expressed itself as disenchanted with aid policy. Reorganization plans were considered in committee and then postponed. The same sequence recurred in 1969. While Congress did enact a number of new programs, serious revision was again postponed. Congress succeeded in 1973 in making several revisions to the overall policy, although critics called them cosmetic merely and the overall disenchantment remained. With renewed optimism Congress began a major revision in 1978, but the bill as it finally emerged was routine. Through all this time Congress repeatedly asked the President for help in defining and rationalizing aid policy, but the guidance was not forthcoming. By the time of the Reagan administration, aid bills had become so unpopular that no separate authorizations were made. In all the Reagan years with the exception of 1985, foreign aid was merely incorporated into omnibus continuing spending resolutions.

The growing disillusionment with foreign aid has several explanations. First, there are problems with measuring the benefits and costs of the policy, problems that transcend any particular donor nation, as Britisher John White so ably points out.[12] In the absence of such justification, however, it is difficult to build support: no one knows who it is that has been aided. In addition, neither President nor Congress can rationalize a policy that is inherently contradictory. Since aid has been used to fulfill a number of different foreign policy objectives, the giving of aid in one case might cancel the benefits derived from another. If we were fighting Communism in the 1960s, why should we then have wished to aid the countries of Eastern Europe, who had Communist governments at the time? If we are trying to make the world safe for democracy, why are we supporting fascist dictatorships? If we wish to be humanitarian, should we not support the poorest countries whether or not their governments have violated human rights? Critics have pointed out that most of the top recipients of U.S. development aid have not been low-income nations, and that nearly 50 percent of the countries receiving military aid have been under some kind of nondemocratic military rule.[13] No one in government has wanted to take on these questions.

Changes in the international setting have also contributed to the American dilemma. Foreign assistance was easier in a world seen as bipolar, with containment of communism the overriding security goal. As the world became more fluid and multidimensional, the rationale—and the consensus—for any particular policy has been lacking. Nations can shift alliance patterns at very short notice, and the policies might need to shift accordingly. It consequently has been more difficult to form a consensus and to maintain one. Finally, Congress's own budgetary problems, growing with the federal deficit, has made it more difficult to authorize anything. Not only did the process of allocating money become more complex with the budgetary reforms of the 1970s, there has been increasingly less money to allocate. Once the government bound itself to balance a budget that could not be balanced, the only possible outcome for many programs, and not merely foreign assistance programs, was the omnibus continuing resolutions.

Nevertheless, we have to distinguish making foreign aid policy from making foreign policy via the foreign aid bill. Both President and Congress have found the legislation useful as a kind of all-purpose foreign policy instrument. The conflicts are less about who will make aid policy than about who will make foreign policy—who will use this instrument for what effect.

THE CONGRESSIONAL ROLE

When we compare the White House draft bill to the final public law that emerges from Congress, the congressional role appears substantial. Looking at specific changes within each section—what we can call the level of a "provision," or section subhead[14]—we can distinguish between legislative and nonlegislative changes. Legislative changes involve alterations in (1) the countries designated as aid recipients, (2) the policy, such as the restrictions applying to a particular program, and (3) the monetary amounts allocated to the program, or the maximum and minimum amounts set. Nonlegislative changes involve (1) requests for oversight, such as reporting requirements served on the President or the Secretary of State, (2) statements expressing the sense of Congress about goals or particular policy objectives, and (3) technical changes in the language or organization of the bill. Using these divisions, we see that Congress makes changes in at least half of the provisions consistently across the years, with about one-third of the changes overall having to do with legislation. This is not "amending" the President's bill—it is at least partially rewriting it. This chapter concentrates on what Congress has done with the authorization bill on matters of legislation, while the next chapter looks at what it did not do.

Activism

Congressional policy through the 1960s was consistent in several ways. It limited allocations to one year when the executive asked for two, encouraged multilateral aid programs as opposed to bilateral aid, loans as opposed to outright assistance, and attempted to provide for more favorable balance of payment conditions for the United States. All this was accompanied by cuts in the overall program which became routine and expected as the decade progressed.

The overall changes from the requests to the authorizations are shown below. It should be understood that while the authorizing committees cut the presidential requests, the appropriating committees would cut them still further, usually in consultation with the substantive committee's experts. Kennedy's economic assistance requests were routinely cut, while the lower requests for military assistance were in large part preserved. Johnson, who tried to continue the Kennedy assistance policies for the most part,[15] had more variable success, depending on how much he "pre-shrunk" the request. Again, only the economic aid—not the military aid—was cut in the Johnson years:

	Request	Authorization	Amount Cut (Billions)
1961	4.9	4.8	.1
1962	4.8	4.3	.5
1963	4.7	4.6	.1
1964	4.5	3.6	.9
1965	3.6	3.6	-
1966	4.2	4.1	.1
1967	4.3	3.5	.8
1968	3.4	2.8	.6

These overall cuts are less important in themselves than in providing a context for interbranch bargaining. At a time in the 1960s when congressional goodwill could mean the difference of millions of dollars for programs, the members' views on foreign policy were taken seriously.

By far the largest number of substantive changes the Congress made at this time concerned the balance of payments problem. As early as 1961, in the bill that would become the cornerstone of the aid program, Congress added limits to the use of foreign currencies in repaying loans, prohibited aid to any enterprises that competed with U.S. enterprises, said that shipment of goods would be made by American-flag vessels and that arrangements must be made to defray part of the shipping costs. All of these changes appeared in the final Foreign Assistance Act of 1961 and stayed in one form or another in subsequent bills. Congress warned Kennedy again in the 1963 authorization that "the President shall consider the possible adverse effect" of the programs on the U.S. balance of payments (Public Law 88:205; hereafter "Public Law" will appear as "PL"). It also restricted loans to countries that could give some guarantees of repaying them, for example by instituting an investment guaranty program. While Johnson kept the congressional changes in his draft bills, Congress then added more refinements on investment guarantees and occasions for the use of foreign currencies. Pilot programs that Nixon added to the foreign assistance bill in 1969 brought congressional changes in cost-sharing and currency restrictions, new insurance provisions, and limits on the total amount of loans that could be made to any country.

In addition to watching the balance of payments, Congress early on kept an eye on the military impact of aid. It set ceilings on military aid in the 1961 act and added restrictions later, terminating aid to countries that could afford to arm themselves, limiting amounts that could be used for the peaceful development of atomic energy, and finally prohibiting any form of aid for the development of sophisticated weapon systems.

During the same time Congress showed itself willing to add or delete countries as aid recipients. In the 1961 bill it prohibited aid to Cuba or any other Communist nations and repeated the provision in 1962, with a list of eighteen countries to be sure the executive branch understood. Kennedy had taken the 1961 restrictions out in his draft bill of 1962, and Congress put them back in. Restrictions on aid to Indonesia and military aid to Africa followed in 1963. By the end of the decade Congress had instituted the practice of earmarking amounts to be spent for particular countries: Israel, for example, and countries in Latin America. Thus as the total aid budget shrank and the earmarking increased, the executive was increasingly limited in the amount of aid it could offer any one nation.

Kennedy and Secretary of State Rusk had protested these country amendments, saying that the specific targeting was no way to make foreign policy.[16] Congress apparently disagreed since it continued the practice. Nevertheless, the restrictions usually included the proviso that the President could designate aid to any one country if it were found essential to national security and if he reported the action to Congress. Often the proviso stipulated that he must "promptly report" to Congress any such action with a fairly detailed treatise of explanation. This was not the kind of throwaway provision that it would come to be later, when Congress would give back with one hand what it was taking away with the other. Here, while providing an escape hatch for exceptional circumstances, Congress was offering no invitation to presidents to see how far they could go. Since the aid program itself depended on Congress's grudging support, presidents were not tempted to abuse the proviso.

An example of the type of proviso used in this period is shown in the prohibition of aid to Communist nations in the 1962 act (PL 87:565):

This restriction may not be waived . . . unless the President finds and promptly reports to Congress that: (1) such assistance is vital to the security of the United States; (2) the recipient country is not controlled by the international Communist conspiracy; and (3) such assistance will further promote the independence of the recipient country from international communism.

In effect, aid could not be given to a Communist country unless it showed signs of not being Communist.

All of these changes, it is important to remember, are in the final public law. They became the nation's foreign policy, with its variable allocations of aid, limits on military aid, and balance of payment provisions. While Congress gave the President the necessary escape hatch for reasons of national security, it remained clear about what it did and did not want.

It is also important to see the role of the committees in this activist period. Most of the congressional changes to the final public law were committee changes, made in the Senate or House foreign affairs committees or else approved by the same committee members serving in the conference. Foreign policy was not made by floor amendments. In the 1965 bill, for example, the House voted down all proposed amendments, with the committee members speaking on the floor to defeat them. The more individualistic Senate adopted two and defeated more than a dozen. One of the adopted amendments was a late administration request and one was an amendment offered by committee member Wayne Morse (D., Ore.), a strong critic of foreign aid legislation. Morse offered ten amendments: he was given one and defeated on the other nine. Even in 1968 when the Senate committee's chairman J. W. Fulbright (D., Ark.) had joined the minority opposing the bill, amendments to cut and to increase the authorization were defeated on the floor. The compromising had already been done in committee and in the House. The House accepted floor amendments from committee Republicans who added cuts to the bill and the House then defeated fifteen other amendments.

The Post-Vietnam Era

The signs of a change in foreign aid policy in Congress can be seen as early as 1969. With the program steadily decreasing in popularity in both the executive branch and Congress, Nixon requested the lowest amount in the history of the legislation and even tried to shift some of the remaining budget to a new emphasis on military aid. By the Nixon policy, which would be expanded greatly in the years of the Reagan administration, the foreign aid bill would help finance military and quasi-military projects which could also be funded elsewhere: most notably in the far more generous budgets of defense and the classified intelligence authorizations. This emphasis on military aid disrupted the party alignments in Congress, both in the committees and in the two chambers. Liberal Democrats who had been the main supporters of foreign aid in the past balked at the military aid provisions, especially in a time of protest against the Vietnam War. Although the House roll call in 1969 of 176 to 163 was still a party vote, the narrow margin showed how many Democrats had defected and voted against the bill. Republicans also split, some voting with the President and some following their traditional opposition. The Senate vote was not even a party vote, with narrow majorities in both parties supporting the hybrid proposal.

While many of the authorization votes in the decade to come would still show party alignments, the outcomes were less predictable. Coalitions in support of any one bill could disappear rapidly and had to be built anew, often around specific provisions or a combining of several provisions in a typical congressional logrolling. The increasing fluidity of alignments and the possibility of attracting stray defecting members brought a larger role for special interests, especially foreign governments, in lobbying the foreign aid bill. In a speech on the Senate floor as early as 1969 Fulbright warned of this kind of impact. He cited as particularly helpful in passing that year's bill the large sums allotted to Taiwan and South Korea (about $50 million apiece) and a $40 million Israeli desalting plant.[17]

As the 1970s wore on, the committee power was also undercut by the decentralization engendered by the congressional reforms. This meant that the committees would have less of a monopoly of policy making and that attempts to coordinate House and Senate differences could be derailed by amendments on the floor. In the absence of committee agreement and with the vacuum created by the parties' confusion, it is not surprising that some of Congress's advantage in this policy area would fall by the way.

Nevertheless, Congress remained active through much of the 1970s. Indeed, the specific country provisions proliferated well beyond the anticommunism of the decade before. The record for these congressional changes occurred with the 1974 bill, which limited Mideast aid and aid to Turkey; prohibited one program from assisting Chile, Korea, or India; repeated the limits from the year before on aid to Laos, Thailand, and South Vietnam; and gave a very detailed breakdown of the way funds would be spent for Cambodia. In case there was any misunderstanding, Congress added a separate provision prohibiting transfer of funds from other parts of the Foreign Assistance Act for aid to Indochina. In a little-noticed innovation, it prohibited aid to countries in which there were U.S. military bases unless those countries allowed U.S. news correspondents access to the base.

While 1974 was clearly an exceptional year, Congress reduced its activity only partially after the passage of the War Powers Act and the resignation of a president from office. In 1976 it set limits on Turkey, Angola, and Chile again, imposed restrictions on the Mideast Fund, and earmarked funds for relief of Italy and Lebanon. In 1977 the limits on Vietnam, Cambodia, Laos, and Cuba (which Carter had removed) were repeated and in 1978 Uganda was added to the list. Congress also earmarked much of the African funds for a $2 million project of locust control.

During the same period Congress had been busy recasting much of the foreign aid program. Revisions in 1973 marked a shift away from bilateral programs to those that would supply direct help to the needy within a nation. This congressionally written legislation was added to throughout the decade. Congress continued its arms watch via the foreign aid bill by cutting funds for military sales, prohibiting aid funds for the development of nuclear power in Israel or Egypt, and restricting arms and nuclear transfers between nations. In 1976 Congress ended the U.S. military grant program with a few exceptions which would continue to be negotiated with the President. Concern with the U.S. balance of payments from the previous decade continued, although much of the congressionally written legislation was still in place in the programs that remained. While presidents often removed the particular country prohibitions (understanding that Congress would put them back in), they did not meddle with Congress's concern for the U.S. Treasury.

The congressional contribution in these years is still noteworthy. If it is more diffused than in the decade before, U.S. foreign policy in general had become less consistent too, and less capable of any clear rationale. Yet, much of the congressional activity of this time does not pay off in legislation, a fact that becomes increasingly clear by the end of the decade. Members of Congress act, but the Congress as a whole carries only a small fraction of that hard work into legislation. The 1980 bill shows this emerging trend in clearest form. Included in the extensive rewriting that the committees engaged in were adjustments for nine separate countries. Congress levied restrictions on aid to Angola and Nicaragua, changed provisions for Pakistan, Iran, and Kuwait, and added Greece and Somalia to a loan repayment schedule. It changed the amounts of aid for Israel and Egypt. At the same time, it wrote new legislation for the African Development Fund, eliminated another program, and cut foreign military sales substantially. It earmarked some of the Population and Health funds for what was called "natural family planning methods."

All this work, however, took place in a context in which Congress was giving back to the executive considerable discretion, as the floor debate made clear. Carter had asked for an easing of several of the restrictions added in the past years and Congress was giving him what he asked for. In the kind of two-handed legislation typical of the period, Congress stated that the President could provide military aid to nations "even if prohibited by law" as long as the President ruled it was "vital to the national security interests of the United States." In effect, the lawmakers had said that the laws on this subject could now be overruled with a presidential statement. As in the pattern seen in previous chapters, the amount of activity is misleading. When all the work was done and the bill was signed into law, Congress had relinquished some of its hard-fought policy-making power.

This shift is also seen in the overall requests and authorizations through the decade:

Amount Cut (Billions)

	Request	Authorization	Amount Cut (Billions)
1969	3.0	2.0	1.0
1970	2.6	2.0	.6
1971	2.8	2.8	-
1972	continuing	continuing	-
1973	2.8	2.4	.4
1974	3.3	2.7	.6
1975	continuing	continuing	[.6]
1976	4.7	4.7	-
1977	4.8	4.8	-
1978	4.6	4.6	-
1979	5.1	4.8	.3

Requests were no longer routinely cut as they had been in the previous decade. Moreover, with the increase in military assistance *in line with presidential requests,* the overall budget was growing. Military assistance had formed less than half of Kennedy's budget, authorized at $2 billion in 1961. That figure had shrunk to $.4 billion in 1969 and 1970, as the antiwar movement grew. By the Carter years, however, it had climbed back—to $3 billion in 1977 and $2.9 billion in each of 1978 and 1979, far beyond the levels for economic assistance.

Direct comparisons across the decades cannot be made because of two contrasting effects: the change in real dollars, which might exaggerate the growth of programs over time, and the shift of many of the multilateral programs to their own separate budgets, which might understate the growth of the assistance programs. Nevertheless, the change in Congress's response to executive requests is clear. It is no longer the ogre of the foreign assistance program. Indeed, by the end of the decade it is giving Carter all of the assistance he requests.

Signs of the growing disintegration through the 1970s can be seen in the shift from committee to the floor.[18] In the 1973 bill, for example, the House erupted with twenty-nine proposed amendments. While most were rejected, the House succeeded in eliminating a major new program—an export credit fund—that its own committee had written into the bill. The House then passed restrictive amendments for nations interfering with U.S. fishing vessels. It rewrote the committee's legislation concerning the expropriation of U.S.-owned property. It strengthened the restriction against funds for reconstruction in North Vietnam and it questioned Portugal's use of funds to support military activities in Africa. Since the vote on the total authorization was going to be close, the amendments were the price for getting any bill at all. The House finally passed the authorization 188 to 183.

In 1974 it was the Senate's turn. It worked its way through twenty-one proposed amendments, eliminating many of the toughest restrictions that the Senate committee had written in. The bill became so confused in the process of amendment that a vote to recommit to committee was passed. As Congressional Quarterly observed in a fitting obituary, "It died from its own encumbrances."[19] Thus the committee which had already rewritten the legislation from the President's draft bill had to write it again. A compromise draft finally passed the Senate by a one-vote margin, five of the Democrats on the committee voting against the bill.

Foreign aid consistently has been part of Congress's working agenda, as we saw in chapter 2. In the years of the 1970s, however, floor votes became increasingly common in both the Senate and the House. The chambers were making the decisions that the committees had made before, often on very specific subjects. Aid to Turkey, India, Angola, Jamaica, Panama, South Africa, and Syria were the subject of floor votes. So also were cuts in the International Development Fund and the International Monetary Fund and arms sales to particular nations.

Needless to say, all the piecemeal changes were placing an increasing strain on the conference committees that had to reconcile Senate and House drafts. The amendments would increase until by the end of the decade none of Congress's many hands seemed to know what all the other hands were doing. This, however, is a story for the following chapter.

"That Was a Surprise, Wasn't It?"

Passing foreign aid legislation became even more difficult in the 1980s with the growing salience of the federal deficit and balance of payment problems. As the Reagan administration's shift from economic to military assistance further undercut party alignments, aid bills became patched-together products of lobbying in both the executive and Congress for particular countries and programs. No larger stable coalitions could form. Nevertheless, the first authorization that Congress passed looked like the 1980 bill of the Carter period in several ways. Again, a number of countries and regions were targeted for congressional adjustments: Israel, Egypt, the eastern Mediterranean, Tunisia, Costa Rica, Nicaragua, and El Salvador. Minor changes were made in one program for Central America and Taiwan, while earlier changes for Greece and Somalia, taken out by the executive, were put back in. This excludes the numerous countries merely singled out for "sense of Congress" provisions. At the same time, the committees had rewritten the Peace Corps legislation and had written new environment and natural resource legislation, as well as making numerous adjustments in the funding for other programs. All this work, however, accompanied a bill that was giving Ronald Reagan a greatly upgraded military assistance program and new discretion. Congress relaxed funding limits previously set for military assistance, raised the ceilings for military sales, and increased the allowable limits for stockpiling. It also accepted the administration's request doubling the thresholds under which individual arms sales would need to be approved by Congress. The return of congressional power to the executive first seen in the 1980 bill was increased in 1981.

The 1981 authorization (PL 97:113) consisted of forty-seven densely written single-spaced pages, about half again as long as a typical book page. About ten of these pages were given to sense of Congress resolutions: broad statements of principle without specific legislative enactments. A long section, for example, explained that the "Congress . . . finds that the world faces enormous, urgent, and complex problems, with respect to natural resources, which require new forms of cooperation between the United States and developing countries." It asked the President to develop procedures to deal with these problems. Another section described the threats to global security from such factors as shortages in food and natural resources, sickness, population pressure, and desperate poverty. It pointed out that such conditions could create unrest and violence and could increase the likelihood of confrontation between nations which possess nuclear arms. It urged:

> that the Nation's understanding of global and national security
> must be broad enough to include the problems cited in this section,

and that adequate protection of the security of the United States requires effective action on these global problems, and in particular on the problems of hunger, disease, and extreme poverty.

The remaining substantive pages contained a total of fifteen presidential escape clauses: provisos that free presidents from whatever restriction Congress has enacted if (a) they determine it is in the interest of U.S. national security, and/or (b) they report to Congress on why they have made the exception. In this way Congress legislates a restriction, but includes the means by which presidents can override the restriction. Escape clauses were provided on such subjects as arms sales to NATO, leasing of defense articles, stationing of advisers in foreign countries, use of funds for foreign nuclear facilities, restrictions on the use of foreign currencies, and aid to Argentina and El Salvador.

For example, presidents could lease defense articles to certain eligible nations only under a set of specified conditions. They could waive these restrictions, however, if they reported to Congress that the national security required the lease. According to the act, funds could not be used for the construction, operation, or maintenance of any nuclear facility in a foreign country. Exceptions could be made, however, if the President certified to Congress that such funds would serve a nonproliferation objective of paramount importance to the United States. These were not minor matters, it is clear, but key controversial issues of the day that Congress was leaving in the President's hands.

One can compare this document with an act from the 1960s which also combined economic and military assistance: the 1967 authorization (PL 90:137). The 1967 bill was less than half the length, at approximately nineteen pages. It contained a smaller proportion of sense of Congress language—about three pages. Even these broad sentiments were designed to give a sense of congressional priorities: specifically, the importance of self-help for recipient nations and a new emphasis on multilateral aid sources. The act included only one presidential escape clause, and this retained some congressional restrictions. The President could agree to furnish defense articles to another, eligible country if he found this necessary for national security and if he promptly reported to Congress. Congress, however, decided what the eligible countries were. Overall, presidential escape clauses increased from an average of two per act in the 1960s to fourteen in the 1980s. While the length of the bills had more than doubled, the escape clauses grew at an even greater rate.

These devices, of escape clauses and sense of Congress resolutions, will be looked at more fully in the following chapter. For the present, they provide a clearer sense of what delegation means. Much of the impressive statute passed in 1981 consisted of broad consensual provisions, requests for the President to do something, or restrictions that contained their own escape clause for the President's discretion. At the level of the statute we see the same optical illusion we have seen before, a quantity of output that disguises how much of the policy is left in the President's hands.

Congress had passed an unusual two-year authorization in 1981, postponing the problem of returning to foreign aid until 1983. In both 1983 and 1984, however, Congress failed to pass any bill, and the programs were maintained by omnibus continuing resolutions. Nineteen eighty-four brought no appropriations legislation either. In 1983 both Senate and House committees had worked on a bill, but failed to get support from their respective chambers. In 1984, the House acted, but the Senate, influenced in part by administration opposition to the bill, did not. Congress managed to pass two specific restrictions as part of the continuing resolutions. It arrived at a compromise with the administration on aid to El Salvador, and it restricted aid to the Nicaraguan contras. In large part, however, the omnibus resolutions simply continued the status quo with some congressional adjustment in funding. This in effect eliminated Congress's discretion in these years over particular recipients and programs.

The votes limiting aid to the contras need to be seen in this context. They were passed at a time when Congress was for the most part enacting no authorizations—in other words, levying no new restrictions. And they followed a period, in 1980 and 1981, when many of the existing restrictions were repealed. Thus while secretaries of state and national security advisers would accuse Congress of "meddling" in Nicaragua, presidents of the 1960s would have told them they didn't know what meddling was.

A compromise bill was passed in 1985 to the wonderment of all. "That was a surprise, wasn't it?" Speaker Tip O'Neill remarked after the House vote, although he of all members might have been the least surprised. The vote, taken under the auspices of the leadership, was by voice: it was suspected that a roll call might have shown a different division.[20] The committees as well as the leadership had worked hard for the compromise in both chambers. The two-year authorization lifted some additional restrictions that the administration had requested, although it cut the requests and retained limits on weapon sales to Jordan and Central America. To try to stop the indirect channeling of funds to Nicaragua, Congress wanted to prohibit the U.S. from making an agreement with another country to provide aid to the contras. Faced with the threat of a presidential veto because of this restriction, Congress compromised, saying merely that the U.S. should not "force" a foreign aid recipient to give aid to the contras. This satisfied the White House and the veto was averted. Presumably the President would be able to say that no potential aid recipient was "forced."

Notice the shift in bargaining advantage from the Kennedy years. Congress could tell Kennedy that no funds should be given to Communist nations unless they showed signs of not being Communist. Kennedy, desperate for any foreign aid legislation, had to accept the restriction. In the later period, it is the Congress that is desperate for a foreign aid bill after all the embarrassments of not being able to pass one. Thus it is the President who can dictate the restrictions.

The passage of the 1985 bill would be the last such surprise, however, in the Reagan years. In 1987 a bill struggled through the House and the Senate committee, but did not reach the Senate floor. In 1988 again the Senate buried the bill, although the first appropriation since 1981 was passed, showing that it was not only the authorizing committees that were finding new problems with the power of the purse. Except for particular restrictions—for example, on arms sales to some nations and on military aid to Nicaragua—which were passed one by one in roll call votes, foreign aid legislation was buried in the continuing resolutions.

No one has tried to study the actual authorization amounts made for foreign assistance in the 1980s. Some were buried in omnibus spending bills while others were separated into urgent supplemental legislation and special "emergency" aid. The sum of $2 billion was authorized for emergency aid in 1985 alone. Yet, if we compare the normal authorization bills that were enacted— for 1980, 1981, and 1985—the result is startling:

	Request	Authorization	Amount Cut (Billions)
1980	5.3	5.0	.3
1981	6.7	5.9	.8
1982	continuing	[6.0]	[.7]
1985	13.2	12.8	.4

Somehow the foreign assistance budget had doubled during the time that no normal authorizations were being passed.

These totals exclude the $2 billion funded for emergency aid and another $2 billion authorized by a supplemental bill for the Economic Support Fund. The Economic Support Fund was begun in the Carter years, in the wake of Camp David, to provide "assistance to friendly nations with large military budgets." These friendly nations with large military budgets were primarily Israel and Egypt. In 1985 the supplemental bill authorized $1.5 billion to Israel, $.5 billion to Egypt, and about $8 million for other Middle Eastern programs. Counting the emergency aid and the supplemental aid along with the regular authorization would bring the total for foreign assistance to about $17 billion, not counting the multilateral lending programs.

The regular authorization for 1985 broke down as follows:

	Request	Authorization	Amount Cut (Billions)
Military Aid	6.7	6.3	.4
Support Fund	4.0	3.8	.2
Development Aid	1.7	1.8	Increase
Other Programs	.8	.9	Increase

While there is no way of making direct comparisons, the development aid appears in line with previous authorizations, which had been slightly under $2 billion a year for much of the 1970s, down from about $2.7 billion on the average in the Kennedy and Johnson years. In 1985, Congress increased the amounts marginally over the presidential request. The major growth appears in the military assistance and the military-related Economic Support Fund, which Congress cut slightly. Military assistance had declined steadily from the $2 billion in the first Kennedy budget to as low as $.4 billion in 1969 and 1970, a sign of Congress's disapproval with executive policy in Southeast Asia. It began to climb again in the Ford and Carter years, averaging $3 billion, not counting the special programs. It then doubled in the Reagan years to about $7 billion, again not counting the supplemental funding or the Camp David bill, which continued to come due.

It is true that Congress in the 1980s was once again cutting administration requests, but the foreign assistance bill at this point was largely a testament to presidential success: in effect, the military aid to Israel and Egypt, the beneficiaries of the Camp David agreements in the Carter years; and the greatly expanded military assistance programs of the Reagan administration.[21]

The Foreign Policy Purse

In using the foreign aid programs as a kind of microcosm of American foreign policy, Congress showed itself at its most characteristic and most powerful. It reviewed the allocation of money and programs in its substantive committees, thoroughly and frequently, rewriting a substantial portion of the legislation. By holding the purse strings, it had no problem designating friends or foes or policy priorities, enforcing the anticommunism of the 1960s, the demobilization of the 1970s, and the more militant mood of the early 1980s. It watched national interests and pioneered new programs and tried to balance when the President should and should not have a free hand. Indeed, as one scholar observes, Congress may have been even more consistent than the executive in the attempt to articulate U.S. interests abroad.[22]

It is true that presidents could always find funds elsewhere if they really wanted them. Areas of the defense budget and the entire CIA budget are typically not reviewed by Congress. In addition, there remains discretion for presidents to juggle funds in foreign assistance as in other programs. Nevertheless, the inexorable annual or two-year foreign aid review held its own political logic: presidents who wanted a program at all would not stray too far from a position on which Congress had expressed itself strongly.

Here in action is Congress's constitutional power of the purse: according to James Madison the "most complete and effectual weapon with which any constitution can arm the representatives of the people."[23] Congress could influence foreign policy broadly through control of the multipurpose foreign assistance funds. Its influence was increased by the fact that presidents wanted these programs more than Congress did. Yet, this situation shifted in the more recent years. With party alignments weakened and committee control in decline, it became increasingly difficult for Congress to authorize. There was also less money to spend. Congress, in effect, got caught in its own purse strings. The bargaining advantage also shifted. As the program became more unpopular, presidents no longer cared if Congress did pass an authorization; in fact they benefited by way of increased discretion when it could not act. So, Kennedy had to fight for a program he felt strongly about. Johnson tried to pacify Congress with reduced requests. But Presidents Carter and Reagan gained back, year by year, the discretion that Congress had sought to exercise over foreign policy in the years before. In combination, neither branch had incentives to debate foreign assistance policy or to bring potential controversies to public view. Since foreign aid had been the congressional strong point, the net result was to weaken the Congress in foreign policy making.

Certainly the committees continued to work hard on legislation in the later period. They could still say no to particular executive requests and alert the White House to issues that it might prefer not to become entangled in. The power of the purse, however, had become a very heavy burden. Now Congress had to settle for any bill it could get, and reply to veto threats with substantial concessions. Therefore, while much of the current debate assumes the congressional role has increased in recent years, one sees evidence in this chapter that the *opposite* is the case—from the consistency of the 1960s to the more diffused policies of the 1970s to the failure in the 1980s to pass any authorizations at all. This failure continued through the years of the Bush administration. In terms of the introductory typology, foreign aid in the Kennedy-Johnson years gives the clearest illustration of the *reform* pattern, with both President and Congress active in the politics of foreign aid. If Congress had not totally acquiesced by the Reagan-Bush years, it had moved much closer to the *conventional* pattern, where the President proposes and Congress yields, albeit with some complaining, to the White House. The trend appears opposite to what the popular debate suggests.

6

✦ ✦ ✦

THE MISUSE OF
COMPROMISE

B ICAMERALISM IS A WIDELY RECOGNIZED FACT of American
political life. It requires that any clear action on the part of
Congress must gain support in the House, the Senate, and
the conference committees charged with reconciling differences
between the chambers. This means that members who would
oppose the singular President on matters such as foreign policy
must build support in both houses and maintain it through the
conference stage, usually by means of committees or parties or
both. It also means that there will be few occasions when Congress
can be clear and definitive about its opposition. Much more typically, Congress will act by the kinds of compromises it builds, both
within any one piece of legislation and across time. It will prod
and push. It will increase its level of grumbling, and become increasingly single-minded about particular objectives until execu-
tives decide that the fight is not worth the prize. Clearly Congress
in compromise is also Congress at work.

The purpose of this chapter is not to criticize the activity of
compromise, which members do so well and which so much of the
institution is devoted to. It is rather to point out *when the compromises have been misused,* when Congress appears in the awkward position of fooling the public, and perhaps itself, that actions have
been taken when in fact they have not. We will see very specific
devices by which this illusion is carried out and a growth in the use
of these devices over time.

We thus return to the authorization bills of the previous chapter to look at some of the additional changes: the sense of Con-

gress provisions and the language added to presidential restrictions, as well as the oversight requirements written in to the final public law. We will also look at the context within which these changes are made and their impact on legislation. Typically they follow major controversies that find the House and Senate divided. However, the use and frequency of these devices change greatly across the years.

The Changing Nature of Compromise

Language and the Sense of Congress

It is through the language of legislation that Congress makes clear its intent, an intent that can guide the administrators of the program, whether in the White House or in an executive agency. Much of the language therefore that Congress writes into a bill can serve an important purpose of clarification. When, for example, in the 1960s Congress presented a list of eighteen nations prohibited from receiving aid along with a half-page statement of its position toward Communist countries and the (unlikely) conditions under which the prohibition could be lifted, it was trying to make its position perfectly clear. Much of the new legislation that Congress writes is also accompanied by extensive language— about the purposes of the program, its scope and limits, and the nature of the administration. A new development assistance program written into the 1978 public law began with three pages of general language on what "the Congress finds" and what "the Congress declares" the program and its goals and priorities to be.

Yet this language can also be used as a substitute for legislation and a kind of congressional face-saving device. Much of the language against nations violating human rights was written, we will see, when restrictions against the human rights violators failed to pass both houses. The language was accepted, but the restrictions were not. For another example, the Senate committee prohibited military assistance to support Greece's military dictatorship. When floor opposition developed to the restriction, language was substituted in the final bill that "urged the U.S. government to exert all possible effort to influence a speedy return to a constitutional government in Greece." Obviously the government could not exert all possible influence for constitutionalism if it was at the same time providing military assistance to the non-constitutional regime.

This effect is seen most clearly when the sense of Congress resolutions occur without any subsequent provisions. In the 1981 foreign assistance bill, one of only two passed throughout Reagan's terms, several such statements occurred. Congress expressed its concern with global poverty and sickness, made a statement about human rights abuses in the Soviet Union, and denounced international terrorism. None of these statements was followed by any legislation in the bill. In the case of the statement on terrorism Congress did ask the President to submit a report assessing the adequacy of the current legislation. Congress was not venturing to appraise its own legislative products. Since there was no legislation, one cannot say that Congress was trying to clarify its legislative intent. Like the symbolic resolutions passed on the floor, these provisions allow Congress to appear active while taking highly consensual symbolic positions.

Another special device is the proviso, the escape hatch for presidential discretion which is added to a restriction. The prohibition against aid recipients giving assistance to the contras was changed to language that said the government should not "force" aid recipients to aid the contras. Presumably the Reagan administration could find its way through that escape route. In an even more extreme example, the House proposed a $40 million authorization for an Israeli desalting plant which the administration opposed as not being feasible. The final bill made the authorization subject to the President's determination of whether the project was feasible or not. Another compromise had been achieved.

Reports to Congress

Reports to Congress serve many different purposes. At their most serious and straightforward, they provide the basis for congressional oversight, essential to any review by elected representatives of the ongoing activities of government. Thus the annual reports required by the economic development program or the Food for Peace program can serve this important function. Reports to Congress also provide ways to give the President discretion: Congress often restricts assistance subject to exceptions that the President may explain in a report. Thus Congress prohibited development aid for any underdeveloped country which purchased sophisticated weapons unless the President reported that the purchases were important to U.S. national security. Used sparingly, this kind of reporting requirement can be useful too, allowing Congress to state a general principle while still providing leeway for exceptions. In point of fact, however, the reporting provisos have become so frequent and routine as to call in question the general rule. Presidents can evade most of the restrictions at the price of having someone write a memorandum. Finally, reports, like the sense of Congress language, can be used as a substitute for legislation. When the legislation fails, Congress appeases the interests who supported the policy by calling for a report.

Certainly the reporting requirements written into the final assistance authorization have skyrocketed across the years. In the 1960s Congress added about two new reporting requirements each year, taking out some of the previously required reports, for a total of eight reports required by the 1969 public law. New and pilot programs were required to make a report as a matter of course, while the remaining requirements dealt primarily with grants of presidential discretion.

In contrast, in the years between 1973 and 1979, new reporting requirements were added at the average rate of *fourteen* a year. In 1974 there were eighteen, with a record high of twenty in 1978. Counting the new and the old reports, the 1978 authorizations for economic and military assistance asked for a total of twenty-nine reports. In 1979 Congress took out several and combined others; nevertheless, eighteen remained when the final bills for the year were passed.

The reports are no trifle either. One, quite typical for the period, required that the President conduct a "comprehensive" study of technology transfers, complete with nine separate subsections, and report to the Congress within one year. Another dissertation asked the President for his global assessment of food production. "The assessment shall include a comparative cross country evaluation, with no fewer than five countries," encompassing achievements, problems, and prospects. This assignment, too, was due in one year. Some of the provisions are serious, like the one prohibiting any further withdrawal of U.S. ground troops from the Republic of Korea unless the President reported:

> on the effect of any proposed withdrawal plan on preserving deterrence in Korea, the reaction anticipated from North Korea, the ef-

fect of the plan on increasing incentives for the Republic of Korea to develop an independent nuclear deterrent, the effect of any withdrawal on our long-term military and economic partnership with Japan . . . [and] on the United States-Chinese and United States-Soviet military balance . . . [and] on the Soviet-Chinese military situation. [PL 95:384]

Others appear to have little value, except a symbolic one, if that. Congress wrote a paragraph-long declaration of objectives asking for greater efficiency and coordination in development programs. It then called on the President to institute this new coordination and report back to Congress on the steps he had taken.

So the 1981 foreign aid authorization weighed in at nearly fifty pages, with ten pages expressing the sense of Congress, fifteen presidential escape clauses, and twenty-eight demands for presidential reports to Congress. Some of these demands carried over from previous congresses and about half, or thirteen, accompanied the escape provisions. While many of the remainder were merely routine requests to be kept informed of ongoing programs, some appeared to be asking the President to do the legislating. Congress, for example, asked the President to summarize the existing legislation affecting international terrorism, to assess its adequacy, and to propose alternative measures. It also asked him to review the entire foreign aid program and to report his analysis and recommendations in nine subject areas.

Is this the new activism? Clearly it is not the presidents and their advisers who are writing these reports or even keeping track of the twenty-eight different timetables in which some bureaucrats will have to write them. Although the bureaucratic hours demanded in writing the reports are almost incalculable, the legislative activity need not be great. When asked about the many reports, congressional staff people say, "No one reads them." Just as we saw in chapter 2, where the increase in legislation masked a decrease in substantive proposals, here, too, the swelling of statutory pages and provisions can be misleading. While the work increases, the impact declines. The devices can be misleading, too, in suggesting an aggressive Congress which ties the President's hands and keeps a close watch on executive decisions. Yet, behind the stern language of the reporting requirements, Congress is giving the President new discretionary authority and asking for advice on legislation.

Someone has suggested that "hyperlexis is America's national disease—the pathological condition caused by an overactive law-making gland."[1] The disease is seen in the explosion of statutes and regulations at all levels of government. Congress clearly has the disease, but it is important to see that the condition only mimics actual lawmaking and oversight. Possibly it can be treated by greater exposure to light.

The Changing Conference

The reforms of the 1970s affected conference committees in several ways. With the decentralization of influence to the party caucuses and to the subcommittees, committee chairs played less of a role in selecting who would be the conferees. While the party leadership continued to have an influence, decentralization left questions of the composition and balance of the conference increasingly up to the chance combination of who happened to be the subcommittee chairs and the other interested legislators at the time. The multiple referral of bills, practiced more in the House than in the Senate, further diversified the conference, bringing more than the main committees' interests to the negotiations.[2] Foreign affairs authorizations therefore could bring together members not only from the two foreign affairs committees, but also from Banking, Agriculture, and Defense.

The conferences thus grew larger. The mean size of the House and Senate delegates rose from about six from each chamber in 1963–64 up to eleven in the House and nine in the Senate in 1979–80, and up again to twelve in the House and ten in the Senate in 1985–86. (These numbers do not include the mammoth conferences for the omnibus reconciliation bills.[3]) The increased size made the meetings more unwieldy for the declared purpose of trying to reach a compromise that both House and Senate could accept. Conferences were also no longer dominated by members—the chairs and ranking members of the two committees—who had an interest in upholding the committees' work and prestige in managing the legislation. Committee outsiders—i.e., those from outside the major committee initiating the legislation—more frequently appeared as conferees, especially from the House. At the beginning of the 1970s only two of 150 House delegations included members not sitting on the originating committee. By 1979–80, twenty-seven of 154 delegations included outsiders.[4] If a conference failed in these years there was really no one to take the blame.

Beginning in 1975, the conferences were also opened to the public, and it was no longer a matter of trading and splitting the difference behind closed doors. Lobbyists now crowded into the small cramped conference rooms and stood on guard in the halls, on the chance that their presence might alter one small phrase or key provision. While the change probably gave special interests more influence, as interviews with members suggest,[5] it may also have produced changes in the nature of the negotiations. Some conferees suggest they now have to fight harder for small issues, supported by lobbying groups, which previously could have been dismissed or compromised.[6]

Additional changes in the same period complicated the conferees' task. Along with the increasing decentralization, floor amendments to the committee's draft increased, as previously discussed. At times, amendments could be deliberately added as "trading material" for the conference, and at other times amendments could be used to try to narrow the difference between the House and Senate drafts. In large part, however, the amendments imposed an additional burden on the conferees, widening the number of interests that would have to be resolved. The budget austerity taking hold in the late 1970s made things even more difficult. Conference committees liked to "split the difference" in a time-honored congressional tradition, compromising money amounts in order to bring about the necessary House-Senate accord. When these money amounts became very scarce resources indeed, no such splitting was possible in any one conference. As a committee staffer observed, "In the old days, it was not a zero-sum game. You could come up with a package that gave the House and Senate everything they wanted."[7] The new politics of budget austerity was more typically zero-sum.

Thus the problems of compromise became greater as the capacity to deal with them grew less. The conferences, under the watchful eyes of special interests, subject to the chance of floor amendments, and without the monetary means of finding easy solutions, would be grateful for any compromise they could get.

The extremes of conference action are seen in two cases widely apart in time. The 1968 foreign assistance authorization was very controversial. While the committees had slashed the "pre-shrunk" White House request, a conservative coalition in both the House and Senate wanted to cut the amounts still further. Everyone knew that the conference stage would be crucial. It would need to reconcile the forty-five differences between the House and Senate drafts and still report out a bill that could pass both chambers. This, however, was still the time of committee autonomy. The conferees, primarily the most senior members of both Senate and House committees, met for one day and dealt with forty-four of the differences. A second meeting was necessary for the remaining one—an exception proposed by senior Senate committee member Wayne Morse (D., Ore.) about western timber exports.[8] Morse, usually much less locally minded than many of his colleagues, was a potentially serious opponent to the authorization bill. The conference met for an additional day to solve the timber export problem and reported back a bill. It won passage by narrow majorities in both chambers.

No clearer contrast could be imagined than the Case of the Purloined Papers in the South African sanctions bill of 1985. The conference had met and done its work, reconciling the difference between the House bill and the Senate draft which proposed much weaker sanctions legislation. Yet, after the President's last-minute opposition, members of the Senate took the exceptional action of filibustering against the conference report. The undermining of the conference went further. When it appeared that a vote could be forced on the sanctions bill, a committee chair, backed by support of the Republican leadership, removed the report so that no vote could occur. The chair was himself a member of the conference. It is rare for a chamber to overturn any conference report. But in this case, the institution of the conference was opposed by institutional leaders themselves: i.e., a party leader and a committee chair, along with other Senate members, who supported the President against the conference.

Admittedly the extraordinary events of 1985 were aided by the split in party control between the House and Senate, with the Democrats controlling one chamber and the Republicans the other. Such a split, holding from 1981 to 1986, had not occurred since the last years of the Hoover administration. Yet the fact that institutional leaders would break the tradition of the sacrosanct conference says much about the new difficulties to be faced at the conference stage. It is also worth remembering that the key player in the conference defeat was not a member of Congress, but the chief of the executive branch.

A similar setback for the conference occurred in 1991. For the first time in six years it looked like a foreign assistance authorization might pass the Congress. Through long hours of negotiation, committee members and conferees gradually steered the bill through House and Senate, conference, and the Senate acceptance of the conference report. Then the Bush White House announced it would probably veto the bill because of the funds provided for international family planning. Abortion became the issue rather than foreign policy and the House debate that followed centered on the family planning provision. The result, after statements from the White House and the House floor on abortion policy, was that the House defeated its own conferees' report.

Once again we find the President as the key actor in the authorization process and a president willing to focus debate on an issue unrelated to foreign affairs. This recalls the cases of trade policy seen previously where debates on plant closing requirements substituted for the foreign policy issues. Bush did not need the authorization—Congress did; the leverage on foreign assistance had swung to the executive branch.

People used to ask who wins in conference, the Senate or the House, assuming a two-person game of negotiation and compromise.[9] A majority of House conferees and a majority of the Senate members have to agree on the compromise draft. However, with the growth of more decentralized and open conferences in recent years, the two-player assumption no longer holds. There are now many players in the conference—all the relevant committees, factions in support of floor amendments, the interest-group representatives who are attending each of the sessions, and even the President. Who wins is less the issue than how the conference can manage any compromise at all and still report legislation. The growing problems at the conference stage can be seen in the cases that follow.

CASES OF COMPROMISE

Early Cases

Deadlocks in conference were rare in the early years, when forty-four differences between the Senate and House could be reconciled in one day. On two occasions the conferees did let the executive solve the interchamber differences by means of a discretionary proviso. The Israeli desalting plant, pushed by the House in 1969, was left to presidential discretion, with the conferees knowing that the President was opposed. A difference about which countries could be exempted from the sophisticated weapons ban was also left to a presidential determination "in the interests of national security." The House wanted to exempt seven countries while the Senate draft included no exemptions. The House conferees expressed themselves as satisfied with the compromise since the President would know which seven countries were in the House draft.[10]

The more serious cases of conflict arose over the nature of the foreign assistance program itself. The impetus to revise the program originated in the Senate, and especially with such strong committee figures as J. W. Fulbright, Wayne Morse, and Frank Church. After engaging in its own compromises, the Senate committee sent to conference a proposal for a two-year authorization, a full-scale review and report, and the termination of the present aid program at the end of the two years. It requested the President to submit his own proposals the following year for a restructured aid program and it also proposed a Foreign Aid Planning Committee to make its own recommendations. The House committee for its part, facing a tight ideological battle on the floor between the supporters and the opponents of aid, had little interest in such luxuries as revision. The committee majority wanted some aid bill to pass, while a minority opposed the program or wanted large across-the-board cuts. Facing the implacable opposition of the House conferees, the Senate group tried to enlist the White House. Since Johnson did not want to get involved in foreign aid either, the House won and the reform proposal was dropped from the final bill. No review or report was asked for. The Senate reformers comforted themselves that a groundwork had been laid and hoped that the administration would recommend changes the following year.

In 1968 the conflict recurred. The Senate again proposed a comprehensive review and a study committee leading to reorganization of the aid program. The White House continued to keep hands off. Since the House was still opposed to any congressional revision, the conference accepted a compromise provision calling on the *President* to review the aid program and report to Congress. The final bill contained language expressing congressional dissatisfaction with the nation's foreign assistance policy and a request for a presidential report.

Although the House won indefinite postponement of a revision, the language reflects something of the Senate's frustration: The public law stated:

> The Congress declares that . . . there should be a comprehensive review and reorganization of all foreign assistance programs, including economic development and technical assistance programs, military assistance and sales programs, and programs involving contributions and payments by the United States to international lending institutions and other international organizations. (PL 90:555)

It continued by saying that "the President is requested" to make "a thorough and comprehensive reappraisal" of the above-mentioned subjects and submit it to Congress. The interim report was due in ten months and the final study in one year and a half.

While the provisos and the reporting requests do occur in these years as devices of conference compromise, their overall frequency is slight. This is especially true considering the number of controversies that Congress is endeavoring to solve.

The New Congress

As early as 1973 shifts in the conference mode of operation were evident. Pressure was on the conference following two years in which no authorizations had been passed. In 1971 the Senate had voted down the authorization bill, and in the next year the conference itself failed to reach agreement and the bill died. Hence the conferees who met in 1973 were challenged on two fronts. They had to reach agreement themselves and they had to produce a draft that could survive the controversies in both chambers. Another Senate defeat was possible, and the House, after considering twenty-nine amendments, had sent its bill to conference with the uninspiring vote of confidence of 188 to 183. There was the additional pressure of a threat of presidential veto. The folks in the White House were able to count the votes in Congress, and the bargaining advantage was shifting to the executive side.

Some of the work of the committees never made it to conference. An Export Development Credit Fund, one of the attempts by the committees to redirect the foreign assistance program, was taken out by the Senate Finance Committee, who also had a look at the authorization bill. A similar proposal by the House committee was deleted on the House floor. Nevertheless, after the bills had staggered through all their amendments in each chamber, 175 differences between the House and Senate drafts went to the conference to be resolved.[11]

The conference did manage to report back some legislation, including a cutoff of funds for military activities in Southeast Asia. Yet many of the hard-fought provisions did not survive the conference. In a proposal designed to give access to information, the Senate put forth a plan to cut off funds for any agency that did not provide within thirty-five days information requested by the General Accounting Office or a congressional committee. Faced with the threat of a presidential veto, the Senate provision was dropped from the final draft. A Senate amendment prohibiting aid to Chile for its violation of human rights was also deleted. In its place the conference wrote language saying it was the "sense of Congress" that the President should "request the government of Chile to protect human rights." A prohibition on military aid to Portugal, which was being used to support military activities in Africa, was also dropped. Instead, the President was directed to make a report to Congress on whether any non-African nation was using U.S. aid for military activities in its African territories. A Senate provision terminating military assistance to Greece was substituted in a similar fashion by the request for a presidential report. To show its broad support for human rights after making these deletions, the conference approved the language:

> It is the sense of Congress that the President should deny any economic or military assistance to the government of any foreign country which practices the internment or imprisonment of that country's citizens for political purposes. (PL 93:189)

In the spirit of compromise, even the Senate provision calling for a settlement of India's debt to the United States was changed to the requirement that the administration report to Congress on how the debt would be settled. A total of thirteen new reporting requirements would be included in the final public law.

Gone were the old-fashioned one-day sessions. This conference had taken eleven days. When the draft was finally reported back, minus the signatures of some of the conferees, the House passed it narrowly and the Senate agreed by a margin of three votes.

The patterns of the 1973 conference would become increasingly familiar as the decade progressed. So, major controversies in the 1978 assistance bills were compromised in conference by the now routine devices of provisos, reports, or declarations of congressional policy. The Senate and House committees split on whether to lift the arms embargo on Turkey, the House committee voting 18 to 17 in support of the administration request to end the ban. After extensive lobbying by the Carter administration and close votes in both houses, the conference gave Carter his arms for Turkey at the price of a report. He would have to certify that Turkey was "acting in good faith" to achieve a peaceful settlement of Cyprus issues and report to Congress on the state of the negotiations every sixty days. A full page in the public law was devoted to what Congress wished to have included in these reports. Another page was devoted to language expressing how strongly Congress felt about the Cyprus issue.

Meanwhile, the House revisions to the economic-assistance bill were shelved by the conference, since the Senate's schedule with the Panama Canal debates had been too full to consider them. In the absence of these revisions, the conference asked for several reports: on why the food aid program was not more successful; on how contracts were awarded for carrying out assistance programs; and a general report on the effectiveness of foreign assistance. All of these were issues that the House bill had tried to address. This marked the second major attempt by the House committee to revise the foreign assistance program. The previous attempt in 1973 had also died in conference. In both cases the conference added language expressing dissatisfaction with foreign assistance, but all substantive revisions were postponed.

Indeed, the urge to compromise might have become even greater in the Carter years. This is not primarily a matter of a Congress seeking accommodation with a same-party president, for the compromises would continue in the Reagan and Bush administrations. Carter's last year in office shows signs of the time ahead. The 1980 conference agreed to allow the President to provide military aid to countries, even if it was "prohibited by law." Up to $50 million in military assistance could be given to any one country, no matter what, for example, might be its record of terrorism or violations of human rights. The conference weakened the restrictions on third-country transfers of arms, and it loosened a restriction, in place since 1968, barring American military advisers or civilian personnel from engaging in combat activities in behalf of the foreign government they were advising. Certainly, in the wake of the Iranian hostage crisis and the Russian advance into Afghanistan, checks on the President's power to wage foreign policy were less popular. But Congress also was having more difficulty dealing with authorizations and appropriations of any kind. After the conference had been stalled for months over an intelligence oversight provision, the conferees finally banished it to separate legislation. Although the authorization bill was finally passed, the appropriations bill failed for the second year in a row, requiring the funds to be allocated through special emergency provisions.

In any case, the "new Congress," for all of its aura of activity and the hard work of its members, was busily giving back to the executive some of the problems it could not handle. During the same time Carter had to fight for the Panama Canal Treaty in widely publicized votes that showed Congress active and independent. But behind the scenes, in economic and military assistance, discretion had moved back to the Oval Office.

Compromise became even more a congressional priority in the Reagan administration as the large authorization bills became increasingly difficult to pass. In this context the 1981 act becomes more understandable with its many escape clauses and long sense of Congress resolutions. Any restriction of the President could risk a veto from a president who did not need the bill as much as Congress did. The Reagan administration's goals were being met primarily through the defense authorization. If the White House needed any continuing authorization for military assistance, it could be sure of congressional support. Congress, therefore, had to be wary of presidential restrictions, while trying to hold its own fragile coalition together. Not including a restriction could threaten Democratic support of the bill. The compromise, in effect, was to retain the restriction and add the escape clause. Both sides could sign on to the bill.

Human Rights Policy

The human rights debate in the Carter administration needs to be seen in this context. During the 1976 campaign candidate

Carter had spoken forcefully for the central role of human rights in American foreign policy. His inaugural address, too, carried on this theme. "Our commitment to human rights must be absolute," the new President said. "Our moral sense dictates a clear-cut preference for those societies which share with us an abiding respect for individual human rights." So clear was the rhetoric that many people to the present day associate Jimmy Carter with an innovative if not entirely successful human rights policy. Certainly, Ronald Reagan did, in arguing against this initiative in the 1980 campaign.[12] Nevertheless, after a few months in the White House and some criticism of his announced stand, President Carter had to rethink how "absolute" the human rights initiative would be. Indeed, the administration soon argued, *against the human rights legislation that was being written in Congress,* that the President's hands should not be tied by this kind of congressional restriction.[13]

The State Department, of course, made this argument consistently through the Nixon, Ford, and Carter years. Finally complying with a congressional demand for a report on human rights violations, the State Department supplied one in 1977, listing six countries as violators: Argentina, Haiti, Indonesia, Iran, Peru, and the Philippines. It argued, however, that aid should be continued because good relations with these countries were in the "U.S. national interest."[14] The reports were originally classified by the State Department and made public only after Congress's insistence. The presidential position thus came to reflect what had been a long-term State Department position on this issue.

Carter's conflicts in this and other matters of foreign policy have been extensively discussed.[15] People point out how the different styles and philosophies of his various advisers struck sympathetic chords in Carter's own thinking. Each adviser would leave the Oval Office feeling (correctly) that Carter was persuaded to his position. They would then tell their subordinates, and sometimes the public, what they understood as the presidential policy.[16] The contradiction between the theory and practice of human rights policy can be understood by this argument. Nevertheless, when it came to the matter of lobbying Congress, the White House consistently opposed the human rights restrictions.

At the same time, a number of Democrats in Congress, particularly on the House Foreign Affairs Committee, were working hard on the human rights issue. They had managed to include in foreign assistance bills earlier in the decade the sense of Congress language "recommending" that the President deny aid to nations practicing imprisonment of their own citizens for political purposes (1973) and that the President should substantially reduce or terminate aid to those nations following a consistent pattern of gross violations of human rights (1974). Neither of these recommendations were followed by the Nixon or Ford administrations. They had also received a report on six violations. Yet from the standpoint of these human rights advocates in Congress, opposition by the new Carter administration to further human rights restrictions was disappointing. Support was weaker in the Senate and the House position was itself undercut by the administration's stand.

Thus the economic-assistance bill of 1977 after it emerged from conference included only one additional restriction. Food aid would be withheld from nations violating human rights unless the President determined—and made two reports—that the food aid would directly benefit "the needy." Since it is unlikely that the food itself was to go into the mouths of the government personnel, presumably the President could deal with this restriction. Only food was restricted in the 1977 bill—not money or other forms of assistance. The military assistance bill did make one change, cutting off aid to Argentina, one of the six nations listed in the State Department report.

By this time loans through the World Bank and other lending associations were considered in the banking committees and were no longer the primary responsibility of foreign affairs committee members. It is interesting to see that a similar compromise was effected in the banking authorization bill. U.S. representatives to the international lending institutions were directed to oppose loan applications by countries violating human rights unless the President determined that the cause of human rights would be served more effectively by not voting against the loan. The Carter administration had argued that no legal instructions should be given to the U.S. representatives—that they should be allowed to work on a case-by-case basis.[17] This, indeed, is the ultimate proviso. It contains language that cancels its own provision.

The human rights advocates in Congress continued the battle in 1978 and did succeed in gaining broader restrictions. The 1978 act prohibited security assistance to nations showing a consistent pattern of gross violations of human rights unless the President determined and reported to Congress that extraordinary circumstances required the assistance. It also weakened a prohibition of assistance to the police, domestic intelligence, or similar law enforcement agencies of a government engaging in these consistent and gross violations of human rights by allowing assistance if the President determined and reported to Congress that extraordinary circumstances warranted it. Under some circumstances, then, the American human rights policy would be to provide direct assistance to the police who were carrying out the violations.

Given these patterns of compromise, it is not surprising that a study finds no significant relationship between human rights violations and U.S. assistance at any time during the Nixon, Ford, or Carter years. The authors analyze the relationship between the "political terror" engaged in by a country, according to three separate measures, and the annual per capita military and economic aid. For example, one of the three measures evaluates the countries as follows:[18]

> Level A: Countries under a secure rule of law, people are not imprisoned for their views, and torture [or political murder] is rare or exceptional.

> Level B: There is a limited amount of imprisonment for nonviolent political activity. However, few persons are affected, torture and beating are exceptional [and] political murder is rare.

> Level C: There is extensive political imprisonment, or a history of such imprisonment. Execution or other political murders may be common. . . .

> Level D: The practices of Level C are expanded to larger numbers. Murders, disappearances, and torture are a common part of life. . . .

> Level E: The terrors of Level D [are] extended to the whole population. . . .

The correlations for the Carter administration are small, whether negative or positive, and are not statistically significant: in other words, the relationship between the amount of aid and the human rights practices of a country cannot be distinguished from chance.[19]

To look at the Carter policy in another way, in only eight cases during the Carter administration was security aid cut off from a nation violating human rights. All of these cases involved Latin American countries: Argentina, Bolivia, El Salvador, Guatemala, Haiti, Nicaragua, Paraguay, and Uruguay. In five of these cases, however, it was not the Carter administration but the country itself that chose to terminate the aid, reacting negatively to the human rights reports and what its officials saw as interference in their domestic affairs.[20] Although some security aid was stopped, the economic aid continued.

During this period a very liberal use was made of the "extraordinary circumstances" clause that Congress wrote into the legislation. As Stephen Cohen, an Assistant Secretary of State in the Carter years, explains it, "The Administration did require some showing of a substantial and specific interest before the exception for extraordinary circumstances was available. . . . However, once a specific interest of some substantiality was cited, the exception was usually invoked."[21] Specific interests included not only countries close to the Soviet Union or Soviet allies and members of pro-Western security organizations, but also those with U.S. military bases and those with major resources used in the United States.[22] Once these extraordinary circumstances were recognized, only a few Latin American nations remained.

Little difference was seen in particular country restrictions in the Reagan years, although the rhetoric had by now sharpened *against* the so-called Carter human rights policy. There remained no significant difference for the most part between nations violating human rights and the annual per capita amounts of U.S. aid given. There was a growing tendency, some observers felt, to argue that some of the human rights violations could be exempted because they were not "consistent."[23] Congress had specified that nations engaging in a gross and consistent pattern of violations should not be assisted. In other words, an uneven pattern of gross human rights violations stood a better chance at being assisted than an even one. This argument, by the way, based on the importance of the word consistent, continued into the years of the Bush administration. If the Latin American countries did not qualify for the extraordinary circumstances of much of the rest of the world, they could be exempted from the penalty on grounds of their inconsistency.

Since few regular authorization bills were passed in the Reagan years, Congress had little chance to write new legislation. Congress did insert language into the 1981 bill "reaffirming" its human rights commitment:

(a) The Congress reaffirms its support for the various statutory provisions which have been enacted in order to promote internationally recognized human rights. (b) It is the sense of the Congress that a strong commitment to the defense of human rights should continue to be a central feature of United States Foreign Policy. (PL 97:113)

The story of human rights policy says something about both branches. We see the separation of rhetoric and reality in the Carter years and a situation where a president was credited with (or blamed for) a change in policy that did not actually occur. Who was making human rights policy if it stayed virtually stable through three administrations? On the other hand, Congress made a distinction between rhetoric and reality too, adding exceptional circumstance clauses to all the language and restrictions, thus allowing the White House in effect to make any decisions it chose to. Like Carter, Congress was taking a public position in support of human rights that was much stronger than the enacted policy. Carter won presidential discretion at the price of his own campaign plank, and Congress won the success of the conference at the price of undermining the work of its own committees.

Rhetoric might be better than nothing at all, as some people argue. Supporters of human rights might be glad that Carter spoke so forcefully in the campaign, and that Congress worked as hard as it did and wrote the restrictions. From this standpoint, human rights advocates might prefer the rhetoric of Carter's 1976 campaign to the speeches of Reagan in 1980 when he argued against it. They might prefer to have Congress reaffirm its position in support of human rights than not to reaffirm it. On the other hand, rhetoric gives the illusion of a policy where none may exist, giving the public a false impression. It also gives the world a somewhat hypocritical picture of the nation, to say the least, if the public pronouncements are so at odds with the actual practice. Finally, it carries on the sense seen previously that both branches are engaged in struggle and controversy when in fact the positions are highly predictable and the policy stays the same across time.

Implications

The patterns are clear enough, and potentially serious enough in their implications, to deserve wider recognition. We can focus on two.

Paper Oversight

It is widely agreed that oversight is basic to any control by elected officials of the policies of modern democracies. Especially in the American context where legislature and executive share constitutional powers is the activity of legislative oversight deemed important. If Congress must delegate broad powers to the executive bureaucracy to carry out the laws and the programs and the funding it has enacted, then Congress must be able to oversee—to gain information about—what these agencies are doing. Oversight can vary from the demand for formal investigations and reports to the informal activities of a few committee members who "keep a watchful eye" on their favorite programs.

The importance of oversight was recognized in the reforms of the 1970s that increased congressional staff and directed each committee to designate a subcommittee to perform the oversight function. The thinking at the time, very well summarized in a study by Morris Ogul, was that Congress should increase its oversight and be given the necessary staff in order to do so. In Ogul's words, "The easiest step that the Congress can take is to provide the resources that will enable some additional oversight to be undertaken by those who wish to do so."[24] As the years passed, it could be shown that the number of staff people had increased. The number of days and pages devoted to committee oversight had increased correspondingly. Thus a study by Joel Aberbach published in 1990 could point out how oversight had increased across the years and conclude that Congress was now "active and aggressive" in performing its oversight function.[25] The only things left to debate were how the oversight should be conducted and whether the new high levels of oversight constituted unnecessary interference with the executive branch.

Yet we have seen earlier in the review of intelligence policy that there was less oversight than meets the eye (chapter 3). The greatly expanded staff was hired in large part from those who had worked for the intelligence agencies while the expanding pages and days of hearings were filled with administration and agency witnesses. No increased staff or days of formal review will change things if Congress does not to want to know what the agencies are doing. Only the illusion of oversight had increased.

The patterns of this chapter are even more challenging to the active and aggressive oversight notion. What appears to be oversight—the persistent demand for reports to Congress from the executive branch on all aspects of the foreign assistance program—is used for a very different purpose. It is typically added in conference as a substitute for legislation when there is conflict about what the legislation should be. It becomes a routine response, a kind of paper oversight, predictable by the executive and manageable by it. So if Congress wants reports on the extraordinary circumstances requiring assistance to human rights violators, the State Department will write the reports. The reports proliferate, but the human rights policy does not change. Congress in effect is claiming credit for its oversight activity when it is not able to perform its legislating activity. In actuality—if no one reads the reports or if they do not change legislation in any way—neither oversight nor legislation is being performed.

The stately dance around the issues is seen in human rights policy and military assistance. Congress writes its language in support of policies that the executive does not favor, calling for a report if exceptions are made. The executive writes the reports, complaining all the while about congressional meddling, and continues to follow its original course. *Since the pattern is repeated year after year,* presumably the participants know what they can expect.

Why should the State Department complain if it is getting the discretion it asked for, and even gaining some back by the end of the Carter administration and through the Reagan years? Presumably there are people low enough in the bureaucratic hierarchies to write all the reports. There appears to be more than a little hypocrisy on both sides. By complaining, the executive branch keeps the pressure on to gain even more discretion, while the Congress can be gratified that it is doing its job in guiding U.S. foreign policy. The executive gives Congress the compliment of complaining and Congress gives the executive the leeway it wants.

Meanwhile the reports accumulate, in foreign assistance alone at the rate of more than twenty a year. It is a phenomenon that people concerned with congressional oversight should look at more closely. A plague of paper oversight mimics and substitutes for the real thing.

Party Leadership and the Conference

Any concerted congressional action requires the help of the party leadership. This rule holds for the old as well as the new, more decentralized institution and reflects the basic principle that members ultimately are responsible only to the voters in 535 separate states and districts. In the absence of some overwhelming sentiment sweeping the country, the party leadership is the only centripetal structure that can bring these members together into a majority vote. It follows that if Congress is to oppose presidents, with all of their rallying power and prestige, the party leaders must help. Presumably these would be the leaders of the party not in control of the White House. Leaders of the President's party in Congress have the more difficult task of balancing the claims of the institution with their work on behalf of White House programs.

What is striking about these cases is the lack of the party leadership's guiding hand. Admittedly, the leaders have had their own problems, coping with the decentralizing trends of the past two decades and attempting to satisfy the various demands of their party members. Nevertheless, leaders can still influence the conference stage, in selecting some of the conferees and in the bargaining. It is they who arrange the various fast-track procedures that restrict floor amendments and help to streamline the issues that will go to conference. They have the responsibility to muster the floor votes that might counter unfriendly amendments or presidential veto threats. Yet there are few signs, during the Carter or Reagan years, of these activities.

The exceptions stand out—O'Neill arranging the voice vote in 1985 when a roll call would not pass, Majority Leader Jim Wright carrying on a peace proposal for Nicaragua, GOP leader Bob Dole assisting in the mysterious disappearance of the conference report when the South African sanctions bill was at issue. In the debate on lifting the Turkish arms embargo in 1978 Democratic party leaders in both chambers helped move the floor votes closer to the administration's position. In the House a narrow majority of Republicans supported the Democratic leaders' compromise amendment, while a narrow majority of Democrats voted against their leader. In the Senate a narrow majority of Democrats also opposed the compromise, while the Republicans voted for it. The exceptions showed party leaders acting more as individuals than as leaders of their party, and in two cases—the sanctions bill and the arms embargo—they were working for the White House rather than for any independent congressional role in foreign policy.

In the early years of the 1970s, Democrats could oppose Republican administrations and rally majorities on issues of peace and cutbacks in defense. The debate between President and Congress on foreign policy could be organized on party lines. The Democrats' stand in this regard weakened with their own president in the White House, and did not recover in the Reagan years. Meanwhile, the committees who often were willing to take an independent stand were not supported by the leadership. In the face of strong arguments by presidents of both political parties that Congress should allow more discretion, there was no one to organize opinion on the other side.

By the end of the 1980s no major revisions had been accomplished in foreign assistance legislation. The President and Congress were still amending the Foreign Assistance Act of 1961. But behind all the rhetoric and reporting requirements engaged in by both branches, some changes had occurred. The executive branch could now make arms sales or arms transfers in substantial amounts to countries even if "prohibited by law." It could allocate economic and military assistance according to its discretion, citing the extraordinary circumstances clause. It could provide military advisers or civilian personnel in situations that might lead to combat. Gross and fairly consistent violations of human rights did not necessarily bar a country from receiving American aid. It is striking how similar the policy was in many respects to the pre-Vietnam period. One can hardly call it the policy of a specific president, however, since the same position had been argued by executive branch spokesmen through many different administrations, and with presidents of both parties.

Congress had used the foreign assistance bill for a wide-ranging review of foreign policy, making its own contributions to that policy along the way. The contributions are significant. But as the Reagan years drew to a close, the bargaining advantage had shifted. First it had become much more difficult to enact any foreign assistance legislation, as support and overall rationale for the program fell away. Second, it had become more difficult to enact budget legislation of any kind. Thus presidents, aware that they needed an authorization less than Congress did, could bargain for more and more. So in Congress in order to pass a bill that both houses could accept, a high price of compromise had to be paid.

Leadership and Reform

One can now see more clearly the irony of the reforms that decentralized influence in both chambers. Congress appears consistently active; yet its more recent efforts often end short of the desired results. The points for separate activity proliferate but so do the points of blockage and conflict, making coordination and compromise that much more difficult. It is hard to fault the members, working so hard in their particular areas of expertise. Think of the effort invested in human rights legislation in both substantive and budgetary committees, in the House and Senate; the time spent on the Turkish arms embargo; the work on foreign aid authorization bills that did not pass. Laziness is clearly not the issue, but rather the focus and organization of the work.

Nor are the problems the result of divided-party control. Congress may be less likely to oppose presidents under conditions of same-party control. On the other hand, the cases in this and the preceding chapter show Congress has been less able to pass complicated authorization bills under divided-party conditions. From the standpoint of those who would like to see Congress active in foreign policy, each condition has its limitations. More importantly, the devices which appear to substitute for legislation have persisted under both conditions. The escape clauses, sense of Congress resolutions, and reporting requirements used in lieu of legislation proliferated under Democratic and Republican presidents, independent of the party composition in Congress. The dance of trade legislation or particular targeting of an arms sale did not change with these political conditions.

If reforms are needed, the party leaders must play a role. They could return more autonomy to the expert committees and resist the temptations of overly facile compromise. It is surprising that the frustrations of members have not reached the point where they pressure the leaders to do so—to provide more "leadership" and support. Still, the decentralized procedures make the power of the purse an increasingly heavy burden. Foreign assistance, chief tool in the modern arsenal of congressional foreign policy making, yields less support in Congress and less clout in bargaining with the White House. These are problems beyond any particular leader's control. Both leaders and members would have to look more closely to see how they are trapped in procedures of their own making. They will not do so, however, if they feel that the present practices are good enough.

7

• • •

NICARAGUA

N
ICARAGUA IS A SMALL AGRICULTURAL COUNTRY, slightly larger in size but smaller in population than the state of Tennessee. The people live primarily on a narrow volcanic belt extending off the Pacific Ocean. While there is some mining in the country, the principal exports are coffee, cotton, sugarcane, and meat.

Many countries have strategic importance in a tense international setting. Yet the size of Nicaragua might seem somewhat out of line with its importance in United States foreign policy in the 1980s. Indeed the attention given this one country's affairs by both President and Congress sharpens some of the themes developed in previous chapters. Returning to the same data used previously, we can begin to see how and why the illusion of struggle persists while very little is being done. We can also see how the choice of this symbolic activity shapes the kind of actions our elected officials take. The illusion of debate expands while the substance becomes impoverished.

THE PRESIDENT'S AGENDA

Why, asks Latin American expert Eldon Kenworthy, did Ronald Reagan create a new bureau at the State Department—the Office of Public Diplomacy for Latin America and the Caribbean—and a new White House Outreach Working Group on Central America, and a "perception management" team within the National Security Council? Why was Henry Kissinger asked to head a new blue-ribbon bipartisan commission on Central America, and why were there regular "Wednesday briefings" of influential citizens? The short answer, says Kenworthy, was that Reagan's Nicaragua policy required so much selling—among the American public, U.S. allies in the region, and key constituency groups.[1]

Nicaragua's importance to the President's speaking schedule was also clear. His foreign policy addresses to the nation in his first term almost entirely accompanied rally points, usually uses of force by the United States. He spoke twice on Lebanon, once on El Salvador, once on Grenada, and once on the Soviet attack on the Korean airliner. Such speeches could show the public that the President was actively at work in foreign policy, although it was policy of a very narrow kind. One exception was made, however: Reagan spoke three times on aid to Nicaragua. In his second term, the rate of foreign policy speaking declined while the subject narrowed even further. Of eight foreign policy speeches, five concerned Nicaragua or the Iran-contra affair. One was on defense policy generally, one on an economic summit, and one on the Soviet arms-limitation agreement. At the same time Reagan was giving these major addresses, he was also giving minor speeches to Latin American groups, as many as seven a year, and speaking of Nicaragua frequently in his weekly radio talks. Nearly half of Reagan's meetings with minority groups in the White House were with Hispanic groups.[2]

The same emphasis is seen in Reagan's messages to Congress on foreign affairs. We saw previously that Reagan was among the least active in pursuing a legislative agenda in foreign policy. In his foreign policy messages to Congress, Reagan ranked near the bottom in terms of attention given to foreign affairs in both his first and second term. While it is true that for all presidents these messages have declined somewhat across the years, Reagan's priorities in those messages which he did give are striking. Of seven major messages in his second term, three concern Nicaragua, with a fourth on economic assistance to Central America generally. It is not that Reagan is simply "unplugging" Congress, and denying its role in legislation, for during all this time the domestic policy messages continue. In 1983, for example, when Reagan sent no foreign policy messages to Congress, he sent a total of nine on other major issues. These included messages on the budget, the economy, school tuition, federalism, health care incentives, tax reform, an amendment for prayer in schools, employment, and education.[3]

Hence if we were to use the public speeches and messages of the President as an indicator of his own priorities and interests, our picture of Reagan would be very clear. Compared to the domestic agenda, foreign policy messages and speeches received less emphasis. The foreign policy that did receive personal presidential attention was heavily concentrated on the use of force by the United States and assistance to Nicaragua.

Nicaragua of course had even more importance in the Reagan administration than this particular record showed. Each year brought a major battle with the Congress on funding for the contras, requiring meetings with Republican leaders, strategy and bargaining sessions, and special lobbying of uncommitted members. With each setback in Congress, the White House strategists returned to prepare a request for the next budget year. Yet even this was not the whole story. All of the covert events surrounding the Nicaragua policy required their own meetings, strategy sessions, and elaborate subterfuge. There would need to be more meetings and activities of damage control when the covert events came to light.

"Picture the performance of a president trained as an actor, speaking from the Oval Office with its trappings of authority, aided by a map of Latin America that progressively turned red as the president detailed the spread of that 'cancer,' that 'malignancy,' whose vectors lay in Managua."[4] Or picture the septuagenarian President, with his "freedom fighter" T-shirt, solemnly proclaiming, "I am a contra too." It would be difficult to overestimate the place of Nicaragua on the President's agenda during these years.

Certainly Nicaragua was part of a larger concern among many foreign policy advisers. The Cold War interpretation of the Monroe Doctrine, by no means limited to the Reagan administration, held that the political leaning of any country in the Western hemisphere was a matter of the gravest U.S. concern. Nicaragua, like Cuba, represented a challenge to that doctrine. Relations with individual Latin American nations depended on more than ideology, however. The CIA involvement in illegal arms sales and drug trafficking (routing cocaine from Bolivia and Colombia, through Central America, to the U.S.) to finance projects in Central America posed potentially explosive issues, dictating particular actions by intelligence officials as well as particular advice to presidents.[5] Nicaragua, then, was not a mere personal whim on the part of

Ronald Reagan, no matter how much he might have been emotionally drawn to the idea of "fighting communism" on that ground. The issue grew out of considerable institutional support. The point remains that *one* issue could so engross the Reagan White House—and subsequently the Congress and the major news media—that it became defined as "foreign policy." A very small part substituted for a complex totality. Ignoring the forest, people gathered in fascination around one tree.

THE CONGRESSIONAL AGENDA

It should not be surprising that Congress showed something of the same concentration: issues raised with force and consistency by either branch will typically be addressed by the other. We saw in chapter 2 that Congress had fallen back in the 1980s to a working agenda like that of the Kennedy and Johnson years. About thirteen bills on the average made this agenda, when one eliminates the various symbolic resolutions. These thirteen were fairly evenly divided between funding bills and substantive legislation. A look at the major agenda items from within this group is revealing. Nicaragua remained on this very small agenda each year from 1982 through 1988.

In 1982 Congress passed the first Boland Amendment restricting the use of funds to aid the Nicaraguan rebels. In 1983 Congress debated issues concerning Nicaragua, Lebanon, El Salvador, and Grenada while the House also passed a resolution calling for a nuclear freeze. With the exception of the nuclear freeze resolution, all of the items involved some kind of use of force by the United States, whether directly by U.S. troops or indirectly through military support and advisers. In 1984 debate on Nicaragua and a related Central America bill comprised two of the five bills on the agenda. A more severe restriction on Nicaraguan funds was passed, prohibiting any support for military or paramilitary activities by any United States agencies. This legislation, which became known as the second Boland Amendment, would engender more activities on the part of both President and Congress. During the same year Congress also debated the trade bill and a supplemental assistance bill made necessary when no regular foreign assistance bill was passed. In 1985 Congress's attention appeared even more narrowly focused, with two separate bills on aid to the contras, a debate on an arms sale to the country of Jordan, and the question of South African sanctions. While Congress did pass a foreign assistance authorization that year, four of the five major bills concerned specific countries. By 1987, of course, in addition to continuing the debate on aid to the contras, Congress also had to vote to form an Iran-contra investigating committee. Overall, Nicaragua provided almost *half* of Congress's working agenda on major legislation in these years.

The duplication of Nicaraguan votes in some of the years is explained by the multiple committee consideration that developed through the 1970s and 1980s. The foreign affairs committees, the intelligence committees, and the defense committees were all considering aid to the contras and having a look at each other's legislation. This not only added to the controversy, since the various committee majorities had different positions, but also gave the public impression that Congress kept changing its mind. Overall, Congress was fairly consistent at least through 1985 in limiting military aid to the contras while allowing some humanitarian aid. Nevertheless, the number of bills from the various committees and the number of roll calls together created a confusing impression. Congress also appeared very busy this way, and actively engaged in a foreign policy matter.

The same concentration appears when we look at the number of separate roll calls taken. This number gives some indication of the attention given a bill by the chamber as a whole as well as the willingness of the leadership to allow the attention. This is especially true in the House where debate is more controlled. In 1983, for example, the two foreign policy issues leading in number of roll call votes were the nuclear freeze resolution and Nicaragua. Twenty-six roll calls were given to the freeze and eleven to Nicaragua. In 1985 the two leading issues were South African sanctions and Nicaragua, with twelve and eight roll calls respectively taken on these issues. The same two issues led in 1987, this time with Nicaragua leading the sanctions issue.

Congress was pursuing its own agenda, it is clear, in these examples and not merely reflecting a president's interests. The freeze and the South African sanctions were being pushed by Congress against a reluctant White House. Nevertheless, Ronald Reagan's concern with Nicaragua can be seen picked up and reflected in the congressional agenda. Only a few bills can be given that kind of chamberwide attention. Thus while two countries—Nicaragua and South Africa—were getting all this attention, the rest of the world had to be dealt with somewhere else.

It is not only that Congress was spending much of its time on Nicaraguan roll call votes, it had to allocate a good share of its budget-making activity to this one issue as well. The struggle between the President and Congress was waged through authorization and appropriations bills almost exclusively from 1981 through 1986, with defense and intelligence appropriations the primary battlegrounds on which the war for Nicaragua was fought. A turndown in funding for the contras in 1981 brought a renewed administration funding request in 1982. The 1983 defeat prompted the White House to tie the 1984 request to a supplemental appropriation bill which included summer jobs and child nutrition programs, popular issues in an election year. Predictably, the 1984 defeat was followed by another request for funds in the intelligence authorization for 1985. In effect the Reagan White House was attempting to wear the Congress down. Since the House was stronger in its opposition to the Reagan policy than the Senate was throughout the period, each one of these contests had to be hammered out and compromised in conference.[6]

Individual members were also spending enormous time on the issue. Democrat Michael Barnes of Maryland, chair of the Western Hemisphere Subcommittee in the House, used his considerable expertise on Latin American affairs to conduct hearings, direct media and public attention to the problem, and develop proposals. The intelligence oversight committees were deeply involved. As the deadlock wore on, members of Congress spent increasing amounts of time on alternative congressional drafts. The House Democrats drafted a proposal headed by Michael Barnes and Lee Hamilton of Indiana. The House Republicans devised their own proposal, to be sponsored by Minority Leader Robert Michel of Illinois. The Democratic Caucus's Task Force on Central America held regular reviews of the policy and encouraged members to travel to the region to study it for themselves. A Conservative Opportunity Society, led by conservative Republican leader Newt Gingrich of Georgia, was also active. A group of swing members, under the leadership of Dave McCurdy, Democratic representative from Oklahoma, developed their own informal caucus and a set of proposals. Overall, from 1983 through

1988 more than one hundred Senators and Representatives, or about one-fifth of the Congress, traveled to Nicaragua and spent time there.[7]

It was perhaps the Speaker of the House, Jim Wright, though, who attracted the most attention when he emerged as a central participant in the debate in 1987. While Wright had been interested in Nicaragua as early as 1980, when he worked for an economic assistance package that would support political pluralism in the country, his featured role began at the request of the administration, battered by the Iran-contra scandal.[8] Wright agreed to what became known as the Wright-Reagan plan, began to work for a cease-fire and negotiations, and continued even after the White House backed down on its support. Wright forged a compromise plan supported by House Democrats, spoke repeatedly on the issue, and in an unprecedented role for a House leader, engaged in discussions directly with foreign leaders. When the Speaker of the House himself plays a direct role in a foreign policy issue, the congressional priorities appear quite clear.

Is something wrong here? Together, both branches give the illusion of a struggle over foreign policy, while concentrating on one small agricultural country in the world. Congressional agendas have become small and narrow, increasingly so over time. At the same time, all the speeches by the President and all the votes in Congress give the impression of conflict and activity of a very intense kind. How could anyone ask them to do more?

THE OTHER AGENDA

A few of the many things Watergate and Iran-contra had in common were the volumes of testimony, the detail, and the colorful personalities—the Norths and Ulasewiczs, the Deans and Caseys and McCords. As we follow the tortuous chronology and try to retrace who said what to whom, we lose sight of some very simple facts—that illegal and unconstitutional actions were taken, and that the trail of responsibility was fairly clear. It led to the elected officeholders. We are distracted from the main event by the many bizarre sideshows.

While the President was giving his Nicaragua speeches and Congress was conducting its votes, other actions were being taken. Nicaragua occupied even more time than its place in the public agenda showed. We can focus on a few of the activities in this chapter to show President and Congress behind the scenes, still struggling to make foreign policy—for Nicaragua at least.

Congress and the CIA

The relations between Congress and the Central Intelligence Agency in the early years of the Reagan administration followed a common pattern in American politics. The director of the agency, then William Casey, the former Reagan campaign manager, was warned that he would have to "stroke" the Congress and overcome some considerable distrust among the members.[9] The key members involved in behind-the-scenes Nicaraguan discussions were the members of the select intelligence committees, described in earlier chapters. While they had been selected, particularly in the House, in large part as members who would support the agency, they considered themselves responsible members of Congress who would want to see that institutional norms were preserved. Edward Boland, handpicked by his friend Speaker Tip O'Neill, chaired the House committee, and Barry Goldwater, the senior, highly respected conservative, chaired the Senate committee in the early Reagan years. The common pattern, then, was to be one of agency support as long as certain rules of congressional respect were observed.

What became atypical in the Nicaraguan events was that the unspoken congressional rules were broken, not once but many times. Each act by Congress was followed by an administration counteraction to evade the law. In 1982 when it was known that the CIA was supporting a covert revolution in Nicaragua, both O'Neill and Boland brought pressure on the committee to limit CIA activity. A compromise was worked out between Boland's committee and the Senate committee, whereby secret language was inserted in the authorization bill prohibiting the CIA and the Defense Department from furnishing military equipment, training, or support to anyone "for the purpose of overthrowing the Government of Nicaragua." The compromise authorization was approved by both the Senate and the House without their knowing of the secret restriction. In November of 1982, however, these same committee members read a *Newsweek* report of how the covert activity in Nicaragua had expanded into a much larger plan to undermine the Sandinista government. Boland and Goldwater were angered, as was Senator Daniel Moynihan, a member of the committee and one of the stronger critics of the agency. Thus began the "deceive-and-forgive" pattern so pronounced through all of the Nicaragua related events.

At this point the agency, presumably on orders from the White House, had already disregarded a congressional objective. What happened then? The Boland Amendment was passed in December of 1982 by a unanimous vote in the House, this time spelling out publicly that no funds were to be used to overthrow the Nicaraguan government. Casey then lobbied the Senate and appeared himself at Senate intelligence hearings, declaring that stopping the flow of arms from Nicaragua to El Salvador remained the goal, not overthrowing the Nicaraguan government. The official administration position (and Casey's) was that arms were flowing from Nicaragua to the Salvadoran rebels, although some analysts reported they could find no clear evidence of the arms flow. Casey met with his lawyers to draft a way to continue the policy of intervention while merely skirting the edges of the Boland Amendment, and he assured the White House that there was no problem with signing the amendment into law. The lawyers rose to the challenge, agreeing that since the actions the agency wished to take could not be carried out for the purpose of overthrowing the government, all actions must be guaranteed and justified "for other purposes." The proper cautions went to all operatives in the field.[10]

This was of course a fairly direct insult to any legislative process. Yet in the months ahead individual members of Congress, including Goldwater and Boland, the authors of the amendment, would try to see whether funds could be gained for the contras by other means, thereby circumventing their own legislation. In 1985, during the period of the military aid prohibition, secret funding was buried in an authorization bill to supply the contras with "information" and "advice." The funding clearly contradicted the humanitarian aid restriction that had just passed both houses. While secret funding provisions have become typical in recent congresses, they do not occur without support from key committee members and party leaders. Since the same people were instrumental in passing the more public contra-aid policy, Congress appeared in the somewhat silly position of trying to sneak legislation past itself.

The White House was also working on circumventing the legislation. Among some of the initial attempts, the administration tried to obtain secret funds through the Senate Appropriations Committee, working through an Assistant Secretary of State, thus bypassing the intelligence committees. Apparently the thinking was that Senate Appropriations would also be willing to contravene the stated position of the Congress. The attempt was discovered, however, and Goldwater was again angered. He and fellow intelligence committee member Moynihan wrote a secret letter to Reagan protesting this insult. After they were given an apology by the Secretary of State, Goldwater returned to the Senate floor ready to help the contra cause. Now back on the administration side, upon receiving the apology, Goldwater criticized his colleagues for "meddling with the efforts by the President to defend the national security."[11]

The next insult came quickly, when the mining of Nicaraguan harbors became public in April 1984. Goldwater and other intelligence committee members had not known that the mining had taken place, despite the fact that the Intelligence Oversight Act of 1980 required that the committees be "fully and currently informed." It turned out that in the routine secret agency briefings of the intelligence committees, Casey had in fact mentioned mining. The reference involved one sentence in eighty-four pages of transcript, or ten seconds of the more than two hours of hearings. In addition, CIA officials pointed out, it had been the *piers* of the harbors that were mined; hence the administration had been technically correct in denying that the *harbors* were mined.[12] Goldwater wrote another letter, and Moynihan threatened to resign from the committee. Casey was contrite and made apologies as best he could. Casey met with the full Senate committee, agreed that the committee "was not adequately informed in a timely manner" about the mining. The committee and Casey agreed to work out new procedures to guarantee that such a lapse should not happen again.

This interchange recalls a case discussed in a previous chapter. When the provision requiring consultation on the use of force was broken in the Carter administration, White House officials and committee members agreed that perhaps the language should be clarified. Indeed what else could be said to save face: the provision, which had been quite clear, had been disregarded. Here, too, committee and agency agree that it must be the procedures which are at fault after Congress discovers that it has been deceived. The face-saving devices allowed the agency to continue its secret Nicaragua operations while it permitted the committee to carry on the impression that it was watching what the agency was doing.

It is no wonder that the congressional votes to be taken subsequently might be treated lightly by the White House or that the committees would continue to receive perfunctory briefings at best. The pattern suggests the familiar problem in family disorders where the child keeps crossing the line that a too indulgent parent is unable to enforce. In political terms, the committees did not have sufficient power within their own chambers to enforce anything: hence they could only wring their hands and hope for the smallest tokens of respect.

The Deniable President

The modern presidency has well developed the technique of plausible denial, as scholars like John Prados and others point out.[13] As a technique or form of communication, plausible denial should assure that presidents can deny knowledge of covert action being carried out by the government. For example, Eisenhower could deny that U.S. planes were sent to spy over Communist territory. The technique, used to protect the country, can also protect the individual president from responsibility for covert or illegal actions. This works in its extreme forms only if the President is willing to appear stupid or inept, or if he can find someone who will quite literally go to prison for him. The modern record suggests that presidents have been willing to take these risks.

Given this institutionalized aspect of the modern presidency, it is difficult to talk of a hidden White House agenda in foreign policy. The difficulties are relieved, however, by following the definition used throughout these chapters. A presidential issue is something presidents and their closest advisers have paid some attention to; or it is at least something that shows the President's attention by a remark in a news conference or a signature on a message to Congress. Of course, we do not know that presidents know what they are signing or hearing about. But if they can claim credit for part of the activity, they must take responsibility for the whole. We talk of presidents conducting wars and signing treaties or doubling a military assistance budget, and we say that Congress should not limit the President's discretion in such affairs. Ulti-

mately presidents are responsible for all of the actions decided at
the White House level or for none of them. If Reagan could take
credit for Grenada, he must take the burden of Nicaragua too.

We know that as early as the first year of his administration,
Reagan signed a broad top-secret finding authorizing political and
paramilitary operations to curtail the activities of the Sandinistas
and support various rebel movements in Central America. The
White House also expressed concern that the operation be kept
secret, fearing a lack of public and congressional support. We
know further that Casey, with his friendship and personal access
to the President, spoke directly to Reagan on Nicaragua several
times in the same year.[14] While the actual decision to mine the
Nicaraguan harbors taken in the White House Situation Room
occurred without Reagan present, witnesses would later claim
that he knew of the mining. Certainly he helped deflect the news
stories when they appeared in early 1983. At the annual address
to the black-tie dinner for White House correspondents which occurred immediately following the press report, he stated his position with characteristic humor:

> What's all that talk about a breakdown of White House communi-
> cations: How come nobody told me? [Laughter.] Well, I know this:
> I've laid down the law, though, to everyone there from now on
> about anything that happens, that no matter what time it is, wake
> me, even if it's in the middle of a Cabinet meeting. [Laughter.]

After the Senate had voted 84 to 12 in a nonbinding resolution
that no money could be spent for the "planning, directing, or supporting" of mining in ports or harbors of Nicaragua, he also announced publicly that he could live with the vote since it was
nonbinding. What the President meant, or what might have
crossed Congress's mind when it passed the nonbinding resolution, is not entirely clear. Presumably just as Congress passed arms
sales restrictions that did not restrict, allowing the administration
to claim special circumstances, here it expressed its anger at being
deceived by passing a resolution that did not bind.

The White House meanwhile was using small sums under its
own discretion to continue the Nicaraguan offensive, while lobbying Congress for additional funding. Having decided from public
opinion reports that the mining was a blunder, the White House
apparently told Casey to conduct a holding action on the covert
program until after the election when the administration would

go all out in support.[15] At the same time it began to seek alternative funding. The Defense Department secretly donated aircraft to transport supplies to contra bases, and it transferred ships, planes, and guns to the CIA at little or no expense. The CIA in turn began giving the Nicaraguan rebels aid from its secret budget, at the rate of more than $1.5 million a year.[16] The administration gained funds from various other sources: $10 million through the State Department from one country; another sum through the secret congressional funding; help from Saudi Arabia and the various private donors in the network that Lieutenant Colonel Oliver North was now spending full time organizing.[17] At this point, the departments of State and Defense, the nation's Central Intelligence Agency, and the office of the National Security Adviser were all giving some priority to the Nicaraguan affair.

Reagan personally met and thanked the private donors for their "support for democracy in Central America." Some individual contributors met as often as five times with the President, while citizen groups, kept carefully distinct from their other lobbying activities, also met with the President frequently.[18] In addition, Reagan held meetings with contra leaders, assuring them at this point that, although Congress had stopped the funding, the United States would not abandon them.[19] As the need for funding increased, more and more nations in the world—particularly in the Middle East and Central America—were drawn into the Nicaraguan problem. Our relations with each of these countries became more complicated as we asked them for help. Apparently, even South Africa was approached, this during the time of the votes on South African sanctions.[20]

This is not to say that Reagan was involved on any day-to-day basis with the Nicaraguan events, but merely that he was involved more frequently and for a longer period than on most other matters of foreign policy. Some of his closest advisers also had to spend a rather large proportion of their time dealing with this one country. If these included the director of the nation's chief intelligence agency and various national security advisers who might have welcomed such activity, the issue spread to encompass the entire White House. Reagan's own role in encouraging the illegal funding would later be criticized by the congressional investigating committee. We also know that Reagan knew of the Saudi connection, since King Fahd ibn Abdul-Aziz found occasion to tell the

President, in a private meeting at the White House, how pleased he was to be working for democracy in Central America.[21]

The Context for Iran-Contra

All this is far from the usual rhetoric of democratic policy making. The President makes jokes while members of Congress conduct hearings that do not inform them. To the White House the congressional prohibition appeared to mean only that the funding had to be found elsewhere. To the CIA the prohibition was a legal and linguistic challenge merely. Even if officials could not stay within the technical letter of the law, they could always apologize to Congress again and suggest that the procedures were not clear. The seriousness of the issue is underlined by constitutional scholar Louis Fisher, who points out the importance of separating the power of the sword from the power of the purse. Fisher cites British parliamentary tradition and the American framers to show the importance of the legislative power of appropriations. He quotes from James Madison, who argued that "those who are to conduct a war cannot in the nature of things, be proper or safe judges, whether a war ought to be commenced, continued, or concluded." And he points out that presidents who attempted to combine these two constitutionally separated powers would have committed an impeachable offense.[22]

Yet, if the legislative process was being insulted, Congress was also insulting itself. Apparently the CIA had enough secret funding for about *two dozen* covert operations, according to the estimate of its director.[23] The intelligence committees of Congress are largely responsible for this funding. The original support in 1981 for five hundred contras who would infiltrate Nicaragua had been passed in a secret authorization by the intelligence committees. The committees also knew, as did many other people, that unauthorized funds were supporting the American military presence in neighboring Honduras. The events reveal at least several layers of deception and self-deception operating simultaneously. And as late as September of 1985, when Oliver North's activities were already attracting attention in the press, the select intelligence committees admitted that their attempts to carry out vigorous inquiries appeared to be frustrated. They were frustrated, it would become clear later, because three administration witnesses—McFarlane, Poindexter, and North—were still lying to them.

What must the officials think of each other to operate in this way? What could they predict and expect for the future? Note the detail and comprehensiveness of the second Boland Amendment, which reflects a Congress already aware that the White House will try to evade the restriction. Congress attempted to leave no loopholes in the law:

> No funds available to the Central Intelligence Agency, the department of Defense, or any other agency or entity of the United States involved in intelligence activities may be obligated or expended for the purpose or which would have the effect of supporting, directly or indirectly, military or paramilitary operations in Nicaragua by any nation, group, organization, movement, or individual.

Senator Christopher Dodd even asked a witness in hearings the following year whether there would be attempts to circumvent the Boland Amendment. He was assured that there would not be. Yet the law would be broken and witnesses would later argue that it was not sufficiently clear. Members of Congress would then express shock and dismay that they were deceived. It is in this mental context that the events of Iran-contra occurred and followed naturally from what had occurred before. The White House continued to seek covert sources for contra funding, while a growing network of international arms dealers knew that the United States was desperately seeking secret cash. Thus in the same atmosphere and with the same participants, in January of 1986 Reagan signed the secret intelligence finding authorizing the sale of weapons to Iran that became known as the arms-for-hostages deal. According to the now-published sources, the document directly enjoined that Congress should not be informed nor should certain members of the National Security Council. Among the excluded members were Secretary of State Shultz, Secretary of Defense Weinberger, and the Chairman of the Joint Chiefs of Staff, Admiral William Crowe.

It was when this decision threatened to become public that Oliver North began shredding his documents and Casey, MacFarlane, and North met to decide on damage control. Certainly the arms-for-hostages deal could have been concluded without bringing in Nicaragua at all—it was part of the concern for the hostages and the broader secret funding that had been occurring throughout the Reagan years. Nevertheless, the funds were diverted: Nicaragua was still in the game. One of Reagan's National Security Advisers (Robert McFarlane) claimed the President knew of the diversion while one (John Poindexter) claimed he did not know. Poindexter took the blame and the circle of deniability was closed.

In any case, the elected officials found that they had not put Nicaragua behind them. With the disclosures, the President's polls fell more than twenty points, to the lowest point in his presidency. About half the public believed Reagan was "lying" when he said he was not told about the diversion of funds. Speeches and news conferences followed in an attempt to control the damage; there were daily White House conferences and careful tracking polls. Hence more time and effort on the part of the President and his advisers had to be spent. The President gave the memorable lines: "A few months ago, I told the American people I did not trade arms for hostages. My heart and my best intentions still tell me that's true, but the facts and evidence tell me it is not." In the four weeks following the November 1986 revelations, the President gave two major press conferences as well as two speeches to the nation. The Attorney General of the United States began his investigations. The director of the nation's Central Intelligence Agency testified (again) to Congress and admitted deception about the diversion of funds. The Secretary of State began a series of speeches and public statements explaining his opposition to much of the policy. The nation's National Security Adviser could no longer look out for the affairs of government, since he was being asked to resign and had to prepare for investigations into his own activities. Despite all the activity, the administration was considered badly damaged through the remainder of Reagan's second term.

Members of Congress, expressing shock at the disclosures, began to set up machinery for an investigation. The House and Senate select committees conducting the investigation would consist of a majority of members who supported the intelligence establishment and who favored support for the contras. In a final irony, the committee heard the witnesses report that yes, Congress had been lied to again.

Even after all this, the committees were careful to limit the scope of their investigation and to look at particular individuals most clearly: North, Poindexter, the late William Casey. They took care not to probe activities of the President or the Vice President or Congress's own part in the past events. In short, the sharpest rebukes were reserved for the *appointed,* not the elected, officials. Among other sensitive issues, the matter of drug trafficking was left aside. It would not be for another two years (and after Ronald Reagan had left office) that a separate congressional subcommittee would find substantial evidence of drug smuggling through the war zones on the part of individual contras, contra suppliers, and contra supporters throughout the region. The report of the subcommittee (generally called the Kerry Committee) observed that senior U.S. officials might have been aware that drug money was a perfect solution to the contras' funding problems.[24] Rightly or wrongly, these issues did not form part of the congressional Iran-contra investigation. Forced to respond in some fashion to what became the widespread public Iran-contra scandal, Congress acted with extreme constraint.

The final report of the Iran-contra investigation, divided into a majority and a minority document, split on predictable party lines. While some commentators called the majority report a "harsh rebuke for the President," Reagan was told essentially that he did not pay enough attention to what some of his subordinates were doing. This criticism of the President, heard since his first year in office and one the Reagan White House evidently found itself able to live with, hardly required a congressional finding. The minority report criticized the majority document, and by implication its own institution, by upholding the preeminence of the executive in matters of foreign policy. In the minority view, the majority was using "an aggrandizing theory of Congress's foreign policy powers that [was] itself part of the problem."[25]

Congress, then, was divided in its own role and wary of assigning blame to elected officeholders. Certainly it had appeared to work hard—and very visibly—for a year in conducting the limited investigation. A majority were willing to say that something was wrong. The report found "confusion and disarray at the highest levels of Government." It targeted irresponsibility, abuses of secrecy, and "disdain for the law." "Time and again we have learned," the report continued, "that a flawed process leads to bad results, and that a lawless process leads to worse."[26]

The congressional actions had been of a far lesser magnitude than the executive's: nevertheless, the criticism contained in the majority report reflected back on the Congress too. The executive had actively sought to contravene the law, but Congress had shown disdain for it as well when it condoned the spending of secret funds and played deceive-and-forgive with the CIA director. The events pointed to serious flaws in White House decision making and in the office of the National Security Adviser, but it also uncovered congressional flaws: it was clear the two intelligence committees were too weak to do the job they were expected to do. There was indeed confusion and disarray at the highest levels of government, spanning both executive and legislative branches.

THE BASIC ILLUSION

The Iran-contra issues have not gone away. It is not only the amount of mystery remaining but the hauntingly disturbing glimpses of government that linger to plague the American psyche: a government where no means yes, intentions contradict actions, and everything is solved by an apology or a speech. This chapter has taken some of the well-known facts of the period and put them together in a different way. It has highlighted several repetitive patterns of behavior: of apologies demanded and given; of secrecy engaged in by both branches; and of actions taken with the understanding, in both the administration and Congress, that the actions will be contravened. Certainly there were administration figures who opposed these activities and committee members who did the best they could within their constraints. Nevertheless, we retain the impression that basic constitutional and ethical issues were not only challenged but laughed at. Against these implications, it is perhaps inappropriate to add more; and yet there is another finding, closely related and reinforcing.

This chapter helps to show how the illusion of an active interbranch struggle can continue while the substance is narrowed and becomes dangerously impoverished. There is a sense of great busyness in all these activities. The President made speeches to the nation and met with interest-group leaders. White House emissaries prowled the globe. Congress kept on with its hearings and crowded its calendar with roll call votes, many of them dramatic and too close to call in advance. There was vigorous debate, pleas from the White House, and last-minute vote switching. There was even a full-scale congressional investigation for everyone to see.

Congress was visibly assertive. No one could say that the elected officials and their closest advisers were not hard at work. And all for Nicaragua.

Indeed, the surface activities strengthened the impression of a struggle, reinforcing the illusion. The legislature could claim that it was being lied to, while the executive could retort that it was being meddled with. Casey complained of congressional "micro-management" of the two dozen covert projects Congress had secretly provided him the funding for. But Casey had to keep coming to the Hill and Congress had to keep accepting the apologies, so that the illusion could be maintained. The theme culminated and was brought home to the American people in the televised Iran-contra hearings. Here were the executive witnesses facing off against the congressional committee members, one branch against the other. Each side was able to make speeches about the proper foreign policy making power, speeches which could feed the debate for years to come. This debate continued into the committee deliberations and appeared in the final committee report.

The surface dramas narrowed things further, suggesting that a particular roll call vote would make a difference or that the President's specially designed T-shirt helped to rally the American people in support of the contra cause. The Tower Commission Report gave us volumes of minutiae to occupy our attention, while the Iran-contra hearings featured the adventures of Oliver North and colorful Iranian arms dealers and the bizarre mishaps they met along the way. While the committee focused attention on the one unanswerable question of whether the President knew of the contra diversion—unanswerable because of deniability—a great many other questions never got asked.

We need to reconsider the basic illusion that the elected officials are broadly engaged in American foreign policy. Like Congress we accept the fact that we were lied to, but think it probably will not happen again. It will not happen because we will not have an Oliver North or a Ronald Reagan or a Richard Nixon or whoever is the individual personality featured at the time. But this active engagement may be the basic lie, or hypocrisy, that the others breed on, the root of all the other lies that came to light when Nicaragua was the center of the world.

8

✦ ✦ ✦

THE AYES AND
NAYS OF REFORM

BOOKS ON AMERICAN POLITICS often end with prescriptions
for reform. It suits the national spirit of optimism and in-
vention, the belief that even institutions can use a tune-up
and bodywork from time to time. This is especially so with books
about Congress, where a long reform tradition makes such chapters almost obligatory. Congress has been the perennial target of
critics in the press, in the White House, and in Congress itself.
Congress is frequently charged with being too fragmented and
parochial—too slow to act and too closely tied to local interests to
take major responsibility in a vast and changing nation. Somewhat contradictorily, it is also criticized for being too strong and
too capable of obstructing presidents, who have come with fresh
mandates from the people and find their programs blocked by a
little band of willful members.[1] Besides being charged with being
too weak or too strong, it is also accused of being irresponsible.
According to one critic,

> Congress has in our own day become divorced from the general
> mass of national sentiment, simply because there is no means by
> which the movements of that national sentiment can readily be reg-
> istered in legislation. Going about as it does to please all sorts of
> committees composed of . . . the dull and the acute, the able and
> the cunning, the honest and the careless—Congress evades judg-
> ment by avoiding all coherence of plan in its action. . . . At the
> opening of its sessions there was no determinate policy to look for-
> ward to, and at the close no accomplished plans to look back upon.

This contemporary-sounding criticism was written by Woodrow Wilson in 1885.[2]

The presidency, too, has come in for its share of reform attention. Writers from Wilson to Richard Neustadt have sought ways of increasing presidential power. According to much of the writing through the 1960s, the President was not strong enough, especially in relation to the powers of Congress. Ten years later, in the wake of the Watergate abuses, people were concerned that the President was too strong and that Congress must be strengthened to check executive excesses. The presidency was imperial or imperiled. From the 1930s to the 1950s reformers wrote that "the President needs help" and called for ways to strengthen the organization and information of the office. More recently, writers such as Irving Janis and George Reedy have pointed out deep flaws in how the newly available information was processed.[3] A decade of writing in the 1980s tried to separate the illusions surrounding the office from its capacity to make any governmental decisions.[4] Scholars looked more closely at what the presidents actually did.

Through all of this writing run the themes of inability and the lack of unaccountability on the part of elected officeholders. Congress or the President cannot act or does not act in responsible ways. Typically, reformers have looked within an institution or sought to correct one of the branches of government by making changes in the other. Congress, for example, should reorganize itself to check presidential excesses. Or Congress should reorganize so that it will not be tempted to interfere with executive branch affairs.

This chapter deviates from the reform tradition in two ways. First, the need for changes is particularly clear and demanding: this is no obligatory or pro forma set of final remarks. Second, since the same problems are found in two institutions, we will not be able to address them by focusing on one. The book has traced a pattern of foreign policy making that spans both President and Congress. We now need to ask why this should be so and what should be done.

Prescriptions for the body politic can be only as good as the diagnosis is accurate. To debate how President and Congress should make foreign policy, we need to see first what they do. To correct or counter unfortunate trends, we need to distinguish real changes from what people think—at one point in time—the trends have been. So, many people believe that Congress became more active in foreign policy in the mid-1970s, this increased activity being a combined product of internal reforms and reaction against Vietnam and Watergate. Since no equivalent countershift occurred, they assume Congress must still be in the active phase. In addition, people assume that since the President is active, the only question is how active the Congress should be. No one has separated the President from the executive branch, what Congress says from what Congress does, or what has been the actual course of foreign policy over time.

We have looked at the changes in foreign policy making in three areas: the working agenda for legislation; the use of force engaged in by the United States; and foreign assistance policy. Each provides a universe of cases that allows comparison across time. While this approach cannot give the detail of a single-case study or a highly selected set of a few cases, it can help to uncover trends that might otherwise be missed. It can also provide data for other scholars to use. Part of the problem with discussing foreign policy making is that people do not know what the policy enactments have been.

In investigating these cases, the book finds little evidence for an increase in congressional activity across the years. In foreign assistance Congress has shown activity and a willingness to confront the President since the Kennedy administration. From the 1960s and before, Congress used its annual review of foreign assistance authorization to target particular areas of concern, often rewriting much of the bill in the process. These were not minor matters. Balance of payments problems, relations with the Soviet bloc, war powers, human rights policy have been among the subjects targeted. The only clearly observable shift occurs in the 1980s, when Congress became less able to pass any authorizations bills and so less capable of using them as an instrument to make policy. If anything, this is a shift toward *decreasing* activity.

In contrast, in matters of the use of force Congress has consistently supported the executive, with few exceptions across the years. One can go case by case through the thirty-three events listed in appendix B, as provided by Congress's own definition of a use of force. In doing this, one finds few points at which the executive was constrained from pursuing a particular course: Southeast Asia, although not until after 1970; Lebanon, although not until a year after the forces had been dispatched; El Salvador and Nicaragua. There could be grumbling. But Congress's main role in the other twenty-nine cases was, like the public's role, to be informed and to give its support. Three of the exceptions occurred in the Reagan years, but since the overall number of uses of force increased greatly in those years, the percentage of times an exception was made did not change. The typical pattern—across the three decades of the study and before and after Vietnam—was for Congress to support the President as Commander-in-Chief.

Some people argue that the presidential constraints imposed by Congress are primarily indirect. The War Powers Act, for example, need not curtail any particular use of force, but should make presidents think twice before engaging troops in a potential combat situation. Yet we saw in chapter 4 that presidents pick their cases when they will and will not report actions in accord with the War Powers resolution. On only one occasion—the *Mayaguez*—did the President report under the provision that triggers the sixty-day clock. In that case, however, the clock had already stopped, since by the time of the report the affair was over. And we saw Congress willing to try anything—even go to the courts—rather than enforce its own legislation. In only one case —Lebanon—has Congress invoked the sixty-day clock. Even that came a year after the forces were sent and, following compromise with the White House, became an eighteen-month clock. The War Powers Act, passed under very exceptional circumstances, could not be enforced in more normal circumstances. Hence if presidents know that Congress will not enforce the act, the constraints, even indirect ones, do not appear great.

The third set of cases, dealing with the legislative working agenda, shows a more complex set of patterns. While the total number of bills appears to have increased across time, the trend disappears when one removes the nonlegislative resolutions: the kind of symbolic statements showing Congress in favor of freedom, opposed to genocide and international kidnapping, and at work proclaiming Dutch American Friendship Day. The highest amount of legislative activity appears in the 1970s with the decades preceding and following it showing lower rates that are about equal. On the average, from four to seven substantive issues, often very specific ones, are debated each year. These include such matters as the sale of missiles to one nation, the prohibition of aid to another, or what to do about Rhodesian chrome. Since at any one point in time only a few issues appear to gain presidential and congressional attention, presumably the remaining issues are handled elsewhere in the executive bureaucracy or in the authorizing committees, or they are not dealt with at all.

A closer, qualitative look does not change these results. Arms sales and intelligence restrictions emerged periodically on the working agenda across two decades. They were perhaps second in their frequency of appearance after such issues as foreign assistance and the various trade regulations. Yet, congressional impact in these areas was heavily concentrated in the years from 1974 to 1979. The deliberations continued but the impact declined. By the last year of the Carter administration, Congress had given up many of these restrictions. Further weakening would occur in the Reagan years. So, hearings on Central Intelligence Agency activities would continue and indeed increase. But they would now be conducted by congressional staffers who were themselves former agency officials and by members of Congress who typically supported the agency activities. If the morale of the agency was low in the 1980s, as officials liked to point out, it was not because of their treatment at the hands of supportive congressional committees. In both of these issues, action taken in the most recent years cut back the power of Congress exercised in the decade before.

In none of these cases do we find an *increase* in activity, nor would the congressional literature lead us to expect one. Students of Congress point out the growing inability to act produced by such things as the weakening committee system and the difficulty of making budgetary decisions. This growing inability is seen in the Carter and Reagan administrations and in conditions of same-party and divided-party control. The chief differences in congressional action in these two administrations is seen in an increase in symbolic resolutions in the Reagan years along with a decreasing ability to make foreign assistance authorizations. In theory divided-party control should give Congress more incentives to oppose the President or suggest alternative policies. In practice, however, this did not appear to be the case, apart from the continuing and highly publicized controversy over Nicaragua. Those who worry that Congress becomes too assertive in conditions of divided-party control would find little evidence for their worries from the Reagan years.

Why, then, would the impression of congressional activity persist so strongly in popular commentary in the absence of any evidence to support it? Certainly there are partisan and ideological incentives. When Republicans were in control of the White

House, conservatives might have wished to defend its prerogatives against congressional inroads, thus exaggerating the threat from Congress. Reagan conservatives, like Kennedy liberals two decades before, undoubtedly desired more presidential discretion. Yet with a Democrat in the White House, the debate goes on. While no doubt some of the commentary reflects ideological concerns, this cannot explain the breadth of the consensus nor the degree to which the conventional wisdom is taken for granted: as if Congress had hit the ground running in the immediate post-Vietnam era and never stopped running.

Both institutions, this book argues, help to perpetuate this impression. In Congress, a host of surface activities mask the underlying trends. The increase in the number of bills and the number of hearings gives an illusion of activity that masks the poverty of debate. The same effect is produced by the proclamations and symbolic resolutions engaged in by both Congress and the President. The steadily mounting number of reports demanded by Congress hides the fact that the reports are typically substitutes for legislation added in conference. Meanwhile, President and Congress engage in one or two very visible struggles each year, with filibusters and veto threats and last-minute compromises, where debate has narrowed down to a very specific issue, and often a peripheral one, such as a plant closing requirement. Indeed, the notion that there *is* a struggle for influence between the two elected branches is itself the most effective illusion, hiding how small the agenda actually is. Together, the use of symbolic resolutions, increase in roll calls and lengthy hearings, addition of reporting requirements, and selection of particular narrow issues for debate give an impression of great activity. These are Congress's special effects.

Presidents and executive branch officials have their own part to play. While presidents must select issues narrowly for their particular attention, they are pressured by others in the executive branch to maintain executive prerogatives. So, Carter and Reagan were pressured by CIA officials to push for fewer restrictions on agency operation. People at State would prefer to carry on their negotiations independent of external, congressional control. Officials can and do pressure Congress directly, often with considerable success. The President's role is critical, however, as justification for the prerogatives. No one can say that Congress should not meddle with an executive bureaucracy: it is supposed to oversee what the bureaucracies do. The justification becomes one that Congress should not meddle with the President, a very different argument and one much more difficult to dispute. In carrying on this contention, presidents not only support their subordinates in the executive branch, they maintain their own reputation as chief and preeminent architect of the nation's foreign policy. No one needs to ask which particular issues the presidents are engaged in at any one time.

This kind of three-way agreement among the Congress, the President, and executive branch officials has its own special effects. They are seen most clearly in the restrictions Congress imposes in such matters as arms sales or foreign assistance funds. Congress passes the restriction with the proviso that it can be suspended "if the President determines" it is in the nation's best interest. When the escape hatch is used, both President and Congress get credit for acting—Congress has restricted and the President has determined—while officials get the discretion they need. These provisos are now routinely added to bills and routinely invoked in the executive branch. Thus at any one point in time Congress has a good idea of what will happen to its restriction and so do the executive branch officials who complain in the hearings about congressional micromanagement. Why do they complain about a restriction that they know will not restrict? It is a compliment to Congress and a way of keeping their discretion under the guise of action by the elected officeholders.

Thus debate over who holds the foreign policy reins makes both branches appear more responsible and eager to make decisions than they may actually be. People debate the merits of the War Powers Act when neither the President nor Congress use the act, finding all kinds of ways to avoid it. They argue whether Congress should meddle in military assistance when presidents use the "extraordinary circumstance" clause that Congress has passed to get around all the meddling. At the extreme presidents jealously guard their prerogatives to make policy for Nicaragua while Congress righteously demands more reports that will not be read. And the stately dance around the issues goes on.

Much of what we find, then, is symbolic action: the highly stylized substitute for the thing it seeks to represent. A successful symbolic communication typically evokes what people already agree to or what they would like to think of as true. It is the presentation of the actual in terms of the ideal.[5] In this case the ideal is that elected officials are actively engaged in making the nation's foreign policy to the extent that they need to struggle about it; the actual is that they are far less so engaged. Once we recognize this symbolic activity, we see another reason why the conventional wisdom has been so tenacious and convincing. It is what people want to believe is true.

People must believe in the controversy or they would need to ask disturbing questions: about what it means if democratic officials are not involved; about how to balance professionalism with democratic control. If Congress is not interfering with the executive branch, who is watching these officials? And what is Congress doing with its time? Are presidents allocating their priorities correctly or are some kinds of foreign policy receiving undue attention? It is not merely the public officials who carry on the illusion, but the citizens and those who report to them about political affairs. For all the drama and special effects have a very specific audience in mind. By agreeing that there is a struggle for power, the audience cheers on the players and asks for an encore.

Hence the task of reform is twofold. Certainly we need to find ways to bring the actual closer to the ideal, not only encouraging more thought and accountability on the part of our elected branches, but *making it easier for them to be accountable*. But most importantly we need to eliminate the illusion and the reforms that merely feed it. We can therefore start with the reforms that are contraindicated by this analysis.

The Nays of Reform

Staff. Those who would like Congress to take a stronger role in foreign policy making typically call for an increase in congressional staff. If the executive has a near-monopoly of information, so the argument goes, Congress can counter this advantage by compiling its own information. This kind of thinking was behind the staff increases of the 1970s and the forming, for example, of the Congressional Budget Office, to provide a resource to challenge presidential budget proposals. It led many to believe that the foreign affairs committees increased their activity in the 1970s because their staffs had increased. In the absence of any systematic studies across time, staff size was taken as the indicator of interest and activity.

However, in the policies we have traced across the years there is no sign of this increased activity, and in some cases indeed we see cutbacks. The expanded staff hired to oversee intelligence activities was drawn in large part from the agencies themselves. The staff processed information provided by their former superiors, who were the main witnesses at the hearings. Even when staff might work hard for policy innovations, as in some of the foreign assistance reforms, the institution did not provide enough support for its committees to see their work through the conference. At best, the increased staff makes no difference. At worst, it gives the illusion of activity where none may be occurring.

Paper oversight. Related proposals for increased oversight activity on the part of Congress show the same difficulties. Oversight has been a favorite reform topic of both friends and foes of Congress, the friends hoping it will make executive agencies more accountable and the foes imagining it will give Congress something to do once it withdraws from the mainstream of making legislation. A vigorous oversight is certainly a requirement for any active congressional role. Yet a previous chapter has found the forms of oversight carried on as a substitute for legislation, the conference committees demanding a report from the President when they can do nothing else. The request for a report becomes a substitute for compromise on the substance of the legislation. The reporting requirements have increased dramatically—up to twenty new reports added in one bill for one year. Like the staff increases, the number of hearings and number of pages of reports are very misleading indicators. They do not accord with the trends we have seen toward increasing delegation, since the end of the Carter years, in arms control, foreign assistance, and intelligence. Moreover, they disguise the fact that the legislation might be decreasing as the reporting requirements grow.

It is admittedly difficult to say when the forms of oversight might be better than no oversight at all. Executive branch personnel, usually well below the level of presidential appointees, can take the writing of these reports very seriously, even if no one in Congress will read them. Report-writing, then, rather than report-reading is the point through which some accountability of bureaucrats to elected representatives can occur. Yet, when the mining of Nicaraguan harbors (or rather, the piers within the harbors and not, technically, the harbors themselves) can be buried within a long report so that no one in Congress is aware of it, the art of report-writing offers little comfort for those who would like more oversight in fact.

A misdiagnosis is also at work in proposals for less advocacy and more objective oversight. If oversight was already vigorous, say by the committees reviewing arms sales or intelligence activities, then we might wish to temper any negative effects. But students of Congress have long pointed out how rare such vigorous oversight is, on any kinds of policy, and how it tends to occur only under exceptional circumstances: for example, when the committee members are advocates for a policy or when the political circumstances, such as provided by divided party control, favor its activity.[6] There is probably no such thing as objective oversight purely. The foreign policy cases we have reviewed show no exception to this general pattern.

One study of intelligence distinguishes between advocacy oversight and the more responsible activity of the later period.[7] It is interesting that the one clear case of advocacy oversight that the study cites is the Pike Committee's investigation of intelligence abuses in the middle of the 1970s. Yet, the Pike Committee was the one time that a committee of Congress actually tried to report on executive misdemeanors. Even that case found the House repudiating its own committee and refusing to make the report public. Those who want less advocacy oversight in intelligence activity would be hard pressed to find any cases supported by the Congress to use as the negative examples in their argument.

"Consultation." Other suggestions which take the surface struggle at face value also need to be questioned. Writers have called for more consultation between the White House and Congress:[8]

> Collaboration entails consultation with Congress before executive action. . . . It means the president must provide timely information to Congress on major foreign policy developments and demonstrate a capacity to change his mind in the face of reasonable opposition. By dealing honestly and openly with influential and knowledgeable legislators, the president can strengthen the hand of responsible forces in Congress and thereby increase his chance of attracting majority support for his policies and preserving as much discretion as possible over the conduct of foreign policy.

The select intelligence committees are taken as a model for this kind of collaboration as it might be applied more broadly to arms control, war powers, and foreign economic policy. Other select oversight committees might focus on exchange rates and trade issues.

Such proposals are merely an invitation to further cooptation if the argument of this book is correct. Consultation provisions were written in to the War Powers Act so that Congress would have "timely information" and so that the President could change his mind "in the face of reasonable opposition." We have seen, however, that the consultation is not followed by presidents nor demanded by Congress. In the clearest cases of violation, members of Congress merely suggested that perhaps the wording of the consultation provision was not clear enough. Nor are the select intelligence committees, weakened by rotating membership and without prestige in their own institution, a likely model for any real collaboration between the branches. They become dependent for information and support on the very agencies they are supposed to oversee. They are the mushrooms, according to critics of intelligence policy on the committees, kept in the dark and fed manure. The communication goes only one way. We have seen how surface devices are already used to give the illusion of activity and vigorous debate. More such devices do not seem called for.

More select committees. Even more clearly, proposals for joint committees can be seen as weakening congressional power. With only rare exceptions joint committees have not worked well in the Congress, where both houses jealously guard their own influence. A joint select intelligence committee, as some people have proposed, would be about as weak a congressional creature as one could imagine. Without the power of standing committees, and removed from the support of their House and Senate institutions, such committees could perform only the most consensual ceremonial functions. The minority on the Iran-contra investigating committee, which supported the President and felt Congress was too "aggrandizing," recommended that intelligence could be best overseen by a joint select committee.

Term limits. Nor should we turn too quickly to criticize the individual members or the electoral system which brings them to Congress. It is not clear what more a Lee Hamilton or Dave McCurdy or Daniel Moynihan could do or all the other members who work so hard in their respective areas of expertise. One thinks of the time Jim Wright must have spent on the Nicaraguan issue or

Stephen Solarz (D., N.Y.) on the Philippines. In order to make his views widely known, Solarz appeared on thirty-four radio and television shows in a five-month period, according to his staff's count, and was quoted regularly in the major newspapers.[9] For each of these very visible members, there are many more at work behind the scenes. The individuals work, but the institution does not necessarily encourage individual action to form a collective product. Why this is the case is a question this study and others should address. It may be a necessary and continuing part of the congressional structure, which must, after all, represent many diverse constituencies: Congress is not built to have the views of a few individual representatives prevail. Alternatively, it may be a sign of temporary weakness to be corrected by institutional—not individual—reform.

It is thus too easy to stereotype members of Congress as lazy or irresponsible when one does not like the policies or lack of policies coming from the institution. So some people call for term limits or other constitutional tinkering on the curious grounds that the voters like their representatives too much to toss them out. Term limits, of course, would *weaken* the Congress by undercutting precisely the institutional support that the individual members need. Traditionally, senior members could claim expertise—among their colleagues and in committees—because they had worked on a particular problem for so long. They could more easily stand their ground against administrative witnesses because of this experience, pointing out that they had seen these problems before and seen many presidents come and go. A Congress of junior members, making their first visit to the White House or confronted with their first formidable State Department report, would be unable to make these claims. Only if one wants *less* of a congressional role in foreign and domestic policy would one argue for term limits, as well as for more select committees, and for multicommittee conference reports.

These are some of the primary reform suggestions offered today for improving relations between the branches. It can be noted that they ask for changes in Congress and not, as in the period following Watergate and Vietnam, for a change in executive branch organization or decision making. Several, such as the staff and oversight proposals, would have little effect beyond increasing the illusion of activity. Others, however, would clearly weaken the Congress by undercutting its base of power in the committee system.

THE AYES OF REFORM

Congress: Rules and committees—reforming the reforms. Given the poverty of the present foreign policy debate, changes are needed that can invigorate both branches, while controlling some of the superficial symbolism. In Congress the obvious target of this invigorating energy is the committees and the kind of rules changes that would support them. Thus the single most important positive recommendation of the study asks for some reforming of the reforms. Why this could be feasible—that is, why the members could support such changes—should become clear in the argument that follows.

It is ironic that the two reform movements culminating in the changes of the 1970s worked against each other. One sought to strengthen the Congress in policy making in relation to the executive branch, while the other decentralized influence to the extent that it was difficult to make any policy. The first added staff and oversight subcommittees to make Congress more independent of executive branch decisions; the second undercut the source of its independence, the autonomy of the committees.

In the classic committee system of the pre-reform period, committee decisions, supported by norms of specialization throughout the chamber, could survive the floor and conference. Members could remain on the standing committees as long as they could win reelection from their own voters. In this way they were protected from influence coming from the White House and from being removed by party leaders. Members would support each other's committees because they were simultaneously supporting their own basis of power and that of the institution. In the modern Congress committee decisions can be undercut by multiple referrals to other committees, whose members have only particular, and often peripheral, interests in the policy, or by floor amendments by individual policy entrepreneurs. With the advent of large decentralized conferences, subject to lobbying from interest groups and the White House, committees also have less control over the conference stage. On any particular foreign policy issue, then, each individual member of Congress might have more influence in the modern Congress, but the institution itself has less influence. There is no autonomous power base.

With select committees, of course, Congress takes a step even further away from committee power. In contrast to standing committees, select committees have little prestige in the chamber or as an assignment for individual members. Understandably, members might take more interest in—and work harder for—their standing committee assignments. The rotating membership of select committees means that members can develop no long-term experience in a policy to command congressional respect nor can they achieve much morale as a group. It is not surprising, therefore, that the committees become much more dependent on staff and on executive information. Seen in this light, the select committees on intelligence show very clearly how Congress wants to handle intelligence policy: i.e., with deference to the executive branch. More select committees, on the model of the intelligence committees, would merely increase this deference.

Obviously one cannot go back to the classic committee system, and few might want to. Yet, there are shifts in thinking and procedures that should be easier to make than to maintain the current illusion that anything is getting done. Members could begin to see their own interests best served by supporting the other committee experts, and so call for restraint on the floor and less individual showmanship. They could remember when faced with hostile administration witnesses or career professionals, that they have at hand their own claim of expertise: the committee members who know the policy because they have been making it for x number of years. They could pressure the party leaders to cut back the multiple referrals, especially in the House, and take responsibility for forming more workable conferences. If party leaders now try to satisfy everyone by dividing a policy area into dozens of separate interests, they might satisfy the members better by giving them less frustration in their work. No procedural shifts will occur without the support of party leaders, but the leaders themselves are dependent on the members' support. No one in Congress is well served by denying the institution's own source of power and prestige.

Congress's present inability to act may force change of some kind. Actually, these changes might be the most welcome to the members themselves and the easiest to achieve. Given individual power on paper, the members have no institutional power in fact. Demanding rules that gave more payoff in legislation for the very hard work that is done should be a position individual members could support. Thus as Congress undertakes the continuing question of how to reform itself, strengthening the power of committees—and thus the real impact of individual members—should be a matter of urgent attention.

Changing presidential priorities: Defining an agenda. Any reform that targets Congress exclusively, however, is not indicated by these results. The patterns of mutual avoidance we have seen implicate both branches. President and Congress are codependents, really, facilitating each other's dysfunction. It takes two to conduct the stately dance around the issues. One passes the extraordinary circumstance clauses that the other uses liberally. Together they evade the war powers restrictions. Each expresses itself as concerned with human rights policy and the control of arms sales; yet, after a brief highly visible face-off on a few selected issues, the policies in large part are left to normal bureaucratic routines.

To invigorate the presidency we can look to its own power point, the interface with public opinion. People confuse the President with the executive branch and foreign policy with the top news stories. Thus it becomes easy to assume presidents are making foreign policy because we see them making statements about it on at least one item every day. But the top stories are presidential by definition: White House press releases and statements by presidents and other administration figures, deemed the "most important" foreign policy news, become the stories everyone reads and watches. Carter administration officials, for example, used to predict the next day's lead story, with almost perfect accuracy, from that day's press releases. Presumably the skilled public relations people in the Reagan and Bush administrations could improve on even that degree of control. In effect, the presidential story becomes the front page news.

Certainly presidents have the ability to follow one or two foreign policy issues at a time, subject to the quality of the information they receive as channeled through intelligence officials, National Security staff, and State Department sources. These can be very important issues, as widely agreed, or quite narrow and particular issues. The case of the Reagan agenda and Nicaragua can illustrate the point. Certainly also they can be briefed as new issues arise, and provided with statements for the press. But this does not mean they follow all the major foreign policy issues or even that they can determine for themselves which are the most important ones. Meanwhile things continue of their own bureaucratic momentum, while the public assumes the President is watching over the world.

Who, then, should guide presidents as to what particular foreign policy issue they will become interested in? Admitting that events in the world will of necessity shape some of the priorities, we still need to ask whether the American public should have any role in this guidance: in effect, if there should be any democratic input in foreign policy. The question becomes particularly important when we realize that there is a kind of public input now, albeit an unconscious one. On occasions of the dramatic use of force, the public rallies around the flag and the Commander-in-Chief, bringing an immediate upturn in the president's public opinion polls. Other presidential foreign policy acts do not show the same impact.[10] Separate occasions of the use of force, which occur most frequently when the economy is in decline, increased sharply in frequency in the Reagan and Bush administrations. It is doubtful that the American people support wars as their favorite instrument of foreign policy; yet, in the absence of other information from the public, the record suggests this.

Reporters and key constituency groups keep presidents under pressure about their domestic agenda, with the agenda items listed by name: the budget deficit, unemployment, health care, education, the environment, to mention a few. No similar pressure and tracking is provided on foreign policy. So supporters could say George Bush pursued "foreign policy," and thus did not have that much time or interest for domestic affairs. Bush's record, however, was distinctive from other presidents only in the number of uses of force. What was called "foreign policy" was only a particular kind of policy.

Somehow, we need more careful tracking of the nation's foreign policy agenda by media and other groups. At minimum we need a list of foreign policy problems to parallel the list for domestic policy—we need the notion of a foreign policy agenda. Recognizing that key groups now—foreign nations, international businesses, executive department agencies—do have their agendas and do pressure the White House, we need some broader monitoring activity. Such watchdog groups would serve two purposes. They could provide both President and public with an independent monitoring of events and trends. They would also focus the *President's* attention on these issues by the strongest of incentives —because the public was watching them too.

We now have media-monitoring groups that report the kind of coverage and sources found in various media outlets. The same kind of monitoring could be offered for a policy area—in this case, foreign policy—tracking where various issues are being considered and what issues are not being considered at all. Some years ago "public interest" groups were formed which monitored issues in need of attention and tried to focus responsibility of the elected branches. They sought to speak for a broad public interest in policy to counter the narrow interests of particular groups. Foreign policy has its own narrow and special interests: foreign governments lobbying through Washington public relations firms; domestic importers and investors; government agencies, with their own agendas and interests, seeking protection from public view. Public watchdog groups are needed as much in foreign as in domestic policy.

The point can be raised that news conferences, whether formal or informal, help to perform this monitoring function. Reporters raise issues beyond those covered in the standard press releases, giving the public and the presidents a somewhat broader perspective in the process. Nevertheless, news conferences are so under the control of presidents that they cannot perform this function continuously across time. Kennedy enjoyed press conferences and Bush performed well in the short informal exchanges he engaged in on a regular basis. However, most of the presidents in the interim years avoided them as much as they could. If journalists themselves recognized that foreign policy was more than what the White House said it was, the public's opinion could be broadened too. The kinds of guests interviewed on the television news shows and quoted as news sources would expand accordingly, beyond past and present administration sources and the few members of Congress who, coincidentally, adopt the presidents' agenda and appear close to their position.

At this point, even the people who consider themselves well informed in foreign policy could say little about how America decides to sell sophisticated weapons to other nations, the proportion of the nation's aid going to clearly democratic or clearly dictatorial nations, the rules currently governing intelligence agencies acting in this country or abroad. They might be surprised to know how the military assistance budget doubled in the 1980s, the size of the Camp David bill, or the fact that the sixty-day provision of the War Powers Act has been invoked only once. They have focused instead on the symbolic constitutional debate —of which branch should have more or less influence—instead of on the policies or the substantive issues. They have taken the rhetoric as the reality.

Certainly agenda-watching would pressure the presidency indirectly, as it would the Congress, by informing citizens on a wider range of issues. This is a kind of invigoration, although perhaps not one the presidents would seek on their own. Yet there could be a more direct benefit also. We tend to think of presidents as having a monopoly of foreign policy information, whereas it is actually the executive branch construed broadly, and not the presidents as individuals or their immediate advisers, who have this information. Presidents would benefit as much from alternative sources of information and ideas as the public would. Presidents are not foreign policy "professionals," as Henry Kissinger used to take pains to point out. They can forget the details of historic treaties or important communiqués. Faced with conflicts and lobbying from within their own information networks, it is no wonder that their actions are often perfunctory. Presidents are experts, however, in dealing with the public and in finding ways to articulate national goals. Establishing this kind of interface between president and public on foreign policy could thus enhance the President's own influence and grasp on issues.

In short, presidents must find allies if they wish to have an individual impact on policy, and their natural ally is the American public. With an invigorated public discussion, Congress might be an ally too, even more so than at present. The illusion of struggle between the branches combined with little public knowledge of foreign affairs cuts presidents off from these two potential alliances.

The major objection to this kind of increase in information concerns the dangers implicit in foreign policy debate. It is commonly felt that the nation should provide a unified front abroad. So people worried that the congressional debate on the Gulf War, a debate whose outcome was known in advance, might send mixed signals to Saddam Hussein. This is a somewhat disingenuous argument, however. First of all, there are conflicts and mixed signals now—between White House advisers, the various lobbying groups, factions within the intelligence agencies. They are sufficient to tie up conference committees or to make sure that actions in one part of the world will contradict actions taken elsewhere. Second, many of these conflicts engage multinational participants. It is not a matter of Americans facing the world as much as interests from abroad and at home vying for influence on American policy. It is not clear that widening the number of American participants in foreign policy discussions will necessarily widen the gap between opinions. It may even narrow it, forcing more accountability on the part of President and Congress to this opinion. Third, of course, the argument does not distinguish the kind of foreign policy issues it is talking about. It is one thing to hope Americans could present a united front in time of war, although they may not always be able to do this. It is quite another to ask them to form a unified front on matters of arms sales, or trade agreements, or the military assistance budget. Seen in this light, the argument seems more a device to force consensus in areas where real disagreement might exist.

The question itself, as to the scope and limits of foreign policy debate, is a serious one and needs more discussion. If the signals a nation sends are important, then Americans need to weigh the various alternative messages: when to show they are a nation of single-minded opinion, or a democratic nation conducting debate, or a nation concerned with the spread of arms, or human rights, or other issues. At minimum, a broader and more knowledgeable discussion of the issues might help to make some of these decisions.

A research agenda. Political scientists clearly have their own work to do in providing information on foreign policy. More studies are needed that will trace the course of issues across time to see what has changed and what remained the same. Political scientists also need to challenge their interviews and conventional sources and look more closely at particular policy areas; else they will simply repeat the kind of symbolic statements that keep attention on the narrow agenda that their sources prefer. Most importantly, they must come to terms with how little we have in the way of systematic knowledge about the nation's foreign policy making. To give an illustration, one review of congressional foreign policy research lists nine subject areas in need of work: from constituency opinion to the activity of committees and party leaders, to budget decisions and interactions with executive branch personnel. Since the areas cover the full span of activity included in most books on Congress, the reviewers are saying there is little information indeed.[11]

Sufficient material is available in nonclassified sources, although it would take effort to collect. *Congressional Quarterly,* which does an excellent job in tracking some issues, has not been providing the same kind of longitudinal view of foreign policy issues. Congress has the information, as we know from its manifold reports, but little of this reaches public attention. Perhaps we could find ways to make Congress report on its reports! This would not only disseminate much useful information, but help to deter some of the more superfluous reporting requirements. Even the more readily available information from Congress, however, has not been utilized. The Congressional Research Service tracks the uses and violations of the War Powers Act. Yet few of the writers producing the many thousands of pages on this subject appear aware of what the reports say. Annual authorization decisions are available to track particular policies over time or to identify changes in congressional attention and interest. Floor decisions are easily available. In any case the issue of classification of sensitive material need not pose an obstacle to this kind of research. Basic information on trends, on actions taken and not taken, on issues buried or postponed is available. For some reason people simply have not looked.

Several research areas in particular are suggested by this work. Each asks that we try to identify the universe of cases to test questions of influence or change across time. The book has sought to identify a congressional working agenda by looking at bills which reached the floor for a vote in at least one chamber. It thus has tried to delineate what Congress as an institution has had to pay attention to, as distinguished from all bills submitted, many of which have no chance of passage, or the particular set of legislation which is ultimately enacted. Alternative definitions of such a working agenda could also be developed and tested, following the lines of this study or David Mayhew's work.[12] Needless to say, we cannot test the impact of such things as reforms, interest groups, individual members, or other influences until we can take this first conceptual step.

It would also be useful to compare the foreign and domestic policy agendas in Congress to see if one is smaller or more stable than the other, or varies differently across time. Some people might expect that the two agendas would be quite different, given lower levels of public information in foreign policy as well as Congress's traditional deference to the executive branch, Yet, if the reforms of the 1970s have increased the difficulty of the congressional institution in deciding foreign policy issues, they may have had a similar impact on domestic issues, in which case the two agendas should be similar when viewed across time. Clearly, a fuller understanding of how active Congress is in foreign policy requires this comparative domestic policy study.

Students of particular policy areas should develop their own universes of cases—for trade decisions, arms sales, and other policies—thus allowing a combination of detailed and yet systematic research. They could proceed by identifying the years their policy is subject to a floor decision or not (as in chapter 2) or by tracking decisions through the annual authorization process (chapter 5). The currently fashionable proposition suggests an increase in congressional activity over time, an increase presumably holding across various policy domains. An alternative proposition, and one suggested by many of the preceding cases, suggests a periodicity, built in by the statutory provisions or by other presidential and congressional events. Congress's activity in trade policy might be the clearest case in point. The two competing hypotheses and others could thus be tested for each of the various foreign policy domains.

No major study exists of foreign assistance despite the fact that the program is used as a multipurpose tool of foreign policy by both presidents and Congress. At the most concrete and practical level, we cannot at present trace relative spending across time, the changes from economic to military assistance, or the importance given various regions of the world or various activities on the part of foreign nations. In contrast to the many analyses given the defense budget, the economic and military assistance budget remains virtually unknown. Studies of these decisions should have a major priority, not only for the policy area itself but as a way of viewing the agenda of elected representatives. Without information in this area political scientists will underestimate the role of Congress in foreign affairs, but they will underestimate it for all of the post–World War II era. They will be talking about Congress's role in foreign policy without understanding the power of the purse.

Individual activity, too, could be researched more fully. The

Public Papers lists all presidential public activity from George Washington to the present, including the text of all speeches, visits home and abroad with foreign leaders, and key documents issued from the Oval Office. While we cannot uncover the private conversations of presidents or discussions of covert activity (subjects not fully researchable, by definition), we can begin to identify areas of individual presidents' interests—a White House agenda as members of Congress and other interested people could understand it. Such an exercise could begin to separate the activity and interest of the presidents we have elected from the routine and ongoing work of the executive branch. It would also allow us to compare the agendas of the various presidents with each other, against a congressional agenda, and for contrasts between domestic and foreign policy. In this way recent studies of presidential activity could be extended into the foreign policy field.

Individual congressional activities could be examined through what they have to say on the floor, in committee hearings, and in news conferences or talk-show appearances. Interview studies could ask members, selected as experts or nonexperts depending on their committee assignments, the kinds of foreign policy activities they engage in. Unfortunately, such material would probably not enable us to investigate change over time. Floor speaking, as in the *Congressional Record,* is not electronically available for the time period under study, nor have interview studies in the past asked members about their foreign policy activity. Information on talk-show speaking and other appearances is collected now, but would exist only since the middle 1980s.[13] True, there is probably more "grandstanding" now, as James Lindsay describes the very visible and public activity of members,[14] since current radio and television programming encourages this response. Yet, earlier congresses had their share of very visible members; one thinks of Senators Arthur Vandenburg (R., Mich.) and J. W. Fulbright (D., Tenn.) and William Proxmire (D., Wisc.), names that became famous in the first three decades of the post–World War II years. As part of his many oversight activities, Proxmire used to send a staff person to meet military aircraft to see who was riding at government expense. Nor is it clear that grandstanding has more of an impact than other actions taken in committee or behind the scenes. Nevertheless, information on congressional activities could begin to show when, in what policy areas, and under what conditions members of Congress do become active. Activity, moreover, should vary by such characteristics as committee assignment, constituency, seniority, and party. Rather than arguing about the amount of activity, we could then be investigating when significant congressional activity occurs. Ultimately, this would be the more interesting research question.

Any one of these studies might extend or qualify the results of this book. The book, then, is offered merely as a first empirical study of a subject given too much talk and not enough research.

A poverty of thinking. Rules changes in Congress that strengthen the committees and more active agenda-watching groups can help center responsibility on elected officials, discouraging the fake duels and dances that now take place on the national stage. But these instruments can do little in themselves against a deeper underlying malaise that involves a poverty of thinking to which not only officials but journalists, academics, and interested citizens must plead guilty. There is something wrong with the thinking that slides from "President" to "executive branch" and back again, that generalizes from dramatic uses of force to "foreign policy," that debates at length a legislative provision that has never been enforced, or that relies on slogans—"meddle," "micromanage," "usurp," "aggressive"—or issues pronouncements on the role of Congress in foreign policy without collecting any facts on that role.

Why do we do this? There is certainly no lack of serious issues to think about. As Seyom Brown concludes in his history of postwar American foreign policy, the real issue is the "urgent need for new and deeper thinking about U.S. foreign relations."[15] This is more than a matter of watching the agenda, it is basic groundwork for determining what the agenda should be. We have been debating the Constitution rather than foreign policy ideas, asking which branch should have more influence to make policies that we have not defined or thought very much about.

Very basic questions arise once we see that it is foreign policy—and not the Constitution—we should be worried about. With the growth of a large and multilayered professional cadre of foreign policy makers, we need to consider much more fully what should be the scope and limits of their influence: i.e., what should be the role of professionals in a democratic government. It is an old question, but it needs to be asked again as the claims that there should be "professional" foreign policy increase and become more accepted. The general answer—that Congress will oversee these professionals through the authorization process or by special oversight committees—does not seem sufficient in light of the cases in this study. It is also clear that individual presidents along with a few close advisers are not able to conduct this oversight either. Indeed they are protected, in the interests of plausible denial, from being able to.

Another very basic question concerns what an American foreign policy might look like if people tried to define it. We have come from two historical periods when the phrase "national security" had some widely accepted content: the defeat of fascism in World War II and the defense against the spread of communism in the Cold War period. We could pursue these security objectives while feeling in accord with national goals and character. The phrase is still used along with claims in behalf of policies said to be in the interests of national security. But what *is* the national security now and how does it fit with what the nation might like to see itself as doing? In a book first published in 1960, Richard Neustadt spoke of a time of "continuing crisis" as the context for presidential decision making. The crisis involved the threat of Cold War and the immanence of nuclear war. The president elected in that year would face a Soviet wall erected in Berlin and a direct confrontation over nuclear missiles. No one would say that crises are a thing of the past, but we need to ask if the crises are of the same degree and if they call for the same kind of responses. So in 1991 a Republican senator called for support for a presidential appointment because these were "turbulent times." Certainly this is a turbulent period for parts of the world, and it is probably true that most times, since the sack of Rome or before, have been turbulent in some way. But are the senator's turbulent times the same as Neustadt's continuing crisis? Shouldn't we update what we mean by crisis in the present age?

It is no wonder that the foreign assistance program cannot be reformed despite its considerable unpopularity. Since foreign assistance has been used, by both the White House and Congress, as a multipurpose instrument of foreign policy, the programs are being asked to achieve goals that have never been defined. Committee attempts to reform the programs, once in the Senate and once in the House, never survived the conference. When Congress repeatedly asked the President to redefine the program, the White House remained silent. No sign of an interbranch struggle for influence could be seen. If we were clearer on the objectives we would like this instrument to perform, a more rational foreign assistance program might follow. We would at least be better able to evaluate the programs that continue anyway by supplemental or omnibus funding, the arms and military assistance that are provided to a strange variety of countries, and the billions of dollars that are spent.

One could say in justification that the nation has developed a kind of pragmatic case-by-case policy that tries to watch for its own advantage in dealing with other countries of the world. Hence the professionals need the kind of discretion they have won from Congress in using arms, trade, or economic assistance as continuing bargaining tools. And yet without clearer guiding objectives, of a kind that could be provided by elected officials, the actions can be self-defeating. They can contradict each other, miss larger developments in the pursuit of short-term goals, and be generally ineffective since there is no standard of evaluation to compare them against. The point was made earlier that nations need to decide what kinds of signals they send abroad—about what they believe in and what they are trying to do. We have no content for the signals as yet. We have not discussed what they should be saying.

Perhaps we need the illusion, given the stakes—i.e., the perceived importance—of some foreign policy issues compared to those of domestic policy. On the one hand, citizens might prefer not to get involved in issues of war and peace and international arms escalation: the stakes are too high. On the other hand, they might feel the need to say there is *democratic* policy making: it is not lobbying by foreign governments or bureaucratic formalism or any other nondemocratic process that determines such issues. People can keep both of these contradictory notions by assuring themselves that their democratically elected officials are in control. Not only does the President single-handedly watch over the world from his special place in the Oval Office, but Congress and the President *struggle* to be sure the best possible policy is enacted.

It is in the interest of President and Congress to seem active and aware. Hence the symbolic struggle continues, with each serving as partner to the other. The members of both branches are skilled at manipulating symbols, as we know from the fact that they are elected in the first place. President and Congress are not the only codependents, however: press commentators and public are implicated, too, as very willing consumers of the symbolism. Thus the biggest obstacle to any reform, and the biggest cliché, is the notion of this struggle between the branches. It seems that Americans really would like their elected officials to play a major role in foreign policy. They want to believe that what they see on the surface is true.

AFTERWORD

✦ ✦ ✦

CONGRESS AND THE NEW WORLD ORDER

T HE PLAY SEEMED FAMILIAR although the characters had traded lines. A Republican leader argued for curbs on presidential war-making powers, citing a statement from the
American Civil Liberties Union. A Democratic senator reminded colleagues, "We cannot have 535 commanders in chief." In one day's
debate on the deployment of U.S. troops in Somalia, which continued into the early hours of the next morning, nearly one-half of the
Senate (forty-four members) spoke. Before the two-week deliberation on the 1994 defense appropriations bill (HR 3116) was over,
sixty-one senators had spoken for more than sixteen hours of debate on issues pertaining to the use of U.S. troops abroad.

Had anything happened beyond some awkward shuffling of
party lines? Was Congress stirring, if not asserting, itself? The
preceding chapters can help place the events of Fall 1993 in perspective, as to what may have changed and what remained the
same.

In several ways the debate on Somalia on October 14 exhibited patterns seen previously. First, the outcome was known before the debate began. The Byrd Amendment, supported by the
majority leader, George Mitchell (D., Maine), and the minority
leader, Robert Dole (R., Kans.), had already been negotiated with
the White House. A vote for the Byrd Amendment and against an
alternative amendment offered by John McCain (R., Ariz.) thus
prepared for an outcome that was already a *fait accompli*. "Minds
will not be changed," as one senator noted, calling for an early end
to debate.[1] The legislation was referred to as the "leadership
amendment" by several senators on the floor.

Second, the outcome would support the President's position. As in the Gulf War debate in the Bush administration, whose outcome was also known in advance, the lengthy debate in Congress would end by upholding President Clinton's position, in the conventional pattern of support for the Commander in Chief. A defeat for the policy negotiated with the White House would "severely damage the institution of the Presidency," one senator warned. Another, who spoke strongly in criticism of the Clinton policy, concluded by saying, "I will vote against undercutting our Commander in Chief."

Third, there was very little difference between the two amendments that were being debated at such length. Both sought to end the American military presence in Somalia as soon as possible, and differed primarily on whether and how a deadline date could be set. "We are engaged in an extraordinarily narrow debate," Slade Gorton (R., Wash.) observed. "There is no question about our leaving. The only question is when." Minority Leader Dole remarked that "this has been a good debate," adding that "I do not think there are probably fifteen days' worth of difference in the two amendments, maybe thirty, maybe ten, maybe less." There was a difference in the outcomes, however. When the Senate finally voted, the Byrd Amendment was solidly supported, 76–23, while the McCain Amendment was defeated, 61–38. A total of 61 senators supported the leadership amendment and opposed the McCain Amendment, thus following President Clinton's position. Twenty-three senators, 20 Republicans and 3 Democrats, opposed Clinton, voting for the McCain Amendment and against the leadership amendment. The remaining 15 senators supported McCain and went on to support the alternative when their preferred policy was defeated. No senators voted against the two amendments. Everyone wanted some limits placed on the military venture.

Why was this such a "good debate," however? As in the Gulf War deliberations, several speakers congratulated themselves that they were having a debate. Others, also reflecting patterns seen previously, admitted that it was "long overdue" and that "Congress [was] finally getting around to its constitutional responsibility." As William Cohen (R., Maine) remarked,[2]

I must say that while we are casting some stones upon the administration for failure to adopt a clear-cut policy, we in Congress must also accept our share of the responsibility because we did, indeed, pass on resolutions that supported the deployment of our forces to Somalia. . . . And we have been rather indifferent or negligent in not following up and maintaining the kind of oversight that is necessary.

Republican Hank Brown of Colorado, who took the anti-Clinton position on amendments, pointed out that he had also opposed the original deployment in the Bush administration. He reminded his colleagues that he had called for hearings on Somalia in December, a request which was turned down. He called again in early 1993 for hearings which had to be canceled when administration officials asked not to testify. "The simple fact is," he concluded, "we did not do our job as a Government. . . . We did not ask the committees of this Congress to do their job—which is our job under the Constitution. The failure that we talk about tonight is a failure of both the executive and legislative branches."[3]

All of this sounds familiar—from the Lebanon engagements in the Reagan administration, the investigation of intelligence abuses, the observations on Iran-contra. In criticizing executive mistakes, whether of Republican or Democratic administrations, Congress takes some blame for itself. It should have been more vigilant, more assertive perhaps. It should have spoken up earlier, held hearings. There is a failure of both branches. The pressures on Congress, however, are also familiar. It is considered important by major decision makers in any nation to present a united front wherever possible, in critical international affairs. Clearly, a Senate quarreling among its members or demanding reluctant administration witnesses to testify disrupts this impression of unity, just as an amendment supported by the leadership of both parties and the White House upholds it. By this argument one could say that it was only when the Byrd Amendment was agreed on with the White House and with the minority leader that the debate became acceptable to many members. As one senator argued, "This amendment will allow the Congress and the President to present a united front to the world on this difficult issue. America speaks with one voice." Senator Dole therefore could say it was a good debate in part *because* there was so little difference between the provisions being debated.

Why, then, the long and very visible debate? Unfortunately, political pressures were present as well, given the intensive television reporting on casualties and on the American taken prisoner, Army Chief Warrant Officer Michael Durant. Word of Durant's release came only on October 14, the day the debate began and when its rules of proceeding were already in place. That the Senate was aware of the potential negative public reaction to the United States' role in Somalia was clear in the remarks of several speakers. One senator suggested that the majority of Americans were not aware of the complex military situation that existed in Somalia. Another said that Congress should lead, not follow, public opinion, and another sought to "explain to the public why it is important that we [remain until the proposed deadline and] fulfill our mission." Another said he had not taken a poll or counted the mail from his constituents, underlining the importance of this opinion even as he denied its immediate effects. As in the reaction to the situation in Lebanon a decade before, the widespread reporting of American losses brought the Senate into action. The debate thus allowed Congress to walk a fine line: on one side, deflecting a negative public reaction to the American casualties; and on the other side, presenting a bipartisan and united front in support for the Commander in Chief. In these terms it was a very good debate indeed.

The session was different, however, from the immediate past in two rather interesting ways. The senators were not content to mouth broad patriotic statements or invoke the gravity of the issue of sending men and women to war, as they did, for example, in the Gulf War debate. Of the 44 members speaking on Somalia, almost all discussed *policy* for the present or the future. They argued the positive and negative implications of setting target dates for the withdrawal of American forces. More broadly, they set forth the pros and cons of the American commitment to the United Nations forces: including the role of alliances in a multinational peacekeeping era, the economic implications, what U.N. forces seemed most and least able to do. "As the Berlin Wall came down, so too our yardstick for national security began to crumble," James Jeffords (R., Vt.) observed. What would the new yardstick be for military involvement, he asked, outlining the dangers and opportunities he saw ahead. There were policy options that were not being considered. In one attempt to supply this yardstick, William Roth (R., Del.) set forth guidelines that might be used in assessing future military ventures. John Kerry (D., Mass.) also suggested guidelines to argue why in the present situation in Somalia critical national issues were at stake.

This was hardly "micromanaging foreign policy," as the term was originally used to describe specific restrictions Congress attached to large-scale executive requests. Nor could one claim too much congressional "assertiveness" in debating a matter that had already been agreed upon. On the other hand, it was not the empty symbolic display that had become too familiar in recent years. There was substance along with the symbols of policy deliberation as the Senate tried for the first time in public to wrestle with the very large questions of America's role in a post–Cold War era.

In a second unusual feature, Congress reached back to its own more illustrious past, invoking the power of the purse. The debate occurred on the annual defense appropriations bill. This traditional weapon had failed in recent years as a multipurpose instrument of foreign policy, as the previous chapters have described. It might well have failed on this occasion too if it had not been invoked by the efforts of, and in the person of, Senator Robert Byrd. Byrd (D., W. Va.) was not only chairman of the Senate Appropriations Committee, he was President Pro Tempore of the Senate, a member of the chamber for thirty-three years, its informal historian, and staunchest defender. If his rhetorical flourishes seemed anachronistic at times in the contemporary chamber, his mastery of the congressional spending process inspired an admiration mixed with fear.[4] He was Mr. Senate.

Byrd, not usually vocal on foreign affairs, had taken the Somalia issue as his own, and sought to use the congressional appropriations power—the power to raise and support armies as the Constitution states—to influence that policy. He spoke not only for a policy in Somalia but for the power of the purse:[5]

> This is the appropriate bill on which to debate our policy in Somalia, because it highlights the importance of the power of the purse—the ultimate arrow in Congress' quiver—to effect the policy of the Nation in such weighty matters as wars and deployments of American forces. The Framers of the Constitution were well aware that the power of the purse was the key to the power of this institution, and we cannot guard the American people and it too closely.

It is Congress's "exclusive" power, he went on, pointing to Section 9 of Article 1 of the Constitution and giving his colleagues a short and possibly much-needed history lesson: "Read it. It does not double speak. It is clear. It is plain. It is the key to a healthy system of checks and balances." The President is Commander in Chief, he admitted. "But suppose he does not have any army, suppose he does not have any navy—Congress has the power to raise and support armies, to provide and maintain navies. So it is this power of the purse . . . [that] my amendment uses."

Byrd's argument could stand in opposition to a president's policy. What if he did not have an army or a navy to deploy or knew that he would have one only to a definite cutoff date? Byrd did not need to make this argument explicit, however, since the policy had already been negotiated with the Clinton White House. He thus could compliment the particular president in the White House in recognizing that Congress was an "equal branch of the government" and speak of the sharing of responsibility between executive and legislative branches. According to his argument, responsibility had moved to the *United Nations*, to New York and away from Washington:[6]

> [The people] do not expect us to shirk this most fundamental of our responsibilities, and we have been shirking it; not a peep being said around here; nothing. . . . Now we are taking a stand. We are debating it; something we should have been doing months ago.

While Byrd could appeal to the shared responsibility of both elected branches against the somehow foreign "United Nations" and "New York," it was to the Congress in particular that he was speaking.

Byrd's efforts were not sufficient, however. The chorus of congratulations he received from other senators was appropriate in one way: he had made the debate take place and staked the fate of the defense appropriations bill on it. Nevertheless, Byrd had been talking for months on the issue when "not a peep" was being said, to use his own words. The work of the majority leader George Mitchell (D., Maine) was also critical in holding the Democratic lines, both in negotiating with the White House and in the Senate votes. Only three Democrats ultimately took the anti-Clinton position of voting for the McCain Amendment and against the Byrd Amendment. So the debate "finally" occurred. It occurred only after the rising tide of public dismay over the Somalia policy and the negotiation of a White House compromise. And it occurred only after three of the traditional components of congressional power were allied: the party leadership, the power of the purse through the appropriations process, and the efforts of a senior, influential committee chair. Each of the three had been weakened in the post-reform years.

The debate that took place throughout the following week, on the same defense appropriations bill, would be even more reminiscent of several previously described patterns. Only one vote was at all controversial: an amendment by Don Nickles (R., Okla.) concerned with the placing of U.S. troops under U.N. foreign commanders. The amendment would not have applied to training, communications, supplies, or humanitarian units or to those units assigned to NATO or other specific military alliances. It would have required presidents to give Congress thirty days' notice if troops were to be assigned to U.N. commanders and a joint resolution by Congress approving the arrangement. Presidents could waive the requirement in the interests of "national security," in which case the arrangement would continue only if Congress approved it within thirty days.

The amendment, opposed by the Clinton administration and the Democratic leadership, was defeated 65 to 33, the Republicans splitting ranks with 32 senators in favor of the amendment and 11 opposed. A substitute nonbinding resolution was then offered, expressing the sense of the Senate that the President "should consult with Congress" before placing U.S. troops under U.N. commanders. This nonbinding resolution, expressing the Senate's "unease" with the issue of U.N. commanders and urging "consultation" between the two branches, was passed by the overwhelming margin of 96–2.

Other nonbinding sense of the Senate resolutions followed by near unanimous votes: for Bosnia (99–1), for Haiti (98–2), for a Senate hearing inquiring into the lack of U.S. preparation for the battle in Mogadishu, Somalia (voice vote). Defense Secretary Les Aspin (himself a former House member and chair of the Armed Services Committee) had been severely criticized in Congress for refusing to send to Somalia armored vehicles and other support requested by U.S. commanders on the scene. Hearings on this issue had already been called for. The amendment on Haiti urged the President to seek prior authorization from Congress before committing further military forces to that country, *or* to send the Congress a detailed report as to why such forces were necessary.

One of the virtues of the amendment on Haiti, the majority leader argued, was that it was "not legally binding." In addition, as Senator Byrd pointed out in opposing the resolution, the loopholes were so large as to allow any president to report that he had satisfied his own criteria. Byrd was only one of two senators opposing the resolution.

So where did things stand after all the speeches and votes, the long evening hours and constant efforts by both party leaders? Mitchell had held the Democratic lines amid criticism of his own party's president, orchestrating the debate and the various resolutions. Minority Leader Dole was also active, although caught in a three-way political cross fire: between his desire to criticize the policies of the Democratic administration, his past record in support of presidential power, and his need as Senate leader to secure bipartisan support. During the same two weeks of floor management and bargaining, Dole had called four separate press conferences and had spoken on NBC's *Meet the Press* and CBS's *Face the Nation*, all on the subject of the military interventions.[7] The defense appropriations bill finally staggered to its conference with the House, burdened with its new legislation and the nonbinding resolutions. These could be compromised further or eliminated later on.

One the one hand, the Senate had clearly sent a message to the Clinton administration. One commentator called it a "wake-up call." To have the Senate speak at such length on matters of war was exceptional; to seek a legislated end to military action, even with the agreement of the White House, was even more exceptional. The events did not fit fully within the conventional pattern of war making described previously, a pattern of presidential action and congressional support. On the other hand, the sound and fury far outweighed the legislative action, recalling earlier symbolic displays: the long debate which occurred after a decision had been reached in the White House; the lopsided votes for nonbinding resolutions with loopholes; the hand-wringing and self-criticism. Congress, the senators told themselves, should have acted earlier, held hearings: they had been too negligent or unconcerned. . . .

Two historical events cited frequently in the debates can help refine the perspective: the reaction to the casualties in Lebanon in 1983; and the Cooper-Church Amendment in 1973, seeking an end to the conflict in Southeast Asia. The Senate appears to engage in such a historic deliberation once every ten years. Each of these events occurred only after widespread publicity on the casualties of the war and long after the original congressional support for the Commander in Chief. The Cooper-Church Amendment was not actually passed, as a matter of fact: a later restriction on funds for action in Southeast Asia was attached to a spending bill, enacted when the peace negotiations were already underway. These mark the *exceptional* occurrences of Congress's somewhat belated participation in war making. They were unlike the events of 1993 in that the congressional policy opposed the existing administration policy—of Nixon in 1973 and Reagan in 1983. In these earlier cases no agreement had been worked out with the White House before the debates began. *This is as "assertive" as Congress gets*, with the dubious exception of the War Powers Act, and reason enough for avoiding use in the future of such a misleading term as "assertive." In each event, a decade apart, Congress joined a swelling public chorus criticizing a military venture and admitting it should have done so earlier. Maintaining a deference to the Commander in Chief, it nevertheless spoke against the policy while allowing the President time to make plans to withdraw.

And so on to 2003? The reduced tensions of a post–Cold War era may weaken the automatic support provided an American president as commander in chief. Alternatively, the Clinton administration might learn from the year's mistakes, as Kennedy learned after the disaster in the Bay of Pigs. Whether or not such debates become more frequent in future years, Congress can draw some lessons of its own. It must look to its traditional powers if it does wish to enter a foreign policy debate—and not merely give the impression of doing so.

Appendix A

◆ ◆ ◆

Major Legislation

This listing shows the major foreign-policy legislation as debated each year in Congress. To be included legislation must be (a) brought to a vote on the floor of at least one chamber, and (b) featured in *Congressional Quarterly Almanac's* annual review of foreign policy. The list thus excludes from the larger working agenda routine extensions of programs, minor programs, or specific changes or provisions when these are not related to major issues of the day. For definitions and discussion, see chapter 2.

The legislation is listed by the public law number or executive agreement letter when passed; otherwise it is listed by bill number. When both authorizing and appropriating legislation are controversial and occur within one year, only the appropriation is listed.

1961

PL 87–297	Establish the U.S. Arms Control and Disarmament Agency
PL 87–293	Establish the Peace Corps
PL 87–329	Appropriate foreign-aid funds
PL87–311	Guarantee American exports in Export-Import Bank policy
S 1215	Senate bill to amend Battle Act to allow military assistance to Eastern Europe fails to pass House

1962

PL 87–731	Authorize loan to United Nations
PL 87–733	Declare U.S. policy on Cuba
PL 87–490	Authorize loan to International Monetary Fund
PL 87–794	Enact Trade Act
PL 87–872	Appropriate foreign-aid funds
PL 87–442	Authorize Peace Corps funds

1963

Exec M	Ratify Nuclear Test Ban Treaty
PL 88–200	Authorize Peace Corps funds and amend act
PL 88–258	Appropriate foreign-aid funds
PL 88–101	Increase lending authority of Export-Import Bank

1964

PL 88–408	Pass the Gulf of Tonkin Resolution
PL 88–259	Restructure and provide funds for Inter-American Bank
PL 88–285	Authorize Peace Corps funds and amend act
PL 88–310	Authorize funds for International Development Association
PL 88–634	Appropriate foreign-aid funds

1965

PL 89–27	Authorize Arms Control and Disarmament Agency
PL 89–124	Appropriate Peace Corps and restructure
PL 89–241	Revise tariff schedules

1966

PL 89–369	Establish U.S. participation in Asian Development Bank
PL 89–367	Authorize supplemental defense funds for Vietnam War
PL 89–371	Authorize supplemental foreign assistance for Vietnam amending the Foreign Assistance Act
PL 89–691	Appropriate foreign-aid funds
PL 89–808	Enact agricultural assistance program

1967

PL 90–629	Authorize arms sales
PL 90–249	Appropriate foreign-aid funds, with restrictions on arms sales
Exec D	Ratify consular treaty between U.S. and U.S.S.R.
S 1155	Senate bill extending the Export-Import Bank and permitting trade with Eastern Europe fails to pass House

1968

PL 90–267	Establish arms sales restrictions for Export-Import Bank
PL 90–314	Cut funds by half for Arms Control Agency
PL 90–349	Amend IMF Agreement for Special Drawing Rights
PL 90–629	Authorize arms sales and restrictions
PL 90–581	Appropriate foreign-aid funds, with deep cuts

1969

Exec H	Ratify Nuclear Nonproliferation Treaty
PL 91–47	Appropriate supplemental funds, with Vietnam restriction
PL 91–99	Authorize Peace Corps funds, with cuts
PL 91–121	Authorize defense procurement, with cuts

| PL 91–170 | Appropriate military assistance |
| PL 91–175 | Authorize foreign and military assistance |

1970

PL 91–672	Authorize foreign military sales, with repeal of the Tonkin Gulf Resolution (the House version included the Cooper-Church amendment limiting funds for Cambodia)
HJ Res 1355	House passes a War Powers Resolution
PL 91–652	Authorize supplemental foreign assistance, with limits on the use of troops in Cambodia

1971

PL 92–129	Extend the draft
HJ Res 1	House passes a War Powers Resolution
PL 92–126	Expand operations of the Export-Import Bank
HR 910	Senate rejects House authorization of foreign and military assistance

1972

PL 92–403	Require the executive branch to submit to Congress the texts of all international agreements
PL 92–448	Authorize the President to approve a U.S.–U.S.S.R. agreement limiting offensive nuclear weapons
PL 92–264	Authorize funds for Radio Liberty and Radio Free Europe
HR 16705	House and Senate fail to agree on appropriating foreign and military aid
S 2956	Senate war powers bill dies in conference

1973

PL 93–121	Extend the Council on International Economic Policy
PL 93–22	Extend some diplomatic privileges to the People's Republic of China
PL 93–22	Authorize special emergency aid to Israel
PL 93–50	Appropriate military assistance funds, with a ban on combat activities in Southeast Asia
PL 93–52	Appropriate continuing funds, with a ban on combat activities in Southeast Asia
PL 93–148	Enact the War Powers Act

1974

| PL 93–448 | Appropriate continuing funds, barring military assistance to Turkey |

PL 93–475	Authorize State and U.S.I.A. funds
PL 93–559	Authorize foreign assistance with Hughes-Ryan amendment regulating intelligence activities
PL 93–618	Enact the Trade Act
S 3830	House fails to pass Senate bill giving Congress power to veto executive agreements

1975

PL 94–23	Authorize funds for South Vietnamese evacuation
PL 94–104	Lift embargo on arms to Turkey
PL 94–110	Approve American monitors of Egyptian-Israeli peace
PL 94–161	Authorize foreign economic assistance

1976

PL 94–304	Monitor Helsinki Agreement
PL 94–329	Enact the Arms Export Act, restricting arm sales
S Res 400	Establish Senate permanent select intelligence committee

1977

PL 95–12	Give President authority to halt imports of Rhodesian chrome
PL 95–52	Curb U.S. participation in Arab boycott of Israel
PL 95–223	Restrict authority of President to impose economic controls during presidentially declared emergencies
PL 95–105	Authorize State Department funds, with restrictions
PL 95–118	Authorize World Bank funds with compromise on human rights violations
PL 95–148	Appropriate funds for economic and military aid
H Res 658	Establish House permanent select intelligence committee

1978

	Ratify the Panama Canal
	Ratify the Neutrality Treaty (Panama)
PL 95–384	Authorize military aid
PL 95–424	Authorize foreign economic aid, lifting embargo against Turkey
PL 95–426	Authorize State Department funds, deleting an executive restriction
PL 95–435	Revise IMF institution, with embargo against Uganda
S Con Res 86	Senate fails to block Mideast jet sales

1979

PL 96–8	Enact Taiwan Relations Act
PL 96–70	Implement Panama Canal treaties
PL 96–35	Authorize $4.8 billion in special aid to Israel and Egypt
PL 96–53	Authorize foreign economic aid, with reorganization of agencies
PL 96–92	Authorize military aid, with compromise on Turkey
PL 96–60	Authorize State Department funds, lifting ban on Rhodesia
PL 96–39	Enact trade legislation

1980

PL 96–533	Authorize economic and military aid with additions for Israel and Egypt
PL 96–536	Appropriate stopgap funds when foreign-aid appropriations fail to pass
PL 96–257	Authorize emergency economic aid for Nicaragua
PL 96–259	Reduce funds for international banks
PL 96–465	Reorganize Foreign Service
PL 96–450	Authorize intelligence funds, with repeal of Hughes-Ryan

1981

H Con Res 194	Senate fails to disapprove AWACs for Saudis
Pl 97–113	Authorize foreign aid with broader presidential authority
PL 97–121	Appropriate foreign-aid programs
S Res 179, H Res 177	Urge U.S. adopt stronger non-proliferation policy
PL 97–132	Authorize Sinai peacekeeping force
PL 97–89	Authorize secret intelligence funds

1982

PL 97–241	Authorize State Department funds, with cuts
PL 97–257	Appropriate supplemental foreign-aid funds, with a portion for the Caribbean Basin Initiative
PL 97–377	Appropriate continuing foreign-aid funds
PL 97–269	Authorize intelligence funds, with Boland Amendment

1983

PL 98–43	Authorize economic and military aid to Lebanon, with restrictions
PL 98–119	Invoke War Powers Act for troops in Lebanon

PL 98–215	Authorize intelligence funds, with limits on aid to Nicaraguan contras
PL 98–212	Appropriate defense funds with limits on aid to Nicaraguan contras
PL 98–151	Appropriate continuing funds, with limits on El Salvador and Guatemala
HJ Res 402	Senate fails to act on House resolution to invoke War Powers for invasion of Grenada
HJ Res 13	House passes nuclear freeze resolution

1984

PL 98–332	Appropriate supplemental assistance funds, with limits on aid to Nicaraguan contras
PL 98–396	Appropriate supplemental assistance funds
PL 98–473	Appropriate continuing funds, with compromise on El Salvador and new Central American funds
PL 98–533	Authorize intelligence funds
PL 98–573	Enact omnibus trade act

1985

PL 99–83	Authorize funds for economic and military assistance
PL 99–88	Appropriate funds for nonmilitary contra aid
PL 99–169	Authorize intelligence funds with limits on contra aid
PL 99–142	Oppose Jordan arms sale at present time
HR 1460	House and Senate ask for South African sanctions

1986

| PL 99–440 | Impose South African sanctions: veto override |
| PL 99–591 | Appropriate economic and military assistance |

1987

PL 100–202	Appropriate continuing funds with some aid to contras and arms sales limits
PL 100–204	Authorize State Department funds, with restrictions
PL 100–178	Authorize intelligence funds
HR 1630	Authorize foreign assistance; not passed
H Res 12 (S Res 23)	Establish Iran-Contra Committee

1988

| | Ratify INF Treaty, banning intermediate and short-range nuclear missiles |

PL 100–463	Appropriate defense funds eliminating contra aid
S 2763	Both houses vote Iraq sanctions
HR 3651	Senate fails to pass House bill with new arms sales limits
HR 1580	Senate fails to pass new South African sanctions
PL 100–418	Enact Omnibus Trade Act
PL 100–453	Pass intelligence authorization without proposed restrictions

1989

PL 101–179	Pass aid to Poland and Hungary
PL 101–167	Enact foreign-aid appropriation
PL 101–193	Pass intelligence authorization

1990

	German Unification Treaty approved
PL 101–382	Pass Caribbean Trade Act
PL 101–302	Give aid to Nicaragua and Panama
PL 101–513	Pass foreign-aid appropriation
PL 101–246	Pass State Department authorization
S 2834	Pass intelligence authorization

1991

	Treaty Conventional Forces in Europe
PL 102–1	Authorize use of force in the Persian Gulf
PL 102–27 (102–28)	Pass Gulf War appropriations
PL 102–228	Authorize aid to the Soviet Union
PL 102–182	Limit chemical and biological weapons
S Res 78 (H Res 101)	Pass fast-track trade extension
HR 2212	Review trade status for China
HR 2508	Pass foreign assistance authorization

APPENDIX B

+ + +

The following list indicates when the United States has utilized military force abroad in situations of conflict or potential conflict to protect U.S. citizens or promote U.S. interests.[1]

Kennedy:

1962   *Cuba.* In the Cuban Missile Crisis, President Kennedy issued a quarantine on the shipment of offensive missiles to Cuba from the Soviet Union.

1962   *Thailand.* In May, five thousand marines were sent to support the country against Communist pressure from outside. They were withdrawn by July.

1962–75   *Laos.* The U.S. provided military support to Laos.

Johnson:

1964   *Congo.* The U.S. sent four transport planes to provide airlift for Congolese troops during a rebellion.

1964–73   *Vietnam.* After attacks on U.S. destroyers in the Tonkin Gulf, the U.S. escalated its participation in the war, until, by 1969, the number of troops reached 543,000.

1965   *Dominican Republic.* The U.S. intervened during a revolt as fears grew that the revolution was coming under Communist control.

1967   *Congo.* The U.S. sent three military transport aircraft with crews during a revolt.

Nixon:

1970   *Cambodia.* U.S. troops were ordered into Cambodia to attack enemy sanctuaries supporting North Vietnamese and Viet Cong forces.

1974   *Cyprus.* Naval forces evacuated U.S. civilians during hostilities between Turkish and Greek Cypriot forces.

Ford:

1975   *Vietnam.* U.S. naval vessels, helicopters, and marines assisted in evacuation of refugees and U.S. nationals.

1975   *Cambodia.* U.S. military forces assisted in evacuating U.S. citizens.

1975   *South Vietnam.* Helicopters and marines evacuated citizens and others.

1975   *Mayaguez Incident.* President Ford ordered naval, marine, and air force to retake the SS *Mayaguez*, a merchant vessel seized by Cambodian naval patrol boats.

1976	*Lebanon.* Helicopters and naval vessels evacuated U.S. citizens and Europeans during hostilities between Lebanese factions.
1976	*Korea.* Additional troops were sent to Korea when two American military personnel were killed in the demilitarized zone when they entered the zone.

Carter:

1978	*Zaire.* Military transport aircraft supported Belgian and French rescue operations.
1980	*Iran.* Six transport planes and eight helicopters attempted unsuccessfully to rescue American hostages in Iran.

Reagan:

1981–89	*El Salvador.* After a guerilla offensive against the government, military advisers were stationed to assist in training government forces in counterinsurgency.
1981	*Libya.* U.S. planes shoot down Libyan jets over the Gulf of Sidra.
1982	*Sinai.* Military personnel were deployed as part of a Multinational Forces and Observers Resolution.
1982	*Lebanon.* In August, marines were dispatched as part of a multinational force to remain for one month.
1982	*Lebanon.* In late September, twelve hundred marines were sent to Lebanon, to remain for eighteen months.
1983	*Egypt.* An AWACs plane was sent to Egypt after a Libyan bombing.
1983–89	*Honduras.* U.S. troops were stationed and conducted exercises.
1983	*Chad.* President Reagan deployed two AWACs, eight F-15s, and ground support forces to assist Chad against Libyan forces.
1983	*Grenada.* Marines and Army airborne troops landed on Grenada to protect lives and restore order, it was reported.
1984	*Persian Gulf.* The U.S. assisted Saudi fighter jets in shooting down two Iranian fighter planes.
1985	*Italy.* Navy pilots intercepted an Egyptian airliner carrying the hijackers of an Italian cruise ship.
1986	*Libya.* The U.S. engages Libyan forces around the Gulf of Sidra.
1986	*Libya.* U.S. air and naval forces conduct bombing strikes on Libya.
1986	*Bolivia.* Aircraft and Army personnel assist Bolivia in anti-drug operations.
1987–88	*Persian Gulf.* President Reagan increased U.S. Navy forces in the Persian Gulf, and began the policy of reflagging and escorting Kuwaiti tankers through the Gulf.
1988	*Panama.* During instability in Panama and pressure for General Noriega to resign, the U.S. sent an additional thousand troops supplementing ten thousand military personnel already stationed there.

Appendix B1
Speaking about the Use
of Force: Percent of Cases

	Both Chambers	One Chamber	Neither Chamber
N (Cases)			
1960s			
7	43	28	28
1970s			
8	50	0	50
1980s			
18	28	17	56

Speaking is counted as substantial when six or more members speak on the subject, even if only briefly. Speeches were included for the month following the event as indexed in *The Congressional Record.* The index heading is the nation or the event. Both chambers spoke on Thailand, 1962, Tonkin Gulf, 1964, Dominican Republic, 1965, Cambodia, 1970, the Vietnam evacuations, 1975, *Mayaguez,* 1975, El Salvador, 1981, Grenada, 1983, and Persian Gulf, 1987. One chamber spoke on Cuba, 1962, Congo, 1967, Iran, 1980, Italy, 1985, and the events in Libya in 1986. Neither chamber spoke on Laos, 1962, Congo, 1964, Cyprus, 1974, Lebanon, 1976, Korea, 1976, Zaire, 1978, Libya, 1981, Sinai, 1982, Lebanon, 1982, Egypt, 1983, Honduras, 1983, Chad, 1983, Persian Gulf, 1984, Bolivia, 1986, or Panama, 1988. The debate on invoking the War Powers Act for Lebanon, held one year later, is not included.

Appendix B2
Congressional Hearings on the Use of Force

Force	Years Covered	Number of Hearings	Number of Pages
Thailand	1962–64	0	0
Cuba	1962–64	2	162
Laos	1962–64	0	0
Congo (2)	1964–69	1	139
Tonkin Gulf	1964–67	1	36
Dominican Rep.	1965–67	3	326
Cambodia	1970–72	3	736
Cyprus	1974–76	0	0
Indochina (2)	1975–77	7	553
Mayaguez	1975–77	3	535
Lebanon	1976–78	0	0
Korea	1976–78	2	101
Zaire	1978–80	1	125
Iran	1980–82	2	135
El Salvador	1981–83	1	92
Libya (3)	1981–89	2	400
Sinai	1982–84	0	0
Lebanon (2)	1982–84	17	1635
Egypt	1983–85	0	0
Honduras	1983–88	5	384
Chad	1983–85	0	0
Grenada	1983–85	9	532
Persian Gulf (2)	1984–88	19	2148
Italy	1985–87	0	0
Bolivia	1986–88	1	65

NOTE: Hearings are counted for the year of the event and the two succeeding years: hence two cases of force at the end of the Reagan administration are not included. The listing is compiled from the CIS abstracts of published and unpublished hearings. Only full hearings dealing with the subject are included.

Appendix C

◆ ◆ ◆

Foreign Assistance Authorizations, 1961–91

1961	PL 87–195
1962	PL 88–205
1963	PL 88–205
1964	PL 88–633
1965	PL 89–171
1966	PL 89–583
1967	PL 90–137
1968	PL 90–554
1969	PL 91–175 Two Years
1970	Continued from Previous Year
1971	No Authorization
1972	No Authorization
1973	PL 93–189
1974	PL 93–559
1975	PL 94–161 Two Years Economic Assistance
1976	PL 94–329 Military Assistance
1977	PL 95–88 Economic Assistance
1977	PL 95–92 Military Assistance
1978	PL 95–424 Economic Assistance
1978	PL 95–384 Military Assistance
1979	PL 96–53 Economic Assistance
1980	PL 96–533
1981	PL 97–113 Two Years
1982	Continued from Previous Year
1983	No Authorization
1984	No Authorization
1985	PL 99–83 Two Years
1986	Continued from Previous Year
1987	No Authorization
1988	No Authorization
1989	No Authorization
1990	No Authorization
1991	No Authorization

NOTE: Where a single public law (PL) is listed, economic and military assistance is combined.

NOTES

✦ ✦ ✦

CHAPTER 1

1. Edward Corwin, *The President: Office and Powers*, 3d ed. (New York: New York University Press, 1957), 171.

2. Cecil Crabb, Jr., and Pat Holt, *Invitation to Struggle*, 3d ed. (Washington, D.C.: CQ Press, 1988).

3. See Thomas Mann, ed., *A Question of Balance: The President, the Congress and Foreign Policy* (Washington, D.C.: Brookings, 1990); Frank Smist, Jr., *Congress Oversees the Intelligence Community* (Knoxville: University of Tennessee Press, 1990); Barry Blechman, *The Politics of National Security* (New York: Oxford, 1990).

4. L. Gordon Crovitz and Jeremy Rabkin, eds., *The Fettered Presidency* (Washington, D.C.: American Enterprise Institute, 1989); Gordon Jones, ed., *The Imperial Congress* (New York: Pharos, 1988); David Abshire and Ralph Nurnberger, eds., *The Growing Power of Congress* (Washington, D.C.: Sage, 1981).

5. *New York Times,* December 18, 1990, A10.

6. John Lehman, *Making War* (New York: Scribners, 1992), 58.

7. Lehman, *Making War,* 69, 70.

8. Lehman, *Making War,* 265.

9. See Theodore Sorensen, *Kennedy* (New York: Harper and Row, 1965), 672–703; Arthur Schlesinger, Jr., *A Thousand Days* (New York: Houghton Mifflin, 1965).

10. See John Burke and Fred Greenstein, *How Presidents Test Reality* (New York: Russell Sage, 1989).

11. Miroslav Nincic, *Democracy and Foreign Policy* (New York: Columbia University Press, 1992), 74.

12. Loch Johnson, *America's Secret Power* (New York: Oxford, 1989), 223 and 128.

13. For examples of this assumption, see Barry Blechman, "The New Congressional Role in Arms Control Policy," in *A Question of Balance,* ed. Thomas Mann, esp. 109, 110; and Cecil Crabb, Jr., and Pat Holt, *Invitation to Struggle,* chapter 8.

14. Robert Katzman, "War Powers: Toward a New Accommodation," in *A Question of Balance*, ed. Thomas Mann, 55.

15. CNN interview, January 24, 1991.

16. Alexander George, *Presidential Decision Making in Foreign Policy* (Boulder, Colo.: Westview, 1980); Hugh Heclo and Lester Salamon, eds., *The Illusion of Presidential Government* (Boulder, Colo.: Westview, 1981).

17. James Lindsay and Randall Ripley, "Foreign and Defense Policy in Congress: A Research Agenda for the 1990s," *Legislative Studies Quarterly*, August 1992: 418.

18. Holbert Carroll, *The House and Foreign Affairs* (Boston: Little, Brown, 1966); Alton Frye, *A Responsible Congress: The Politics of National Security* (New York: McGraw Hill, 1975); Thomas Franck and Edward Weisband, *Foreign Policy by Congress* (New York: Oxford, 1979); Charles Whalen, Jr., *The House and Foreign Policy: The Irony of Congressional Reform* (Chapel Hill: University of North Carolina Press, 1982).

19. See, for example, Johnson and McCormick, "The Making of International Agreements"; Fred Kaiser, "Oversight of Foreign Policy: The U.S. House Committee on International Relations," *Legislative Studies Quarterly*, August 1977: 255–79; Arnold Kantor, "Congress and the Defense Budget," *American Political Science Review*, March 1972: 129–43; Robert Pastor, *Congress and the Politics of U.S. Foreign Economic Policy, 1929–1976* (Berkeley: University of California Press, 1980). Two more recent studies of specific topics are Loch Johnson's study of intelligence oversight in *America's Secret Power* and James Lindsay's study of nuclear weapons procurement in *Congress and Nuclear Weapons* (Baltimore: Johns Hopkins, 1991). Johnson's study covers the full time period from the 1960s through the 1980s, while Lindsay's study uses selected cases.

20. *Congressional Quarterly Weekly Report,* July 3, 1993: 1751.

21. A good example is Barbara Sinclair, "The Transformation of the U.S. Senate," in *Home Style and Washington Work* (Ann Arbor: University of Michigan Press, 1989), 113–36. See also Whalen, *The House and Foreign Policy*.

22. Irving Janis, *Groupthink*, 2d ed. (New York: Houghton Mifflin, 1982); Alexander George, *Presidential Decision Making in Foreign Policy*.

23. Theodore Lowi, *The Personal President* (Ithaca: Cornell University Press, 1985), 16.

24. Richard Fenno, Jr., *Congressmen in Committees* (Boston: Little, Brown, 1973).

25. Fenno, *The U.S. Senate: A Bicameral Perspective* (Washington, D.C.: American Enterprise Institute, 1982).

26. Fenno, *Congressmen in Committees*, uses goals and environments to discuss committee activity. I am applying the ideas to congressional policy making more broadly.

27. Eileen Bargen, "Representatives' Decisions on Participation in Foreign Policy Issues," *Legislative Studies Quarterly*, November 1991: 521–46.

28. Standard studies on the point, differing only in emphasis, are Jon Bond and Richard Fleisher, *Presidential Success in the Legislative Arena* (Chicago: University of Chicago Press, 1990); George Edwards III, *At the*

Margins (New Haven: Yale University Press, 1989); and Douglas Rivers and Nancy Rose, "Passing the President's Program: Public Opinion and Presidential Influence in Congress," *American Journal of Political Science,* May 1985: 183–96.

29. Michael Mezey, "The Legislature, the Executive, and Public Policy: The Futile Quest for Congressional Power," in *Divided Democracy* (Washington, D.C.: CQ Press, 1991), 111.

30. Catherine Rudder, "Committee Reform and the Revenue Process," in *Congress Reconsidered,* 1st ed., eds. Lawrence Dodd and Bruce Oppenheimer (New York: Praeger, 1977), 124–26.

31. Quoted in Whalen, *The House and Foreign Policy,* 49.

32. Norman Ornstein et al., *Vital Statistics on Congress* (Washington, D.C.: American Enterprise Institute, 1987), 159–64.

33. Louis Fisher, *Constitutional Conflicts between Congress and the President,* 3d ed. (Lawrence: University of Kansas Press, 1991), 287.

34. Barbara Hinckley, *The Symbolic Presidency: How Presidents Present Themselves* (New York: Routledge, 1990), p. 89.

35. Edward Tufte, *Political Control of the Economy* (Princeton: Princeton University Press, 1978).

36. See Charles Ostrom and Brian Job, "The President and the Political Use of Force," *American Political Science Review,* June 1986, 541–66; Paul Brace and Barbara Hinckley, *Follow the Leader: Opinion Polls and the Modern Presidents* (New York: Basic, 1992).

37. *New York Times* staff, *The Pentagon Papers* (Chicago: Quadrangle, 1971); Larry Berman, *Planning a Tragedy* (New York: Norton, 1982), chapter 2.

38. The study which comes closest to doing so is James Robinson, *Congress and Foreign Policy Making,* rev. ed. (Homewood, Ill.: Dorsey, 1967).

CHAPTER 2

1. See Norman Ornstein et al., *Vital Statistics on Congress* (Washington, D.C.: American Enterprise Institute, 1987), 194.

2. John Kingdon, *Agendas, Alternatives, and Public Policies* (Boston: Little, Brown, 1984), 3.

3. Ornstein et al., *Vital Statistics on Congress,* 155.

4. This seems preferable to looking at committee agendas since committees technically consider all bills submitted to them, even those expected to have no legislative future. It is also true that committee hearings serve many purposes beside that of preparing for immediate legislation. A later chapter will look more closely at the agendas of the two chief foreign policy committees.

5. Since many of the bills have multiple roll calls, it is not surprising that the average number of roll calls per year (not shown in the table) has also increased: from about 20 in the 1960s, to 60 in the early 1970s, to a high point of 99 in the Carter years, falling back to about 60 in the 1980s.

6. The total number of bills as well as the number of resolutions was slightly higher in Reagan's second term as compared with the first.

7. A large share of the treaties the Senate votes on, not shown in the table, are also passed unanimously. The rate is about 90 percent. The Senate considers on the average seven or eight treaties a year, typically passing several en bloc with one vote. While a few major treaties require serious attention, it is clear that most of the time this constitutional obligation does not overburden the working agenda.

8. Ornstein et al., *Vital Statistics on Congress*, 149–61.

9. The list accords well with other listings of key legislation such as those found in *Congressional Quarterly*'s annual reviews of major legislation by policy area and their smaller number of key votes (see *Congressional Quarterly Almanac*, Washington, D.C., annual volumes). For a list of the cases, see appendix A.

10. David Mayhew, *Divided We Govern* (New Haven: Yale, 1991), especially chapter 3.

11. Mayhew, *Divided We Govern*, 41

12. See Mayhew, *Divided We Govern*, table 4.1. According to this list one congress in the 1960s (1965–66) passed no major foreign policy legislation; two congresses in the 1970s (1975–76 and 1977–78) passed none; and one congress in the 1980s (1981–82) also passed none.

13. See Paul Brace and Barbara Hinckley, *Follow the Leader: Opinion Polls and the Modern Presidents* (New York: Basic, 1992), chapter 4; see also Gary King and Lyn Ragsdale, *The Elusive Executive* (Washington, D.C.: CQ Press, 1988), 70–75, for the House patterns in foreign and domestic policy.

14. For similar results on the difference between parties, see Lee Sigelman, "A Reassessment of the Two Presidencies Thesis," *Journal of Politics*, November 1979, 1195–1205; LeLoup and Shull, "Congress Versus the Executive: The Two Presidencies Reconsidered," *Social Science Quarterly*, March 1979, 704–19; Richard Fleisher and Jon Bond, "Are There Two Presidencies? Yes, But Only for Republicans," *Journal of Politics*, August 1988, 747–67. The Senate results are similar. In the Fleisher and Bond study, for example, presidents facing same-party Senate control (including Reagan for six of his eight years in office) averaged support close to 80 percent, while presidents facing opposite-party Senate control averaged about 65 percent.

15. See Fleisher and Bond, "Are There Two Presidencies?"

16. Paul Light, *The President's Agenda* (Baltimore: Johns Hopkins,

1982). See also Cary Covington, "Congressional Support for the President: The View from the Kennedy/Johnson White House," *Journal of Politics,* August 1986, 717–28.

17. As listed in the *Public Papers of the Presidents,* various volumes. All speeches broadcast live to a nationwide audience are included. The messages to Congress requesting legislation exclude the many minor reports, which do not request legislation, and all minor treaties. Informal messages to leaders or individuals in Congress are also excluded.

18. According to one writer, the idea for a Peace Corps had originally been circulated in Congress, by Representative Henry Reuss of Wisconsin. See Alfred de Grazia, "The Myth of the President," in *The Presidency,* ed. Aaron Wildavsky (Boston: Little, Brown, 1969), 63.

19. For background, see Theodore Sorensen, *Kennedy* (New York: Harper, 1965), 529–40; Barbara Kellerman, *The President as World Leader* (New York: St. Martins, 1991).

20. See Sorensen, *Kennedy,* 728–40.

21. Congressional Quarterly, *Congress and the Nation,* (Washington, D.C.; Congressional Quarterly, 1969), II:70.

22. Congressional Quarterly, *Congress and the Nation,* II:99

23. Robert Pastor, *Congress and the Politics of U.S. Foreign Economic Policy* (Berkeley: University of California Press, 1980), 179.

24. See Barbara Kellerman, *The President as World Leader,* 167, and Donald Spencer, *The Carter Implosion* (New York: Praeger, 1988), 59. For a fuller assessment of Carter's foreign policy, and his objectives, see Erwin Hargrove, *Jimmy Carter as President* (Baton Rouge: Louisiana State University Press, 1988), chapter 5.

25. See Hargrove, *Jimmy Carter as President,* 123.

26. See Michael Klare, *American Arms Supermarket* (Austin: University of Texas Press, 1984), 143, 144. Klare quotes Proxmire's speech in the *Congressional Record.*

27. See William Hyland, ed., *The Reagan Foreign Policy* (New York: Meridien, 1987), introduction; see also R. Gordon Hoxie, ed., *The Presidency and National Security Policy* (New York: Center for the Study of the Presidency, 1984), 361.

28. See Jentleson, "American Diplomacy: Around the World and along Pennsylvania Avenue," in Thomas Mann, ed., *A Question of Balance: The President, the Congress and Foreign Policy* (Washington, D.C.: Brookings, 1990), 163. See also Cecil Crabb, Jr., and Pat Holt, *Invitation to Struggle,* 3d ed. (Washington, D.C.: CQ Press, 1989), 124.

29. The famous example is Patrick Buchanan's op-ed piece in the *Washington Post,* March 5, 1986, but there were many earlier examples. See Jentleson, "American Diplomacy," 150–55.

30. Congressional Quarterly, *Congress and the Nation*, VI(1985):127.

31. Jentleson, "American Diplomacy," 171.

32. Blechman, "The New Congressional Role in Arms Control," in Thomas Mann, ed., *A Question of Balance*, 133.

33. See *Congressional Quarterly Almanac* (Washington, D.C.: Congressional Quarterly, 1990), 800.

Chapter 3

1. The first postwar legislation, and foundation of the Central Intelligence Agency, comes from the National Security Act of 1947.

2. See, for example, John Prados, *Presidents' Secret Wars* (New York: Morrow, 1988), 108.

3. Gregory Treverton, "Intelligence: Welcome to the American Government," in Thomas Mann, ed., *A Question of Balance: The President, the Congress, and Foreign Policy,* (Washington, D.C.: Brookings, 1990), 73. See also Loch Johnson, *America's Secret Power: The CIA in a Democratic Society* (New York: Oxford, 1989), 108.

4. Quoted in Treverton, "Intelligence," 72.

5. For a review of this period see Barbara Hinckley, *Stability and Change in Congress,* 4th ed. (New York: Harper and Row, 1987), 296–300; and Frank Smist, Jr., *Congress Oversees the U.S. Intelligence Community* (Knoxville: University of Tennessee Press, 1990), 5–9. The Clifford quotes are from interviews by Smist.

6. See Smist, *Congress Oversees the U.S. Intelligence Community,* 26.

7. See Smist, *Congress Oversees the U.S. Intelligence Community,* especially chapter 4.

8. Loch Johnson, *A Season of Inquiry: Congress and Intelligence,* (Chicago: Dorsey, 1988), 203.

9. Legislation was passed in 1978 clarifying procedures under which electronic surveillance could be conducted. For legislation during this period, see Smist, *Congress Oversees the U.S. Intelligence Community.*

10. Smist, *Congress Oversees the U.S. Intelligence Community,* 248, 249.

11. John Oseth, *Regulating U.S. Intelligence Operations* (Lexington: University of Kentucky Press, 1985), 153–57.

12. See Treverton, "Intelligence," 70–108.

13. Johnson, *A Season of Inquiry,* 263.

14. Johnson, *A Season of Inquiry,* 70.

15. Johnson, *A Season of Inquiry,* 102.

16. Johnson, *A Season of Inquiry,* 263.

17. Johnson, *America's Secret Power,* 212.

18. Johnson, *America's Secret Power.*

19. See *Congressional Quarterly Almanac*, 1988, 498. See also Treverton, "Intelligence," 90.

20. *Congressional Quarterly Almanac*, 1988, 499.

21. This has now been well documented by writers both supportive and critical of the intelligence agencies. See, for example, John Prados, *Presidents' Secret Wars;* and Rhodri Jeffreys-Jones, *The CIA and American Democracy* (New Haven: Yale, 1989), among other sources.

22. See, for example, Jeffreys-Jones, *The CIA and American Democracy*, 201–204.

23. These specific policies are not included in the list of legislation in appendix A, as the decision rules for the appendix make clear. They are, however, included in the number of bills shown in tables 2.1 and 2.2.

24. Italics added. *Wall Street Journal*, July 27, 1988, as quoted in Roger Porter, "The President, Congress, and Trade Policy," *Congress and the Presidency*, Autumn 1988, 169.

25. See Porter, "The President, Congress, and Trade Policy," 172.

26. As quoted in *Congress and the Nation* (Washington, D.C.: Congressional Quarterly, 1973), III:123.

27. For a good discussion of this and Bush's policy generally in maintaining relations with existing heads of state, see Michael Duffy and Dan Goodgame, *Marching in Place: The Status Quo Presidency of George Bush* (New York: Simon and Schuster, 1992).

28. Pietro Nivola, "Trade Policy: Refereeing the Playing Field," in Thomas Mann, ed., *A Question of Balance*, 201. For the same use of the work in Japanese trade negotiations, see Clyde Prestowitz, Jr., *Trading Places: How We Allowed Japan to Take the Lead* (New York: Basic Books, 1988), 253.

29. Robert Pastor, "The Cry-and-Sigh Syndrome: Congress and Trade Policy," in Allen Schick, ed., *Making Economic Policy in Congress* (Washington, D.C.: American Enterprise Institute for Public Policy Research, 1983), 159–95. See also Nivola, "Trade Policy," 215, 216.

30. Nivola, "Trade Policy," 241, 242.

31. *Congressional Quarterly Weekly Report*, May 8, 1982, quoted in Nivola, "Trade Policy," 220.

32. Prestowitz, *Trading Places*, 251.

33. *Congressional Quarterly Weekly Report*, October 13, 1984, 2716.

34. Prestowitz, *Trading Places*, 323.

35. *Congressional Quarterly Weekly Report*, August 6, 1988, 2215.

36. Raymond Vernon et al., *Iron Triangles and Revolving Doors* (New York: Praeger, 1991), 27–32.

37. Vernon et al., *Iron Triangles*, 32, 33.

38. See Michael Klare, *American Arms Supermarket* (Austin: University of Texas Press, 1984), 11, 41.

39. *Congress and the Nation*, IV(1977):877.

40. See *Congressional Quarterly Almanac*, V(1981):108.

41. *New York Times*, June 24, 1976.

42. See *New York Times*, October 11, 1977.

43. *Congress and the Nation*, V(1981):109, reports figures from the Defense Security Assistance Agency.

44. See Klare, *American Arms Supermarket*, 47.

45. Quoted in *Newsweek*, December 15, 1980, 53.

46. *Congressional Quarterly Almanac*, IV(1977):877.

47. Barry Blechman, "The New Congressional Role in Arms Control," in Thomas Mann, ed., *A Question of Balance*, 109–45.

48. Klare, *American Arms Supermarket*, 248.

49. Barbara Hinckley, *Stability and Change in Congress*, 4th ed. (New York: Harper and Row, 1987), 192–96.

50. Barry Blechman, "The Congressional Role in U.S. Military Policy," *Political Science Quarterly*, Spring 1991, 27–31; Thomas Mann, *A Question of Balance*, 32, 33.

CHAPTER 4

1. Ellen C. Collier, ed., "Instances of Use of United States Armed Forces Abroad, 1798–1989," Congressional Research Service, The Library of Congress, December 4, 1989. For a discussion of the various lists, see Francis Wormuth and Edwin Firmage, *To Chain the Dog of War: The War Power of Congress in History and Law* (Dallas: Southern Methodist University Press, 1986).

2. James Robinson, *Congress and Foreign Policy Making*, rev. ed. (Homewood, Ill.: Dorsey, 1967), 50.

3. See Theodore Sorensen, *Kennedy* (New York: Harper and Row, 1965), 672–703.

4. See Charles Ostrom and Dennis Simon, "Promise and Performance: A Dynamic Model of Presidential Popularity," *American Political Science Review*, June 1985, 1096–1119; Paul Brace and Barbara Hinckley, *Follow the Leader: Opinion Polls and the Modern Presidents* (New York: Basic, 1992), chapter 2; Michael MacKuen, "Political Drama, Economic Conditions, and the Dynamics of Presidential Popularity," *American Journal of Political Science*, May 1983, 165–92.

5. John Mueller, *War, Presidents, and Public Opinion* (New York: Wiley, 1973), 54, 55. For the impact of the Vietnam war on public support, see

also Michael Sullivan, *The Vietnam War* (Lexington: University of Kentucky Press, 1985), chapter 4; Daniel Hallin, "The Media, the War in Vietnam, and Political Support," *Journal of Politics*, February 1984, 2–24; and Benjamin Page and Richard Brody, "Policy Voting and the Electoral Process: The Vietnam War Issues," *American Political Science Review*, September 1972, 979–95.

6. For a good discussion of the relation between public opinion and congressional action in Vietnam, see Barry Hughes, *The Domestic Context of American Foreign Policy* (San Francisco: W. H. Freeman, 1978), 38–40.

7. A fifteen-page bibliography is supplied by Sherry Shapiro, *War Powers: Selected References*, Congressional Research Service, Library of Congress, May 1988. The Congressional Research Service keeps up to date on responses to the act and presidential compliance. See Ellen Collier, *The War Powers Resolution: Fifteen Years of Experience*, Congressional Research Service, Library of Congress, August 3, 1988; and Collier, *War Powers Resolution: Presidential Compliance*, Congressional Research Service, Library of Congress, March 10, 1989.

8. Collier, *The War Powers Resolution: Fifteen Years of Experience*, 15–26.

9. See Michael Rabner, "The Reagan Administration, the 1973 War Powers Resolution, and the Invasion of Grenada," *Political Science Quarterly*, Winter 1985/86, 631.

10. *The Situation in Iran*, Hearings before the Senate Committee on Foreign Relations, 96 Congress, 2d Session (Government Printing Office, 1980), 4.

11. See, for example, Barry Blechman, "The Congressional Role in U.S. Military Policy," *Political Science Quarterly*, Spring 1991, 27–28.

12. Kenneth Sharpe, "The Post-Vietnam Formula under Siege: The Imperial Presidency and Central America," *Political Science Quarterly*, Winter 1987/88, 557.

13. Quoted in Robert Katzman, "War Powers: Toward a New Accommodation," in Thomas Mann, ed., *A Question of Balance: The President, the Congress, and Foreign Policy* (Washington, D.C.: Brookings, 1990), 56.

14. See Louis Fisher, *Constitutional Conflicts between Congress and the President*, 3d ed. (Lawrence: University of Kansas Press, 1991), 275–77.

15. Goldwater v. Carter, 444 U.S. 996, 998 (1979), quoted in Fisher, *Constitutional Conflicts*, 279.

16. Rabner, "The Reagan Administration, the War Powers Resolution, and the Invasion of Grenada," 645.

17. Subcommittee on International Security and Scientific Affairs, Committee on International Relations, House of Representatives, 94th Cong., 1st Session, *Hearings*, June 4, 1975, 18. The speaker was Representative Paul Findley, R. Ill. In his introduction subcommittee chair

Clement Zablocki, D. Wis., remarked, p. iv, that he felt the War Powers Act had worked reasonably well.

18. Collier, *The War Powers Resolution: Fifteen Years of Experience*, 30, 31.

19. Collier, *War Powers Resolution: Presidential Compliance*, 12.

20. Collier, *War Powers Resolution: Presidential Compliance*, 45–50.

21. Clyde Wilcox et al., "Before the Rally: The Dynamics of Attitudes toward the Gulf Crisis before the War," a paper presented at the annual meeting of the American Political Science Association, Washington, D.C., September 1991. The polls were conducted by the Wirthlin group in behalf of "Citizens for a Free Kuwait": i.e., the White House position. Mr. Wirthlin also conducted daily tracking polls for the Reagan administration.

22. *Proceedings and Debates of the 102nd Congress, First Session, The Congressional Record,* January 12, 1991, 137:8, S367.

23. Louis Fisher, "War Powers: The Need for Collective Judgement," in James Thurber, ed., *Divided Democracy* (Washington, D.C.: CQ Press, 1990), 215.

24. *Congressional Record,* U.S. House of Representatives, May 15, 1975, 14077ff.

25. The fullest account is Mark Hertsgaard, *On Bended Knee: The Press and the Reagan Presidency* (New York: Farrar,.Straus, Giroux, 1988), chapter 10.

26. *Congressional Quarterly Weekly Report,* October 1983.

27. Committee on Appropriations, House of Representatives, Hearings on Appropriations for the Department of Defense, Part IV, April 28, 1980.

28. See Fisher, "War Powers," 206, 207.

29. Sharpe, "The Post-Vietnam Formula under Siege," 559.

CHAPTER 5

1. Robert Pastor, *Congress and the Politics of U.S. Foreign Economic Policy* (Berkeley: University of California Press, 1980), 253.

2. See Pastor, *Congress and the Politics of U.S. Foreign Economic Policy,* 252. See also Holbert Carroll, *The House of Representatives and Foreign Affairs* (Boston: Little, Brown, 1966), chapter 1.

3. Quoted in *Congressional Quarterly Almanac 1975,* 336. At the time Bundy appeared as a witness, he was president of the Ford Foundation.

4. See Pastor, *Congress and the Politics of U.S. Foreign Economic Policy,* 257.

5. Hans Morgenthau, *American Political Science Review,* 1962. Thus his

six purposes are (1) humanitarian, (2) subsistence, (3) military, (4) bribery, (5) prestige, and (6) economic development.

6. The authorization provides the statutory authority for the spending, or appropriation, of government money. A foreign aid bill would go first to the authorizing committees, and then to a conference committee if necessary, and only then to the appropriating committees. In practical terms, members anticipate and prepare for the decisions at each of these stages.

7. Presidential draft bills are not designated with the congressional documents that show the history of the legislation. The bills were traced by document number, provided by the Office of Management and Budget. Using the document number, bills could then be located in the National Archives, Civil Reference Branch; and also in documents included in the legislative history of the public law in *United States Code Congressional and Administrative News* (Brooklyn, Edward Thompson Co., various years).

8. *Congressional Quarterly Almanac 1969,* 440.

9. And see Judith Tendler, *Inside Foreign Aid* (Baltimore: Johns Hopkins, 1975), 38, 39, for the lack of presidential support.

10. See Barbara Hinckley, *Stability and Change in Congress* (New York: Harper and Row, 1987), 302.

11. Hinckley, *Stability and Change in Congress,* 301–6.

12. John White, *The Politics of Foreign Aid* (New York: St. Martin's, 1974), especially chapters 1 and 2. See also Robert Packenham, *Liberal America and the Third World* (Princeton: Princeton University Press, 1973).

13. See, for example, Frances Lappe et al., *Betraying the National Interest* (New York: Grove Press, 1987), 31, 58. The authors cite statistics for the mid-1980s.

14. The section subhead, or provision, is a standard unit in the bill, designated by a, b, c, and so forth following the section number. Its length can vary from a few lines to a page or more. Thus everything in a section 202, subhead a, for example, constitutes one provision.

15. See, for example, Packenham, *Liberal America and the Third World,* 87, 88.

16. *Congressional Quarterly Almanac 1963,* 255, 258.

17. *Congressional Quarterly Almanac 1969,* 446.

18. Steven Smith and Christopher Deering, *Committees in Congress,* 2d ed. (Washington, D.C.: CQ Press, 1990), 182, 184, show the change committee by committee in the average number of floor amendments the committee's bill received. The House Foreign Affairs Committee showed

an above-average number of amendments in the 1970s compared to the other committees and an average amount in the 1980s. The Senate Foreign Relations Committee showed about the average number of changes compared to the other committees.

19. *Congressional Quarterly Almanac 1974*, 537.

20. *Congressional Quarterly Almanac 1985*, 51.

21. *Congressional Quarterly Almanac 1985*, 47, points out that while some of the increase was due to "bookkeeping" changes in arms-related programs, the bulk of the increase consisted of military programs Reagan had won from Congress.

22. Pastor, *Congress and the Politics of U.S. Foreign Policy*, 282.

23. *Federalist* #58. The Constitution lodges this power exclusively in the hands of Congress, in article 1, section 9.

Chapter 6

1. Bayliss Manning, "Hyperlexis: Our National Disease," *Northwestern University Law Review* 71 (1977), 767, as quoted in Roger Porter, "The President, Congress, and Trade Policy," *Congress and the Presidency*, Autumn 1988, 171.

2. See Lawrence Longley and Walter Oleszek, *Bicameral Politics: Conference Committees in Congress* (New Haven: Yale University Press, 1989), 65. The authors estimate that the House, where the Speaker has been able to make multiple referrals since 1975, might refer 25 percent of its bills in that fashion. The Senate, using a long-standing unanimous consent rule, might refer 10 percent.

3. Steven Smith and Christopher Deering, *Committees in Congress*, 2d ed. (Washington, D.C.: CQ Press, 1990), 194.

4. Smith and Deering, *Committees in Congress*, 194.

5. See Longley and Oleszek, *Bicameral Politics*, 149.

6. Longley and Oleszek, *Bicameral Politics*, 54.

7. Longley and Oleszek, *Bicameral Politics*, 70.

8. See *Congressional Quarterly Almanac 1968*, 432.

9. For the large literature on the subject, primarily coming from the 1970s, see Longley and Oleszek's summary in *Bicameral Politics*, 78–85.

10. *Congressional Quarterly Almanac 1968*, 433.

11. According to Hubert Humphrey (D., Minn.), the Senate floor manager of the bill. See *Congressional Quarterly Almanac 1973*, 833.

12. See David Carleton and Michael Stohl, "The Foreign Policy of Human Rights: Rhetoric and Reality from Jimmy Carter to Ronald Reagan," *Human Rights Quarterly*, May 1985, 208.

13. For the congressional initiative, see also Carleton and Stohl, "The

Foreign Policy of Human Rights," 207; and David Forsythe, *Human Rights and World Politics* (Lincoln: University of Nebraska Press, 1983).

14. *Congressional Quarterly Almanac 1977*, 364.

15. See, for example, Erwin Hargrove, *Jimmy Carter as President: Leadership and the Politics of the Public Good* (Baton Rouge: Louisiana State University Press, 1988); Betty Glad, *Jimmy Carter: In Search of the Great White House* (New York: Norton, 1980); Seyom Brown, *The Faces of Power: Constancy and Change in United States Foreign Policy from Truman to Reagan* (New York: Columbia University Press, 1983), 451–63.

16. Brown, *The Faces of Power*, 456, 457.

17. *Congressional Quarterly Almanac 1977*, 370.

18. Carleton and Stohl, "The Foreign Policy of Human Rights," 212, 213. And see Raymond Gastil, *Freedom in the World: Political Rights and Civil Liberties* (Westport, Conn.: Greenwood Press, 1980), 37.

19. See Carleton and Stohl, "The Foreign Policy of Human Rights," 216. See also Stohl et al., "Human Rights and U.S. Foreign Assistance: From Nixon to Carter," *Journal of Peace Research* 21 (no. 3, 1984), 215–26.

20. Stephen Cohen, "Conditioning U.S. Security Assistance on Human Rights Practices," *American Journal of International Law* 76 (April 1982), 270–75. See also Carleton and Stohl, "The Foreign Policy of Human Rights," 216.

21. Cohen, "Conditioning U.S. Security Assistance on Human Rights Practices," 270.

22. Cohen, "Conditioning U.S. Security Assistance on Human Rights Practices," 270.

23. Carleton and Stohl, "The Foreign Policy of Human Rights," 217, 218. On one measure, based on State Department reports, the Reagan administration seems somewhat *stronger* than the Carter administration in restricting aid for human rights violators. The authors point out, however, that this is probably more a matter of bringing the reports in line with the allotments than vice versa.

24. Morris Ogul, *Congress Oversees the Bureaucracy* (Pittsburgh: University of Pittsburgh Press, 1976), 199.

25. Joel Aberbach, *Keeping a Watchful Eye* (Washington, D.C.: Brookings, 1990). And see especially 193, 194.

CHAPTER 7

1. Eldon Kenworthy, "Selling the Policy," in Thomas Walker, ed., *Reagan versus the Sandinistas: The Undeclared War on Nicaragua* (Boulder, Colo.: Westview, 1987), 159.

2. Barbara Hinckley, *The Symbolic Presidency: How Presidents Present Themselves* (New York: Routledge, 1990), 97.

3. Messages to Congress are included in *The Public Papers of the Presidents,* various years.

4. The words are Kenworthy's: "Selling the Policy," 163.

5. See Peter Dale Scott and Jonathan Marshall, *Cocaine Politics* (Berkeley: University of California Press, 1991).

6. For good studies of the congressional role in Nicaragua, see Philip Brenner and William LeoGrande, "Congress and Nicaragua: The Limits of Alternative Policy Making," in James Thurber, ed., *Divided Democracy* (Washington, D.C.: CQ Press, 1990), 219–47; and Cynthia Arnson, *Crossroads: Congress, the Reagan Administration, and Central America* (New York: Pantheon, 1989).

7. Brenner and LeoGrande, "Congress and Nicaragua," 234.

8. Arnson, *Crossroads,* 203.

9. Bob Woodward, *Veil: The Secret Wars of the CIA: 1981–1987* (New York: Simon and Schuster, 1987), 211–15.

10. Woodward, *Veil.*

11. Woodward, *Veil,* 319, 320.

12. Loch Johnson, *America's Secret Power* (New York: Oxford, 1989), 223.

13. John Prados, *Presidents' Secret Wars* (New York: Morrow, 1988), 108.

14. Woodward, *Veil,* 174ff.

15. Woodward, *Veil,* 323, 336.

16. Kenneth Sharpe, "The Post-Vietnam Formula Under Siege: The Imperial Presidency and Central America," *Political Science Quarterly,* Winter 1987/88, 563.

17. And see Mark Hertsgaard, *On Bended Knee: The Press and the Reagan Presidency* (New York: Farrar, Straus, Giroux, 1988), 323.

18. Theodore Draper, *A Very Thin Line: The Iran-Contra Affairs* (New York: Hill and Wang, 1991), 62–67.

19. Hertsgaard, *On Bended Knee,* 308.

20. Hertsgaard, *On Bended Knee,* 328; Draper, *A Very Thin Line,* 84.

21. Draper, *A Very Thin Line,* 81, 82.

22. Fisher, "War Powers," 210–12.

23. Woodward, *Veil,* 373.

24. Report of the Subcommittee on Terrorism, Narcotics, and International Operations as discussed in Scott and Marshall, *Cocaine Politics.*

25. See *Congressional Quarterly Weekly Report,* November 21, 1987, 2847–53. The minority report is summarized on pages 2900ff.

26. *Congressional Quarterly Weekly Report,* November 21, 1987, 2893.

CHAPTER 8

1. For a summary of this literature, see Barbara Hinckley, *Stability and Change in Congress*, 4th ed. (New York: Harper and Row, 1987), 11, 12.

2. Woodrow Wilson, *Congressional Government* (New York: Meridian, 1956), 132. Originally published in 1885.

3. Irving Janis, *Groupthink*, 2d ed. (Boston: Houghton-Mifflin, 1982); George Reedy, *The Twilight of the Presidency* (New York: World, 1970).

4. See Hugh Heclo and Lester Salamon, eds., *The Illusion of Presidential Government* (Boulder, Colo.: Westview, 1981); Godfrey Hodgson, *All Things to All Men* (New York: Simon and Schuster, 1980); Thomas Cronin, *The State of the Presidency*, 2d ed. (Boston: Little, Brown, 1980).

5. See discussion in Barbara Hinckley, *The Symbolic Presidency* (New York: Routledge, 1990), chapter 1. See also Murray Edelman, *Politics as Symbolic Action* (New York: Academic Press, 1971); Jeffery Tulis, *The Rhetorical Presidency* (Princeton: Princeton University Press, 1987); and Henry Tudor, *Political Myth* (New York: Praeger, 1972).

6. See, for example, Morris Ogul, *Congress Oversees the Bureaucracy* (Pittsburgh: University of Pittsburgh Press, 1976).

7. Frank Smist, Jr., *Congress Oversees the Intelligence Community* (Knoxville, University of Tennessee Press, 1990).

8. The arguments are well summarized by Thomas Mann, *A Question of Balance*, 30.

9. Hedrick Smith, *The Power Game: How Washington Works* (New York: Random House, 1988), 140.

10. Paul Brace and Barbara Hinckley, *Follow the Leader: Opinion Polls and the Modern Presidents* (New York: Basic, 1992), chapter 5.

11. James Lindsay and Randall Ripley, "Foreign and Defense Policy in Congress: A Research Agenda for the 1990s," *Legislative Studies Quarterly*, August 1992, 417–50.

12. See discussion in David Mayhew's *Divided We Govern* (New Haven, Yale, 1991), especially chapter 3.

13. At the C-SPAN Video Archives at Purdue University.

14. James Lindsay, "Congress and Foreign Policy: Why the Hill Matters," *Political Science Quarterly*, Winter 1992/93, 607–28.

15. Seyom Brown, *The Faces of Power: Constancy and Change in United States Foreign Policy from Truman to Reagan* (New York: Columbia University Press, 1983), 628.

AFTERWORD

1. All references to the Somalia debate are taken from 103rd Congress, First Session, *Congressional Record* (October 14, 1993), S13431–S13480.

2. *Congressional Record,* October 14, 1993, S13445–6.

3. *Congressional Record,* October 14, 1993, S13451.

4. And see *Congressional Quarterly Weekly Report,* October 16, 1993, 2824.

5. *Congressional Record,* October 14, 1993, S13432.

6. *Congressional Record,* October 14, 1993, S13432.

7. Information supplied by the Public Affairs Video Archives of Purdue University. My thanks to Robert Browning for making this and other information available.

APPENDIX B

1. Based on the CRS report "Instances of Use of United States Armed Forces Abroad, 1798–1989," ed. Ellen C. Collier, Congressional Research Service, Library of Congress, Washington, D.C., December 4, 1989. The report accords closely with other lists. See, for example, Francis Wormuth and Edwin Firmage, *To Chain the Dog of War: The War Powers of Congress in History and Law* (Dallas: Southern Methodist University Press, 1986), 133–49.

Major References
+ + +

Aberbach, Joel, *Keeping a Watchful Eye* (Washington, D.C.: Brookings, 1990).

Arnson, Cynthia, *Crossroads: Congress, the Reagan Administration, and Central America* (New York: Pantheon, 1989).

Bargen, Eileen, "Representatives' Decisions on Participation in Foreign Policy Issues," *Legislative Studies Quarterly*, November 1991, 521–46.

Bartels, Larry, "Constituency Opinion and Congressional Policymaking: The Reagan Defense Buildup," *American Political Science Review*, June 1991, 457–74.

Berman, Larry, *Planning a Tragedy* (New York: Norton, 1982).

Blechman, Barry, *The Politics of National Security* (New York: Oxford, 1990).

———, "The Congressional Role in U.S. Military Policy," *Political Science Quarterly*, Spring 1991, 27–31.

Bond, Jon, and Richard Fleisher, *Presidential Success in the Legislative Arena* (Chicago: University of Chicago Press, 1990).

Brace, Paul, and Barbara Hinckley, *Follow the Leader: Opinion Polls and the Modern Presidents* (New York: Basic, 1992).

Brenner, Philip, and William LeoGrande, "Congress and Nicaragua: The Limits of Alternative Policy Making," in James Thurber, ed., *Divided Democracy* (Washington, D.C.: CQ Press, 1991), 219–55.

Brody, David, *Assessing the President: Media, Elite Opinion, and Public Support* (Stanford: Stanford Univerity Press, 1991).

Brown, Seyom, *The Faces of Power: Constancy and Change in United States Foreign Policy from Truman to Reagan* (New York: Columbia University Press, 1983).

Burke, John, and Fred Greenstein, *How Presidents Test Reality* (New York: Russell Sage, 1989).

Carleton, David, and Michael Stohl, "The Foreign Policy of Human Rights: Rhetoric and Reality from Jimmy Carter to Ronald Reagan," *Human Rights Quarterly*, May 1985, 205–29.

Carroll, Holbert, *The House and Foreign Affairs* (Boston: Little, Brown, 1966).

Cline, William, ed., *Trade Policy in the 1980s* (Cambridge: MIT Press, 1983).

Cockburn, Leslie, *Out of Control* (N.Y.: Atlantic Monthly Press, 1987).

Cohen, Stephen, "Conditioning U.S. Security Assistance on Human Rights Practices," *American Journal of International Law* 76 (April 1982), 270–75.

Collier, Ellen, ed.,"Instances of Use of United States Armed Forces Abroad, 1798–1989" (Washington, D.C.: Government Printing Office, Congressional Research Service, The Library of Congress), December 4, 1989.

Collier, Ellen, ed., *The War Powers Resolution: Fifteen Years of Experience* (Washington, D.C.: Government Printing Office, Congressional Research Service, The Library of Congress), August 3, 1988.

Congressional Quarterly Almanac (Washington, D.C.: Congressional Quarterly), various volumes, 1961–88.

Corwin, Edward, *The President: Office and Powers*, 3d ed. (New York: New York University Press, 1957).

Covington, Cary, "Congressional Support for the President: The View from the Kennedy/Johnson White House," *Journal of Politics*, August 1986, 717–28.

Crabb, Cecil, Jr., and Pat Holt, *Invitation to Struggle*, 3d ed. (Washington, D.C.: CQ Press, 1988).

Cronin, Thomas, *The State of the Presidency*, 2d ed. (Boston: Little, Brown, 1980).

Destler, I. M., *Making Foreign Economic Policy* (Washington, D.C.: Brookings, 1981).

Draper, Theodore, *A Very Thin Line: The Iran-Contra Affairs* (New York: Hill and Wang, 1991).

Duffy, Michael, and Dan Goodgame, *Marching in Place: The Status Quo Presidency of George Bush* (New York: Simon and Schuster, 1992).

Edwards, George III, *At the Margins* (New Haven: Yale University Press, 1989).

———, "The Two Presidencies: A Reevaluation," *American Politics Quarterly*, July 1986, 247–63.

Fenno, Richard, *The U.S. Senate: A Bicameral Perspective* (Washington, D.C.: American Enterprise Institute, 1982).

Fenno, Richard, Jr., *Congressmen in Committees* (Boston: Little, Brown, 1973).

Fiorina, Morris, *Divided Government* (New York: Macmillan, 1992).

Fisher, Louis, *Constitutional Conflicts between Congress and the President*, 3d ed. (Lawrence: University of Kansas Press, 1991).

———, "War Powers: The Need for Collective Judgement," in James

Thurber, ed., *Divided Democracy* (Washington, D.C.: CQ Press, 1991), 199–218.

Fleisher, Richard, and Jon Bond, "Are There Two Presidencies? Yes, But Only for Republicans," *Journal of Politics*, August 1988, 747–67.

Forsythe, David, *Human Rights and World Politics* (Lincoln: University of Nebraska Press, 1983).

Franck, Thomas, and Edward Weisband, *Foreign Policy by Congress* (New York: Oxford, 1979).

Frye, Alton, *A Responsible Congress: The Politics of National Security* (New York: McGraw Hill, 1975).

Gastil, Raymond, *Freedom in the World: Political Rights and Civil Liberties* (Westport, Conn.: Greenwood, 1980).

Gaubatz, Kurt, "Election Cycles and War," *Journal of Conflict Resolution*, June 1991, 212–44.

George, Alexander, *Presidential Decision Making in Foreign Policy* (Boulder, Colo.: Westview, 1980).

Hallin, Daniel, "The Media, the War in Vietnam, and Political Support," *Journal of Politics*, February 1984, 2–24.

Hargrove, Erwin, *Jimmy Carter as President: Leadership and the Politics of the Public Good* (Baton Rouge: Louisiana State University Press, 1988).

Heclo, Hugh, and Lester Salamon, eds., *The Illusion of Presidential Government* (Boulder, Colo.: Westview, 1981).

Hertsgaard, Mark, *On Bended Knee: The Press and the Reagan Presidency* (New York: Farrar, Straus, Giroux, 1988).

Hinckley, Barbara, *Stability and Change in Congress*, 4th ed. (New York: Harper and Row, 1987).

———, *The Symbolic Presidency: How Presidents Present Themselves* (New York: Routledge, 1990).

Hoxie, Gordon, ed., *The Presidency and National Security Policy* (New York: Center for the Study of the Presidency, 1984).

Hughes, Barry, *The Domestic Context of American Foreign Policy* (San Francisco: Freeman, 1978).

James, Patrick, and John Oneal, "The Influence of Domestic and International Politics on the President's Use of Force," *Journal of Conflict Resolution*, June 1991, 307–32.

Janis, Irving, *Groupthink*, 2d ed. (Boston: Houghton Mifflin, 1982).

Jeffreys-Jones, Rhodri, *The CIA and American Democracy* (New Haven: Yale, 1989).

Johnson, Loch, *America's Secret Power: The CIA in a Democratic Society* (New York: Oxford, 1989).

————, *A Season of Inquiry: Congress and Intelligence* (Chicago: Dorsey, 1988).

Johnson, Loch, and James McCormick, "The Making of International Agreements: A Reappraisal of Congressional Involvement," *Journal of Politics,* May 1978, 468–78.

Kaiser, Fred, "Oversight of Foreign Policy: The U.S. House Committee on International Relations," *Legislative Studies Quarterly,* August 1977, 255–79.

Kantor, Arnold, "Congress and the Defense Budget," *American Political Science Review,* March 1972, 129–43.

Kegley, Charles, Jr., and Eugene Wittkopf, eds., *The Domestic Sources of American Foreign Policy* (New York: St. Martin's, 1988).

Kellerman, Barbara, *The President as World Leader* (New York: St. Martin's, 1991).

King, Gary, and Lyn Ragsdale, *The Elusive Executive* (Washington, D.C.: CQ Press, 1988).

Kingdon, John, *Agendas, Alternatives, and Public Policies* (Boston: Little, Brown, 1984).

Klare, Michael, *American Arms Supermarket* (Austin: University of Texas Press, 1984).

Kotz, Nick, *Wild Blue Yonder: Money, Politics, and the B-1 Bomber* (Princeton: Princeton University Press, 1988).

Lappe, Frances, et al., *Betraying the National Interest* (New York: Grove, 1987).

Lehman, John, *Making War* (New York: Scribners, 1992).

Light, Paul, *The President's Agenda* (Baltimore: Johns Hopkins Press, 1982).

Lindsay, James, *Congress and Nuclear Weapons* (Baltimore: Johns Hopkins, 1991).

————, "Congress and Foreign Policy: Why the Hill Matters," *Political Science Quarterly,* Winter 1992/93, 607–28.

Lindsay, James, and Randall Ripley, "Foreign and Defense Policy in Congress: A Research Agenda for the 1990s," *Legislative Studies Quarterly,* August 1992, 417–50.

Longley, Lawrence, and Walter Oleszek, *Bicameral Politics: Conference Committees in Congress* (New Haven: Yale University Press, 1989).

Lowi, Theodore, *The Personal President* (Ithaca: Cornell University Press, 1985).

MacKuen, Michael, "Political Drama, Economic Conditions, and the Dynamics of Presidential Popularity," *American Journal of Political Science,* May 1983, 165–92.

Mann, Thomas, ed., *A Question of Balance* (Washington, D.C.: Brookings, 1990).

Mayhew, David, *Divided We Govern: Party Control, Lawmaking, and Investigations* (New Haven: Yale, 1991).

McCormick, James, and Michael Black, "Ideology and Senate Voting in the Panama Canal Treaties," *Legislative Studies Quarterly,* February 1983, 45–64.

McCormick, James, and Steven Smith, "The Iran Arms Sale and the Intelligence Oversight Act of 1980," *PS,* Winter 1987.

Mezey, Michael, "The Legislature, The Executive, and Public Policy: The Futile Quest for Congressional Power," in James Thurber, ed., *Divided Democracy* (Washington, D.C.: CQ Press, 1991), 99–122.

Morrow, James, "Electoral and Congressional Incentives and Arms Control," *Journal of Conflict Resolution,* June 1991, 245–65.

Mueller, John, *War, Presidents, and Public Opinion* (New York: Wiley, 1973).

New York Times staff, *The Pentagon Papers* (Chicago: Quadrangle, 1971).

Nincic, Miroslav, "America's Soviet Policy and the Electoral Connection," *World Politics,* April 1990.

———, *Anatomy of Hostility* (New York: Harcourt, 1989).

———, *Democracy and Foreign Policy* (New York: Columbia, 1992).

Nivola, Pietro, "The New Protectionism: U.S. Trade Policy in Historical Perspective," *Political Science Quarterly,* Winter 1986, 577–600.

Ogul, Morris, *Congress Oversees the Bureaucracy* (Pittsburgh: University of Pittsburgh Press, 1976).

Ornstein, Norman, et al., *Vital Statistics on Congress* (Washington, D.C.: American Enterprise Institute, 1987).

Oseth, John, *Regulating U.S. Intelligence Operations* (Lexington: University of Kentucky Press, 1985).

Ostrom, Charles, and Brian Job, "The President and the Political Use of Force," *American Political Science Review,* June 1986, 541–66.

Ostrom, Charles, and Dennis Simon, "Promise and Performance: A Dynamic Model of Presidential Popularity," *American Political Science Review,* June 1985, 1096–1119.

Packenham, Robert, *Liberal America and the Third World* (Princeton: Princeton University Press, 1973).

Page, Benjamin, and Richard Brody, "Policy Voting and the Electoral

Process: The Vietnam War Issues," *American Political Science Review*, September 1972, 979–95.

Pastor, Robert, *Condemned to Repetition: The United States and Nicaragua* (Princeton: Princeton University Press, 1987).

———, "The Cry-and-Sigh Syndrome: Congress and Trade Policy," in Allen Schick, ed., *Making Economic Policy in Congress* (Washington, D.C.: American Enterprise Institute, 1983).

———, *Congress and the Politics of U.S. Foreign Economic Policy, 1929–1976* (Berkeley: University of California Press, 1980).

Pfiffner, James, "Divided Government and the Problem of Governance," in James Thurber, ed., *Divided Democracy* (Washington, D.C.: CQ Press, 1990), 39–60.

Porter, Roger, "The President, Congress, and Trade Policy," *Congress and the Presidency*, Autumn 1988, 165–84.

Prados, John, *Presidents' Secret Wars* (New York: Morrow, 1988).

The Public Papers of the Presidents (Washington, D.C.: Government Printing Office), various volumes, 1961–88.

Reedy, George, *The Twilight of the Presidency* (New York: World, 1970).

Rivers, Douglas, and Nancy Rose, "Passing the President's Program: Public Opinion and Presidential Influence in Congress," *American Journal of Political Science*, May 1985, 183–96.

Robinson, James, *Congress and Foreign Policy Making*, rev. ed. (Homewood, Ill.: Dorsey, 1967).

Rourke, John, Presidential Wars and American Democracy (New York: Paragon, 1993).

Rubner, Michael, "The Reagan Administration, the 1973 War Powers Resolution, and the Invasion of Grenada," *Political Science Quarterly*, Winter 1985/86, 627–48.

Russett, Bruce, *Controlling the Sword* (Cambridge: Harvard, 1991).

Schlesinger, Arthur, Jr., *A Thousand Days* (New York: Houghton Mifflin, 1965).

Scott, Peter Dale, and Jonathan Marshall, *Cocaine Politics* (Berkeley: University of California Press, 1991).

Sharpe, Kenneth, "The Post-Vietnam Formula under Siege: The Imperial Presidency and Central America," *Political Science Quarterly*, Winter 1987/88, 549–69.

Shull, Steven, ed., *The Two Presidencies: A Quarter Century Reassessment* (Chicago: Nelson-Hall, 1991).

Sinclair, Barbara, *Majority Leadership in the U.S. House* (Baltimore: Johns Hopkins, 1983).

————, "The Transformation of the U.S. Senate," in Morris Fiorina and David Rohde, eds., *Home Style and Washington Work* (Ann Arbor: University of Michigan Press, 1989).

Smist, Frank, Jr., *Congress Oversees the U.S. Intelligence Community* (Knoxville: University of Tennessee Press, 1990).

Smith, Steven, and Christopher Deering, *Committees in Congress,* 2d ed. (Washington, D.C.: CQ Press, 1990).

Sorensen, Theodore, *Kennedy* (New York: Harper and Row, 1965).

Spencer, Donald, *The Carter Implosion* (New York: Praeger, 1988).

Stohl, Michael, et al., "Human Rights and U.S. Foreign Assistance: From Nixon to Carter," *Journal of Peace Research* 21:3 (1984), 215–26.

Stubbing, Richard, *The Defense Game* (New York: Harper, 1986).

Sullivan, Michael, *The Vietnam War* (Lexington: University of Kentucky Press, 1985).

Tendler, Judith, *Inside Foreign Aid* (Baltimore: Johns Hopkins, 1975).

Tidmarch, Charles, "Presidential Leadership Change and Foreign Policy Roll Call Voting in the U.S. Senate," *Western Political Quarterly,* December 1972, 613–25.

Tulis, Jeffery, *The Rhetorical Presidency* (Princeton: Princeton University Press, 1987).

Vernon, Raymond, et al., *Iron Triangles and Revolving Doors: Cases in U.S. Foreign Economic Policymaking* (New York: Praeger, 1991).

Whalen, Charles, Jr., *The House and Foreign Policy: The Irony of Congressional Reform* (Chapel Hill: University of North Carolina Press, 1982).

White, John, *The Politics of Foreign Aid* (New York: St. Martins, 1974).

Wilson, Woodrow, *Congressional Government* (New York: Meridian, 1956).

Woodward, Bob, *Veil: The Secret Wars of the CIA: 1981–1987* (New York: Simon and Schuster, 1987).

Wormuth, Francis, and Edwin Firmage, *To Chain the Dog of War: The War Powers of Congress in History and Law* (Dallas: SMU Press, 1986).

INDEX

✦ ✦ ✦